The Composition of *Four Quartets*

also by Helen Gardner

A READING OF *PARADISE LOST*
RELIGION AND LITERATURE
THE BUSINESS OF CRITICISM

(*Edited by*)
A BOOK OF RELIGIOUS VERSE
THE METAPHYSICAL POETS
THE NEW OXFORD BOOK OF ENGLISH VERSE

The Composition of
Four Quartets

HELEN GARDNER

NEW YORK
OXFORD UNIVERSITY PRESS
1978

First published in Great Britain 1978
by Faber and Faber Limited
First published in America
by Oxford University Press
Printed in Great Britain
at the University Press, Oxford
by Vivian Ridler
Printer to the University
All rights reserved

Library of Congress Catalog Card Number 77-92749
ISBN 0-19-519989-8

Preface

My first sight of the drafts of *Four Quartets* and of the correspondence with John Hayward about them was in 1947, when, as the result of a query from me over a Donne manuscript, he asked me to come to tea and showed me the volumes he had bound up. This was the beginning of a close and affectionate friendship to which my labours on this book have been a kind of tribute. For I knew, as I worked, that what I was doing would have given him pleasure.

That it would have given pleasure to Eliot is more doubtful. In February 1941, he wrote to the Librarian of Magdalene College, Cambridge, of which he was an Honorary Fellow, to enquire whether the college library took 'any interest in "contemporary manuscripts"', adding 'I don't see why it should', and offered it the 'mss.' of *The Dry Salvages* with the option of refusal: 'if you *do* like to have such mss. I shall be glad to hand over this and future ones; but if you don't there is no need to take them just to be kind.' When the Master (A. B. Ramsay), to whom the Librarian had handed the letter, wrote to express the College's pleasure in accepting the gift, Eliot expanded his uneasiness:

> From the point of view of an author, I am not sure such papers should be preserved at all; from the point of view of a librarian, they seem to me a nuisance: but if they are to be preserved, I should be sorry to think that they should be divided only between the Bodleian and Eliot House and that none should be at Magdalene.

Some eighteen months later he wrote again to the Master to say it 'would be a pleasure' to add 'the manuscripts and papers' of *Little Gidding* to those connected with *The Dry Salvages*, with a qualification:

> When I say that this would be a pleasure, I do not wish this quite truthful assertion to be construed as expressing general approval of the preservation of my own or indeed of most manuscripts. As a general rule, to which I cannot perceive my own work to provide any exception, it seems to me that posterity should be left with the product, and not be encumbered with a record of the process, of such compositions as these. Their presentation, however, affords an author one of the few means at his disposal for showing his gratitude and appreciation, such as I owe towards Magdalene: and it is in this spirit that I have proposed subtracting these papers from the national supply of pulp.

Although I share some of Eliot's apprehension that the current interest in
poets at work may distract attention from what finally emerged from all
their toil, and believe, with him, that the study of the creative process, however interesting, has far less to give us than a study of the object created,
I am reassured by the fact that four years spent with abandoned fragments,
discarded readings, and what Eliot called the 'Litter' of composition has not
diminished my love for these poems or my conviction of their greatness.
It has, indeed, contributed to an increase of that 'understanding and enjoyment' which Eliot in later life thought it was the prime function of criticism
to promote.

The length of the poems and the amount of material, particularly for
Little Gidding, has posed problems of presentation. Although Eliot was not
unique among poets in inviting and accepting criticism of 'work in progress'
from his friends, it is rare—in my experience unique—to find such discussion committed to paper. It seemed to me imperative for readers' comfort
that they should have the final text before them, with the process of revision
attached and the comments and queries with Eliot's replies immediately
presented. This has involved cutting up the text and the letters, which
I regret; but the alternative would face the reader with continually flipping
to and fro to remind himself of the wording of the passage being discussed.
I have, however, printed in full the first draft of *Little Gidding* with Hayward's
letter upon it in an Appendix, to allow a reader the shock of reading a familiar
poem in an unfamiliar form and, if he wishes, to play the game of what
comment he would have made if faced by it as Hayward was.

I was tempted at the beginning to be selective and to print only those
passages and readings from the drafts which seemed to me to be significant,
fearing that they might be buried under a mass of trivialities. But I decided
that it was my duty to make the material available and not to impose my own
criterion of significance upon it. The correspondence shows Eliot so
scrupulous over the minutest details in his 'wrestle with words and meanings'
that I came to the conclusion that all changes in the drafts should be noted.
I have made an exception in dealing with the working typescripts, as distinct
from the drafts, of *Little Gidding* and not noted punctuation variants in
them. Eliot's manuscript drafts are very lightly punctuated, or not at all,
and his working typescripts are erratically punctuated. It is in those drafts
which are in the nature of 'fair copies' that he gave his mind to problems of
punctuation. For the benefit of those who are not interested in changes in
a preposition or alterations of punctuation I have signalized by an asterisk
readings which are the subject of discussion in the commentary.

As this book is not 'an edition of *Four Quartets*' many passages that an
editor would annotate are left without annotation. What annotation I have
provided arises usually out of hitherto unpublished material. I have attempted
in Part I to provide a background to the study of the drafts by giving informa-

tion about the progress of the poem, the circumstances in which it was written, and the major sources. Both here and in the commentary I have quoted, sometimes extensively, from articles that are not easily available, including uncollected articles by Eliot. Far more people than scholars with access to university libraries cherish these poems and I have tried to bear their interests in mind.

My greatest debt is to Mrs. Valerie Eliot for giving me access to all the unpublished material with a bearing on *Four Quartets* and for giving me freedom to use it as I thought best. She has also given me information I might otherwise not have found and been most generous in answering my questions. After her, I owe most to the late Dr. A. N. L. Munby. As the Librarian in charge of the Hayward Collection in King's College Library, and as an old friend of Hayward's, he was enthusiastic over the whole enterprise and nobody could have been more helpful. His death, before I had brought the work to a conclusion, was both a personal and professional loss. I am very grateful to his assistant, Mrs. Penelope Bulloch, for helpfulness throughout and especially after Dr. Munby's death. I have also to thank the Librarians at Magdalene College, Professor J. A. W. Bennett and Mr. Pepys Whitely, for kindness in allowing me to work in the Library and for supplying me with photocopies, and Professor Bennett and his son, Piers, for reconstructing the torn-up manuscript pad there. Like all who work on Eliot I am indebted to Dr. Donald Gallup. He sent me photocopies of the manuscript of *East Coker* IV and showed me Eliot's letters to Mrs. Perkins, his hostess at Chipping Campden, as well as being always ready to answer queries. I have also to thank the Librarian of the Houghton Library, Harvard, for supplying me with copies of the drafts for 'Lines for an Old Man' and for permission to publish them, and Mr. David Farmer, Assistant Director of the Humanities Research Center at the University of Texas at Austin, for telling me of the typescript of *The Dry Salvages* there, for supplying me with a photocopy, and for permission to quote its readings and to quote from a letter from Eliot to Philip Mairet. I owe my knowledge of this to Mr. Paul Anderson. I am grateful to the late Rear-Admiral Samuel Eliot Morison and the Editors of *The American Neptune* for permission to quote *in extenso* from his article on 'The Dry Salvages and the Thacher Shipwreck' and to Professor Harry Levin for calling my attention to this article.

Mr. George Every, formerly of the Society of the Sacred Mission at Kelham, gave me information about Eliot's visits to Kelham and his sight of a kingfisher in flight there in the summer of the year in which he wrote *Burnt Norton* and also, most kindly, lent me the first draft of a verse play of his on King Charles's visit to Little Gidding after Naseby which Eliot read and discussed with him in 1936, the year he went there. Mrs. Oakeley, John Hayward's sister, gave me personal information about him. Among many with whom I have discussed the work I should like particularly to thank Mr. Vivian Ridler for his kindness in giving me expert advice on methods of presentation, Mrs. Anne Ridler, at one time Eliot's secretary and a friend of Hayward's, who read some of the material in early stages, and Mr. Jon Stallworthy, who gave me the benefit of his advice drawing on his experience in working on the rather different problems of the papers of Yeats and Wilfred Owen. I am greatly indebted to Mr. R. E. Alton for help in deciphering some difficulties in manuscript. I was more than fortunate in having the assistance of Mrs. Bridget Bertram as a research assistant, whose skill in typing and setting out the material saved me hours of labour. Miss M. E. Griffiths of St. Anne's College enabled me to have my typescript xeroxed in the deadest depth of the long vacation. Finally, I must acknowledge the skill and care of the staff at the Oxford University Press in dealing with very difficult copy, and their patience and helpfulness over the proof-reading.

I would like to add that I owe much to the classes I have given in the last few years on *Four Quartets* in Oxford. Members both gave me information and made suggestions, and also, by asking questions I could not answer at the time, stimulated enquiry. Most of all, by their obvious love for the poems they confirmed my belief that these poems that spoke so powerfully to our condition in the dark years when they first appeared still speak with power to a later generation.

HELEN GARDNER

Contents

Abbreviations and References

EHC   Eliot–Hayward Correspondence in King's College Library, Cambridge

HMC   News-letters from John Hayward to Frank Morley in King's College Library, Cambridge

D   Typed drafts of the four poems bound up by John Hayward, referred to as D1, D2, etc., in King's College Library, Cambridge

M   Typed drafts of *The Dry Salvages* and of *Little Gidding*, referred to as M1, M2, etc., in Magdalene College Library, Cambridge

MS   Remains of a writing pad, with some loose leaves from other pads, in Magdalene College Library, Cambridge

Letters from Eliot for which no reference is given should be assumed to have been bound up by Hayward with his drafts.

Typing errors in both Eliot's and Hayward's letters have been silently corrected; but Eliot's occasional mis-spellings are noted. The use of single and double quotation marks in the correspondence has been standardized to English practice. In typing, both Eliot and Hayward at times used capitals instead of underlining for italicization or quotation marks. These are represented by small capitals, to avoid over-emphasis.

Other references:

Gallup   *T. S. Eliot: A Bibliography*, by Donald Gallup, second, revised edition, 1969

Grover Smith   *T. S. Eliot's Poetry and Plays: A Study in Sources and Meaning*, by Grover Smith, Jun., University of Chicago Press, 1956

Quatre Quatuors   *Quatre Quatuors*, Editions du Seuil, Paris, 1950. Translation of *Four Quartets* with notes by John Hayward, by Pierre Leyris. Quotations are from Hayward's notes (in English) in King's College Library, Cambridge

Tate   *T. S. Eliot: The Man and his Work*, essays collected and edited by Allen Tate, *Sewanee Review*, Jan.-Mar. 1966, reprinted by Chatto and Windus, London, 1967. Page references are to the London edition

PART ONE

CHAPTER I

The Documents in the Case

The minute changes made in their compositions by eminent
authors are always a matter of both curiosity & instruction to literary
men, however trifling and unimportant they may appear to block-
heads. EDMOND MALONE[1]

Any who share Malone's curiosity over changes made by eminent authors
in the process of composition can hardly anywhere find more to gratify their
curiosity than is to be found in the material that has survived from Eliot's
work on *Four Quartets*. Manuscript and typed drafts display both major,
substantial changes and minute alterations in phrases, words, and pointing;
and, up to the very last moment, in corrected proofs, he can be seen changing
his mind, sometimes finding a new word, sometimes reverting to a word he
had earlier rejected but now found more satisfactory than its substitute. In
addition to the surviving drafts, there is a mass of other information about
the progress of the poem. In correspondence Eliot discussed words and
phrases, explained his meaning or gave a reference, justified a choice of one
word rather than another, proposed various alterations before making a
choice, and accepted or rejected suggestions. Taken together the drafts
and the correspondence allow us to see his mind moving towards his final
text, give information about the sources and the concerns that lay behind
the poem, and clarify the poet's intentions.

One reason for the abundance of material and information about *Four
Quartets* is that Eliot, who was often evasive in comments on his earlier
poetry, was never evasive about *Four Quartets*. He was willing to talk about
the poem and to give direct answers to questions. In speaking of it he never
employed the defensive irony that marks so many of his references to *The
Waste Land*. He never suggested that he did not himself know 'what he
meant' and that a reader's guess was as good as the author's. If asked to
explain a reference he did so. The poet who refused to divulge whether Pipit
was 'a little girl, an inamorata, a female relative, or an old nurse'[2] was quite

---

[1] See James M. Osborn, *John Dryden: Some Biographical Facts and Problems* (revised edition,
University of Florida Press, Gainesville, 1965), 147.

[2] Eliot's own summary, in a letter to me, of the debate on 'A Cooking Egg' in *Essays in Criticism*
(January and July 1953) which he thought touched 'the nadir of critical futility . . . so far as my own
work is concerned'.

ready to say which shrine 'on the promontory' he had in mind and what places he had thought of as being 'the world's end'.

In his *Paris Review* interview with Donald Hall, Eliot agreed that there had been a 'general tendency' in his work, even in his poems, to 'move from a narrower to a larger audience'. He thought there were two elements in this:

> One is that I think that writing plays (that is *Murder in the Cathedral* and *The Family Reunion*) made a difference to the writing of the *Four Quartets*. I think that it led to a greater simplification of language and to speaking in a way which is more like conversing with your reader. I see the later *Quartets* as being much simpler and easier to understand than *The Waste Land* and 'Ash Wednesday'. Sometimes the thing I am trying to say, the subject matter, may be difficult, but it seems to me that I am saying it in a simpler way.
>
> The other element that enters into it, I think, is just experience and maturity. I think that in the early poems it was a question of not being able to—of having more to say than one knew how to say, and having something one wanted to put into words and rhythm which one didn't have the command of words and rhythm to put in a way immediately apprehensible.
>
> That type of obscurity comes when a poet is still at the stage of learning how to use language. You have to say the thing the difficult way. The only alternative is not saying it at all, at that stage. By the time of the *Four Quartets*, I couldn't have written in the style of *The Waste Land*. In *The Waste Land*, I wasn't even bothering whether I understood what I was saying.[3]

Eliot assented to his interviewer's asking him whether he felt the *Four Quartets* was his 'best work', adding 'I'd like to feel that they get better as they go on. The second is better than the first, the third is better than the second, and the fourth is the best of all.'[4] This expression of satisfaction is unparalleled in Eliot's comments on his own work. A critic need not accept his judgement; but it explains his readiness to discuss the poem. Further, the strongly autobiographical element in all his poetry appears undisguised in *Four Quartets*; but the painful and deeply troubling experiences which lie behind the earlier poetry, and to which he could not give direct expression, were now in the past. The questions that *Four Quartets* provokes are not

---

[3] *Writers at Work: the Paris Review Interviews*, Second Series (New York, 1965), 104–5.

[4] Although Eliot was less satisfied when he wrote to John Hayward sending him a proof copy of *Four Quartets*, he took the same view that the poems 'got better' as they went on: 'Going through them again, I am depressed by a certain imprecision of word and phrase, especially in Burnt Norton but also in East Coker: my only solace is that I *do* think the writing improves toward the latter part of the book.' (Letter of 12 June 1944, EHC.) Eliot's twice expressed view that *The Dry Salvages* improves on its predecessors explodes Donald Davie's extraordinary suggestion that the 'badness' of the poem was deliberate. His article, 'T. S. Eliot: the End of an Era', first printed in *Twentieth Century* (1956), has been given unfortunately wide currency in Bernard Bergonzi's Casebook on *Four Quartets* (1969).

painful. It is a confessional poem, but not in the same sense as *Ash Wednesday* is a confessional poem.

A second reason for the abundance of material on *Four Quartets* is the circumstances in which the poem came to completion. There is comparatively little material available for a study of *Burnt Norton*, written during 1935 in peace time; but with the war the circle of Eliot's friends was broken. Correspondence had to take the place of conversation and drafts had to be sent by post and commented on by letter.[5] The most important of these friends was John Hayward, scholar, bibliographer, and collector. His friendship with Eliot developed during the thirties and he constituted himself in some measure 'Keeper of the Eliot Archive'. Eliot himself had from the beginning preserved many of his manuscripts and typed drafts. In 1922, along with the drafts of *The Waste Land*, he sent to Quinn a notebook containing his early poems, many of them unpublished, all carefully dated either at the time of copying, or by the addition of dates to poems copied earlier. He also included typed drafts of some of the poems in his 1920 volume. Hayward collected such material systematically and dated it carefully. He bound up with his drafts of the *Four Quartets* relevant letters from Eliot, supplying dates on the drafts and dates for letters from Eliot which had not been dated by the writer. All this material, plus Eliot's correspondence with him, he bequeathed to the Library of King's College, Cambridge.[6]

Since Eliot acknowledged his indebtedness to John Hayward's criticisms, some account of him and of their friendship seems required here.[7] John Davy Hayward was born 2 February 1905. He was the son of a distinguished surgeon living at Wimbledon. He suffered from a progressively crippling congenital disease: facio-humero-scapular muscular dystrophy.[8] This causes

---

[5] Eliot's habit of trying out his poems on his friends is well known. Mr. Simon Nowell-Smith has sent me a jotting he found among the papers of William Plomer, which must refer to a reading of *East Coker*. Virginia Woolf was in London in the middle of February and again at the end of the month in 1940, according to the Appendix to Quentin Bell, *Virginia Woolf*, vol. ii (1972):

> Leonard said that when Tom Eliot was living in Emperor's Gate ('surrounded by curates') he sent the Woolves a typescript of one of his longer poems (I think one of the *Four Quartets*) and sent copies to Mary Hutchinson and McKnight Kauffer. He invited them all to read it critically and then assemble and make their opinions known to him. Whatever Mary Hutchinson and Kauffer said he dismissed as of no interest, but when it was Virginia's turn she said she thought too many lines ended with a present participle. 'That's a *good* criticism, Virginia', he said. Leonard remarked sardonically that, all the same, 'Tom only made one or two alterations'. Rodmell, 28 January 1965.

[6] Under the terms of Hayward's will Eliot's letters are reserved until the year 2000. I quote from them by courtesy of the literary executor, Mrs. Valerie Eliot.

[7] This account is based on the obituary in the King's College *Annual Report*, the memorial number of *The Book Collector* (Winter, 1965), information from John Hayward's sister, Mrs. Oakeley, information from the Eliot-Hayward Correspondence, and personal knowledge.

[8] Dr. Henry Oakeley of St. Thomas's Hospital, John Hayward's nephew, kindly gave me this information, adding that the disease is 'the synonymous eponym of the limb-girdle muscular dystrophy of Landouzy-Dejerine. It may occur randomly, as a dominant or a recessive gene, but not usually as a sex-linked gene.'

the muscles gradually to wither away. The disease is one for which there is no cure and no alleviating or arresting treatment. The condition was first diagnosed when he was about ten years old, although it had been noticed earlier that he slept with his eyes only partially closed. After a round of visits to specialists and a week of prayer by the nuns of the neighbouring Ursuline convent, it had to be accepted that there was nothing that could be done, and, as the effects of the disease did not become marked for some time, he led a normal schoolboy's life at Gresham's School, Holt. He concentrated there on modern languages and developed a passion that became lifelong for France and French literature. As a schoolboy he was introduced to Saint-Évremond, whose letters he was to edit, and he spent a time of study in France before going up as an exhibitioner to King's College, Cambridge, in 1923.

By this time he was partially crippled; but he got about in a Baby Austin which gave him great pleasure, and he was not so severely handicapped as to be unable to enjoy the various activities of an intelligent and sociable undergraduate. He sang with musical societies in a fine bass voice and in later life would refer with pride to his performance as Fourth Madman in the Marlowe Society's production of *The Duchess of Malfi*. Intellectually he was formidably precocious. In addition to taking the English Tripos in 1925 and the second part of the Modern Languages Tripos in 1927, he produced in 1926 an edition of the works of Rochester.[9] Three years later there appeared his famous Nonesuch edition of the complete poems and selected prose of Donne: a book that was an astonishing feat for a young man of twenty-four. It showed skill and judgement as an editor, sense and sensibility in succinct comments, and genius as an anthologist able to extract the ore from the 'weighty bullion' of Donne's prose. It also revealed his extraordinary capacity for hard, long, and sustained work.

This remained with him until the end of his life. The long list of his publications only represents a fraction of the work he undertook. Partly this can be accounted for by the fact that for most of his life he was confined to his desk; partly, I imagine, he felt when young that his time might be short and developed the habit of filling every minute; but, chiefly, it was his determination to be independent and to make a career as a man of letters in defiance of a cruel fate that drove him on. As an undergraduate he spent his vacations in his parents' home in Wimbledon. The first of Eliot's letters to him (2 October 1925) is addressed to him there, thanking him for an invitation to address the Heretics and refusing with polite regrets. On going down from Cambridge he was unwilling to live with his parents and settled in

---

[9] It is fair to note that in later life he was rather embarrassed at references to this edition, not because of any *pudeur* at the subject-matter, but because he regretted his treatment of the canon and text. In spite of its defects, the edition was a remarkable feat for an undergraduate, being the earliest twentieth-century attempt to print all Rochester's works.

London. At first he lived with friends in Queen's Gate, moving, when they had to leave London, to a ground-floor room in Uffington House, Wetherby Gardens, and then to 22 Bina Gardens, S.W.7, where his flat became a rendezvous for literary friends and a port of call for many from abroad. His fondest boast, as Cyril Connolly recalled, was a message from Paul Valéry: '*Je n'oublierai jamais* Bina Gardens.' When he first came to London he was still able to walk, though with great difficulty, and to drive his car. But in two or three years he had to give this up and take to a wheel-chair. This did not prevent him from getting about London with extraordinary gaiety and courage, with the help of co-operative taxi-drivers, porters, and stalwart friends. He would give directions with wonderful unselfconsciousness and displayed a total absence of panic as he was heaved in and out of taxis or hoisted up and down stairs. He very rapidly settled down in London to the busy life of an all-round free-lance literary man: editing, anthologizing, reviewing, and advising editors and publishers, combining this with a full social life as a host and guest.

In September 1927, just down from Cambridge, he re-introduced himself to Eliot. Eliot's second letter to him (28 September 1927) is a cordial note, saying that he remembered him very well and would be glad to have some reviews from him. It ended with the invitation: 'Come to tea.' Hayward reviewed for the *Criterion* in 1928 and 1929 and his diary records lunching with Eliot. Their friendship began to grow close in 1930 when Hayward wrote in praise of *Ash Wednesday*, and Eliot replied with warmth.[10] By 1931 they were on Christian-name terms and in February of that year Eliot wrote him an unusually intimate letter on suffering. After Eliot's return from his visit to America of 1932-3, a group of friends, all directors of Faber and Faber, began to meet regularly at Bina Gardens. The host, John Hayward, was nicknamed Tarantula, being at the centre of the web and having, as all his friends were aware, considerable power of stinging; Eliot was the Elephant, presumably because he 'never forgot', though he retained his old nickname of Possum; Faber was the Coot, presumably because of his baldness; and Frank Morley, for reasons I cannot guess at, was the Whale or Leviathan. Much of the Eliot-Hayward Correspondence is concerned with this group, who shared a passion for Sherlock Holmes. A good deal of the correspondence would be obscure to anyone not acquainted with the Holmes cycle. A memorial of the meeting of these friends is *Noctes Binanianae*, a collection of their verses privately printed in 1939. A manuscript note in John Hayward's copy, now in King's College Library, explains the origins of this rare volume, of which only twenty-five copies were printed:

The following poetical effusions were composed for the most part in the summer and autumn of the year 1937. The pieces in French, Latin

[10] For a quotation from Eliot's letter, see p. 39.

and German belong to the latter part of the following year. The authors were Mr. Geoffrey Faber, Chairman of the publishing house of Faber and Faber Ltd., Mr. T. S. Eliot & Mr. F. V. Morley, partners in the same, & Mr. John Hayward, their friend.

Another memorial of Eliot's friendship with Hayward at this time is *Old Possum's Book of Practical Cats*, published in 1939 and in the illustrated edition a year later. Hayward's endearing dandyism is affectionately mocked by the gratitude expressed for the help of 'the Man in White Spats'.

Another manuscript note by Hayward, written against the title of Eliot's poem '*Abschied zur* Bina', records that he left Bina Gardens in November 1938. He moved to a flat in Chelsea. By this time the war clouds were gathering and it was obvious that London was going to be no place for someone who was by now totally immobile. In the autumn of 1939 Lord Rothschild found him alone in his flat with nobody to care for him and carried him off to Merton Hall, Cambridge, where he remained for the duration of the war. Morley went to America, to work for Harcourt Brace in New York. To keep himself in touch with friends and with literary affairs in London, he commissioned Hayward to write him a regular news-letter. 'Tarantula's Special News Service', written with Hayward's characteristically lively blend of news, gossip, and literary comment, contains much information about Eliot's varied activities during the war, his wretched health and the discomforts of his life, and reports on his progress with his poem. The letters are now in the Library of King's College, along with the Hayward bequest.[11]

At some time before the outbreak of the war Eliot gave Hayward a typescript of *Burnt Norton*. It is the copy sent to the printer containing corrections and directions for printing. It is authenticated by a manuscript note in Eliot's hand: '"Burnt Norton" / printer's copy, / from the T. S. Eliot bequest / to John Hayward Esq.' Hayward had this handsomely bound up. In a letter written 23 June 1940 Eliot reported to Hayward that he had found the drafts of *East Coker*.

> I can now report that I have discovered the early drafts of 'East Coker', and as there are five copies all of which appear to have different alterations, I might as well send you the lot. There is also the proof from the N.E.W. authenticated by a letter from Mairet. There was no ms. except of section IV, and that I gave to Hugh Walpole to try to sell for the Red Cross.

Hayward replied on 27 June:

> Thank you very much indeed for sending the drafts of the poem, which have been carefully placed with the Archives (the most important of which I've got here) for safe keeping. Or rather, they will be as soon as Mr. Gray has bound them together to match 'Burnt Norton'.[12]

[11] They are referred to as HMC (Hayward–Morley Correspondence).　　　[12] EHC.

The volume bound up by Hayward contains a sheet on which two snapshots of East Coker taken by Eliot have been mounted, followed by four typed drafts (D1, D2, D3, D4), a final typed draft (D5),[13] which has been marked with directions to the printer, the first proof, with Eliot's corrections, and the first printing of the poem in the *New English Weekly* (Supplement), Easter 1940. On a final sheet there is mounted a poem headed '1904–1940' by Sir Robert Vansittart. Whether Eliot sent this poem to Hayward with the drafts, or whether Hayward had it bound in as expressive of their feelings in the tragic summer of 1940, it is impossible to say. Both men, as lovers of France, would have shared Vansittart's grief that the *Entente Cordiale* had ended

In sorry separation at Bordeaux.

The poem is not a distinguished one, but its presence bound up with drafts of *East Coker* is a moving reminder of the circumstances in which Eliot's poem was first read.[14]

The first four drafts consist of two typescripts, each with its carbon. D2 was sent to a friend and has a few pencilled comments by him. D3 is the draft which was sent to Hayward. His letter of comment is not extant; but a letter from Eliot, of 27 February 1940, thanking Hayward for his 'prompt comment on E. Coker', and expressing gratitude to him for 'encouraging me to believe that the poem is worth the trouble', makes clear what Hayward's criticisms, queries, and suggestions were.[15] All the points that Eliot replies to are marked in D3 in pencil by a light underlining and a pencil cross in the margin, and the word 'sickness', supplied in the margin against line 156, is in Hayward's hand. A reference in the same letter to 'Herbet' as making the same objection as Hayward had made identifies the reader of D2 as Herbert Read.

The manuscript of Part IV, which Eliot wrote that he had given to Hugh Walpole to sell for the Red Cross, is now in the possession of Dr. Donald Gallup. It consists of four leaves torn from a scribbling pad on which Eliot has jotted down the scheme for the four verses of the lyric.

Eliot gave Hayward only one draft of *The Dry Salvages*. Hayward kept the draft he had been sent and it is marked with his lightly pencilled queries and crosses in the margin. He bound up with this draft a letter from Eliot replying to his queries.[16] Dr. Munby extracted from the Eliot–Hayward Correspondence some relevant items and placed them within the covers of Hayward's volume. They are a sheet containing Hayward's queries and

[13] They are marked in pencil as 1, 2, 3, 4, 5 by Hayward.
[14] The Hayward–Morley Correspondence contains references to Vansittart in the summer of the following year, with the comment 'V. likes and admires Tom'.
[15] EHC.
[16] Eliot wrote in this letter, 4 January 1941, 'please keep the copy you have'.

comments; a photograph of the Dry Salvages sent to Eliot by his brother and sister-in-law with Christmas greeting; and a postcard sent by Charles Olson to Ezra Pound, St. Elizabeth Hospital, Washington, D.C., post-marked 14 June 1947, to which Eliot has attached a typewritten note.[17]

Four other drafts of *The Dry Salvages* Eliot gave to Magdalene College, Cambridge.[18] They are labelled by him 1st Draft, 2nd Draft, 3rd Draft, 4th Draft. The fourth draft (M4), which Eliot at first mistakenly labelled as the third, is heavily annotated in the neat, small hand of Geoffrey Faber. It is the same text as was sent to the printer. Eliot also gave to Magdalene College the first proof for the printing of the poem in the *New English Weekly*, dated 'Jan. 29'. This is very heavily corrected, partly in response to Faber's criticisms. Hayward's draft is a carbon of the second draft in Magdalene (M2). A carbon copy of the third draft (M3) is in the library of the Humanities Research Center at Austin, Texas.

The *Little Gidding* volume is by far the richest of the Hayward volumes. It has five drafts, which are bound to face each other to facilitate comparison. They are identified by Hayward as 'First Draft', 'First Revision', 'Second Revision', 'Second Complete Draft', and 'Final Recension'. Hayward has dated each draft. The drafts are followed by the *New English Weekly* 'First Proof', on which Eliot has written 'Corrected T.S.E. 28. ix. 42', and by the *New English Weekly* text. Hayward's letter commenting at some length on the first draft is extant in the Eliot-Hayward Correspondence.[19] Eliot's reply to it, as well as nine further letters replying to comments and criticisms on the later drafts, is bound up with the drafts. Hayward's letters, to which these are replies, are not extant, but their gist can be deduced from his pencilled markings on the drafts and from Eliot's replies.

In addition to the five drafts that Eliot sent to Hayward, there are thirteen typescripts of all or parts of *Little Gidding* in the library of Magdalene College, Cambridge. By sorting, these can be put in sequence and related to the Hayward drafts. With the exception of the first revision of Parts II and III, the Hayward drafts are carbons of which the top copies are at Magdalene.[20] These Eliot worked on, retyping from them, and working on the retypings. Thus, while the Hayward drafts are fair copies, the Magdalene typescripts are working papers. Many are scrawled with suggestions and queries, crossings out, and reversions to what had been crossed out; and in retyping Eliot made alterations as he typed.[21] As he

---

[17] See p. 34.

[18] The first three drafts are typed by Eliot. The fourth is the carbon copy of a professionally typed typescript, presumably the carbon of the copy sent to the printer.

[19] The first draft and Hayward's letter commenting on it are printed in Appendix A, pp. 225-36.

[20] The 'First Revision' of Parts II and III sent to Hayward is a top copy. The carbon of this, on orange flimsy paper, is at Magdalene.

[21] See pp. 153-4 for descriptions of the typescripts arranged in a chronological sequence with Hayward's drafts.

wrote when sending the second complete draft to Hayward on 2 September 1942:

> I think that it is much easier to judge of changes when you have a fresh copy incorporating them, and moreover I find it advisable, as did Virginia, to type out anything again and again. Each time I find something that I had previously overlooked and this time I think I have picked up two points which neither you nor I noticed.

These eighteen typescripts by no means exhaust the available material for a study of the growth of *Little Gidding*. As well as the typed drafts, Eliot gave to Magdalene College the remains of a cheap, little scribbling pad, along with some loose leaves from two, or probably three, other pads. These humble objects contain manuscript schemes and drafts for parts of *The Dry Salvages* and for most of *Little Gidding*. The first leaves, well over half the original pad, have been torn out neatly along the line of the perforations; the following leaves have been torn out roughly, leaving irregular stubs, and only the last nine leaves are still in place on the pad. I have to thank Professor J. A. W. Bennett, Librarian of Magdalene College, and the neat and skilful fingers of his son, Piers Bennett, for making a reconstruction of the main pad, by matching the irregular stubs against the irregular tops of the torn-out leaves. In addition there are four loose leaves from a much smaller pad, four from a pad of almost the same size as the first but with slightly different ruling, and two others which may be leaves torn out from the beginning of the main pad along the line of the perforations or, more probably, belong to a different one.[22]

Finally, the Hayward Bequest contains inscribed copies of all four of the poems as published separately, that of *The Dry Salvages* being inscribed: 'for John Hayward whose suggestions somewhat altered this poem T. S. Eliot 10. ix. 41'; the proof of the first edition of *Little Gidding* with corrections, and the proof of the first (English) edition of *Four Quartets*, with corrections.

The American edition of *Four Quartets* contained a prefatory note acknowledging Hayward's help: 'I wish to acknowledge a particular debt to Mr. John Hayward for general criticism and specific suggestions during the composition of these poems. T.S.E.' In the English edition the note was modified, Eliot remembering that others had had a share; but Hayward was still singled out: 'I wish to acknowledge my obligation to friends for their criticism, and particularly to Mr. John Hayward for improvements of phrase and construction.' Hayward wrote to acknowledge his copy of the New York edition on 4 June 1943. Characteristically, he could not help mingling

[22] For a full description of this manuscript material and a reconstruction of the pad, see Appendix B, pp. 237-9.

with his gratification at Eliot's tribute to his assistance his dismay at the
wretched appearance of the volume:

> I must tell you that a copy of FOUR QUARTETS has arrived from New
> York & that I am more pleased and touched by your note of acknowledge-
> ment than I can say. It is far the biggest compliment that I've ever had
> paid me and I am correspondingly delighted. I suppose you've seen the
> book. It is, to judge by my copy, the most wretchedly printed book pro-
> duced by a firm with all the resources of modern typography I've seen.
> Even the amateur Hogarth *Waste Land* is hardly worse. The choice of
> type on cover and for the text is deplorable. The inking is bad. The lay-
> out is contemptible—just look at the spacing of the textual paragraphs.
> The imposition is appalling. Poor Frank! I take it that he is in no way
> responsible; but it is a horrible reflection of American taste and tech-
> nique. It is all the more deplorable because poetry gains much by being
> skilfully presented to the reader's eye. . . . However, these faults cannot
> abate my pleasure in having a copy of a wollum I've looked forward to
> for so long—or my gratitude to you for associating me with it. . . .[23]

As early as 1935, when Eliot was without a home, Hayward suggested
that they should set up house together. Eliot was at this time unwilling for
personal reasons to make any permanent arrangements. By the end of the
war his circumstances had changed and the plan was revived. They found
a flat at 19 Carlyle Mansions, Cheyne Walk, Chelsea, and Eliot moved into
it in February 1946, Hayward joining him a month later. The ménage lasted
until Eliot's marriage in January 1957.[24] Hayward's large and beautiful
room, with its massive desk in the window overlooking the river, became,
as John Carter wrote, 'a place of pilgrimage for every bibliophile visitor to
London', as well as a place where trembling authors had to take their place
on 'the stool of repentance' to have their errors and infelicities of expression
pointed out. It was also a place where friends would come for those long
tea-time visits he loved, when he gratified his taste for imparting and
imbibing gossip, as well as for showing some recently acquired treasure or
mocking at some monstrous piece of ignorance and folly. The story of his
life from the ending of the war until his death in 1965 does not belong to this
book. Perhaps the most striking of his achievements were his share in the
National Book League's Exhibition of first and early editions of English
poetry, in 1947, for which he produced an illustrated catalogue, variously
described as 'famous', 'exemplary', and as 'a permanent landmark in bibliographical scholarship'; his work in organizing the exhibition *Le Livre*

---

[23] EHC.
[24] A witty and affectionate account of the joint household and of the housekeepers who reigned over
it was given by Christopher Sykes in *The Book Collector* (Winter, 1965).

Anglais at the Bibliothèque Nationale in 1951; and, most of all, his brilliant editorship of *The Book Collector* from its first appearance in the spring of 1952 until his death. But he himself once said to me that, of all his activities, his share in bringing *Four Quartets* to its conclusion gave him the most satisfaction.

CHAPTER 2

The Growth of *Four Quartets*

The little girl had the makings of a poet in her who, being told
to be sure of her meaning before she spoke, said: 'How can I know
what I think till I see what I say.' GRAHAM WALLAS, *The Art of
Thought*.

Like *The Waste Land*, 'The Hollow Men', and *Ash Wednesday*, *Four
Quartets* was not planned but grew. It became in the writing the unified
poem which the four separate poems finally came together to create. In an
interview with John Lehmann in 1953,[1] and again in an interview with me
in 1958,[2] and in the long *Paris Review* interview with Donald Hall in 1963
Eliot explained how *Burnt Norton* began 'with bits that had to be cut out of
Murder in the Cathedral', adding 'I learned in *Murder in the Cathedral* that
it's no use putting in nice lines that you think are good poetry if they don't
get the action on at all'. In reply to the consequent question whether any of
the minor poems were actually sections cut out of longer works, since there
are two that sound like 'The Hollow Men',[3] Eliot answered that those were
'the preliminary sketches'. The interviewer went on: 'You seem often to
have written poems in sections. Did they begin as separate poems? I am
thinking of "Ash Wednesday" in particular.' Eliot replied:

> Yes, like 'The Hollow Men', it originated out of separate poems. As
> I recall, one or two early drafts of parts of 'Ash Wednesday' appeared in
> *Commerce* and elsewhere. Then gradually I came to see it as a sequence.
> That's one way in which my mind does seem to have worked throughout
> the years poetically—doing things separately and then seeing the possi-
> bility of fusing them together, altering them, and making a kind of whole
> of them.

Later in the same interview, having been asked whether it was true that he
'composed on the typewriter', Eliot replied:

> Partly on the typewriter. A great deal of my new play, *The Elder*

---

[1] *New York Times Book Review*, 29 November 1953.   [2] *Sunday Times*, 21 September 1958.
[3] 'Eyes that last I saw in tears' and 'The wind sprang up at four o'clock', printed as 'Minor Poems'
in *Collected Poems 1909–1935* (1936), were first published, along with what became the third part of 'The
Hollow Men', as 'Doris's Dream Songs' in *Chapbook*, 39 (November 1924).

Statesman, was produced in pencil and paper, very roughly. Then I typed it myself first before my wife got to work on it. In typing myself I make alterations, very considerable ones.[4] But whether I write or type, composition of any length, a play for example, means for me regular hours, say ten to one. I found that three hours a day is about all I can do of actual composing. I could do polishing perhaps later.

The interviewer asked whether any of the non-dramatic works were thus written 'on schedule', adding 'Perhaps the *Four Quartets*?' To which Eliot answered that 'The *Quartets* were not on schedule':

> Of course the first one was written in '35, but the three which were written during the war were more in fits and starts. In 1939 if there hadn't been a war I would probably have tried to write another play. . . . The form of the *Quartets* fitted in very nicely to the conditions under which I was writing, or could write at all. I could write them in sections and I didn't have to have quite the same continuity; it didn't matter if a day or two elapsed when I did not write, as they frequently did, while I did war jobs.[5]

The circumstances of the war acted in rather the same way as overwork and personal distress operated on the composition of *The Waste Land* and its successors, 'The Hollow Men' and *Ash Wednesday*. These were none of them works which Eliot sat down to write, as a play has to be written, to a coherent scheme with regard to 'continuity'. Nor were they written by a man who could work to a regular schedule of work, 'regular hours, say ten to one'. For all his devotion to the theatre, and his lifelong ambition to write a great play, in writing plays Eliot was writing, to some extent, against the bent of his natural genius. Essentially he was an explorer, not an expounder, discovering truth of feeling, and the truths that feelings point to, in the process of exploration; and discovering also connexions and new meanings in poems or passages of poems written without thought of their coherence with each other.

Murder in the Cathedral was commissioned by George Bell, Bishop of Chichester, in the summer of 1934, and was first performed in the Chapter House of Canterbury Cathedral on 15 June 1935. During the autumn and winter of 1934 Eliot was drafting and discussing his play with Martin Browne, who Eliot had insisted was to produce it, and with Ashley Dukes and Rupert Doone, who were anxious to have it for their new venture of poetic plays at the Mercury Theatre. By 25 February 1935 Eliot was able to send Martin Browne, who was at York for a winter repertory season, 'the revised version of Act I', asking him for 'criticism from a dramatic point of view'. Browne obliged with a long letter, 2 March, to which Eliot replied

---

[4] The manuscript rough drafts and many typed drafts of *Little Gidding* show this process of composition with great clarity.

[5] *Writers and their Work: The Paris Review Interviews*, Second Series (New York, 1965), 99–101.

three days later. Browne's main complaint was that the act was too static. He also found the Tempters' speeches obscure and not sufficiently differentiated in their rhythms, and, among other suggestions, he wrote 'we need the reactions of Chorus and Priests' to the Tempters' speeches. Eliot's reply showed a certain amount of resistance: 'I don't deny that the play as you outline it would be a good play; it might be a better play than mine; but it wouldn't be MY play.' But he set to work to meet some of the detailed criticism. His efforts to do so can be seen in a typed draft which was sent to Miss Stella Mary Pearce, who was to design the clothes, some time shortly after 3 April when it was settled that she should be the designer. One suggestion that Eliot took up was that there should be comments by Chorus and Priests on the Tempters' speeches. He supplied interpolations for the Chorus and salvaged from his first rough draft a short passage which he gave to the first Priest after the exit of the first Tempter. To provide a comment from the second Priest, after the exit of the second Tempter, he wrote a passage of thirteen lines. These, with slight alterations in wording, became the opening paragraph of *Burnt Norton*.[6] As Martin Browne owns, 'All these additions turned out to be unnecessary: Eliot's play proved itself dramatically right as he conceived it.' But in this 'unnecessary' attempt to liven up Act I of *Murder in the Cathedral* there lies the germ of *Burnt Norton* and consequently of *Four Quartets*.[7]

Burnt Norton was then a poem that came quickly. It was written in the latter part of 1935 in an interval between the completion of *Murder in the Cathedral* and Eliot's beginning work on his new play, *The Family Reunion*, a draft of which was read to the Brownes in November 1937. Enigmatic and beautiful, it appeared as the last poem in the *Collected Poems 1909–1935*, which was published 2 April 1936, less than a year after Eliot had drafted the passage that was to provide it with its opening.

The first reference to *East Coker* is in a letter from John Hayward to Frank Morley, No. XI in 'Tarantula's Special News-Service', dated February 1940:

> I am relieved to hear that Tom has picked up his tablets again after all these months—almost a year—of silence. . . . He now writes to say that he is making a little progress with a new poem in succession to 'Burnt Norton'—the second of three quatuors—provisionally entitled 'East Coker', of which he has drafted the first two out of five sections. 'It may be quite worthless', he adds, 'because most of it looks to me like an

---

[6] See p. 39 for discussion of the passage which is printed on p. 82.

[7] See E. Martin Browne, *The Making of T. S. Eliot's Plays* (1969, reprinted with supplementary material 1970), 34–79 and particularly the Supplement to Chapter 2, 345–52. The author only discovered carbon copies of his correspondence with Eliot as his book was being published and shortly afterwards Mrs. Stella Mary Newton 'unearthed' the typed draft she had been sent, the only draft to contain the *Burnt Norton* passage. Mrs. Newton's draft is now in the McKeldin Library of the University of Maryland. Mrs. Valerie Eliot kindly supplied me with a typed copy of the passage in question.

imitation of myself, and, as for the rest, well, Blake and Clough keep on getting into it, and I have been trying to rub them out; I *have* got rid of the line 'The Archer's Bow and Taurus' ire', which, however, did not look quite so silly as all that in its context.'

Eliot must have worked very fast, since in his next letter, Letter XII, also dated February 1940, Hayward was able to report the completion of the poem:

> Well, the old master, Tom, polished off his poem more quickly than he expected or led me to expect, and a copy reached me for comment yesterday. He says 'You might keep it to yourself', but I don't think this applies to you, who, for this purpose, I count as myself. So, I will tell you that I think that this poem—'East Coker'—is prodigiously fine. Just over 200 lines in five sections. It has moved me a good deal more deeply than 'Burnt Norton' (of which it is a kind of sequel), one explanation of this being, perhaps, the outstanding beauty of the lyrical verses. It is also poignantly self-revealing—such confessions, for example, as: 'Leaving one still with the intolerable wrestle / With words and meanings'; or: 'So here I am, in the middle way, having had twenty years— / Twenty years, largely wasted, the years of *l'entre deux guerres*. . . .'

Hayward went on to quote further from Part V, ending 'Here is something to which to look forward with great expectation.' *East Coker* was printed in a Supplement to the *New English Weekly* Easter Number, 1940 on 21 March. The poem made an enormous impression, coming as it did at the dreariest moment of the war. Hayward wrote to Morley, Letter XVI, April 1940:

> Tom's 'East Coker' has been received with the greatest possible applause by the few people who knew, or who were told that it could be found in that obscure weekly in which Tom is interested. I wish it could be given a wider circulation without delay—that the world should not have to wait until it is incorporated in a new edition of his collected Poems. Is it possible that your Board would consider the idea of printing it separately in the manner of an outsize 'Ariel' poem? Tom, presumably, would say that if this is to be done at all, you should wait until you can print 'East Coker', 'Burnt Norton' and the two other pieces he has in mind to complete the series with, all together in one volume.

The Supplement had to be reprinted in May and June, and in September Hayward's suggestion of separate publication was taken up and the poem was published in pamphlet form by Faber and Faber at the price of one shilling.

Hayward's letter to Morley announcing that Eliot was at work on a 'new poem in succession to "Burnt Norton"—the second of three quatuors' shows that the poems were already conceived of as 'quartets'. More interesting is his reporting in February that Eliot was planning only two more poems on the model of *Burnt Norton*, while in April he speaks of Eliot having it in mind to complete the series by writing two more after *East Coker*. This confirms what Eliot stated more than once: that the notion of four poems based on the symbolism of the four elements and the four seasons, which seems so fundamental to the conception of *Four Quartets*, was a notion that came to him during the writing of *East Coker*. Professor Kristian Smidt reports that in 1948 Eliot told him that it was 'during the writing of *East Coker* that the whole sequence began to emerge, with the symbolism of the four seasons and the four elements. *Burnt Norton* then had to stand for spring in the sequence, though its imagery was perhaps more summery.'[8] It is rather strange that, announcing the arrival of *The Dry Salvages* on his desk on the following 1 January, Hayward referred to it as 'the third poem of Tom's trilogy'; but a note in the margin by Morley against Hayward's suggestion of separate publication of *East Coker* suggests that Morley had some doubt whether the sequence was to be three or four poems. It may be that Eliot had conceived the notion of four poems, but, while feeling pretty clear what material and experiences he would draw upon for the third, was doubtful whether he could find a place or experiences that could focus his meditation on Fire. That is to say, he might have wished to write four but felt certain only that he could write three. Another point of interest is Eliot's rueful confession that Blake and Clough kept 'getting into' *East Coker*. The influence of Blake and Clough, masters of the long line, is obvious when one reads it, particularly the reference to Clough, an example of the pervasiveness of Victorian poetry in Eliot. It now seems extraordinary that it has not been noted that the opening of Part V might have come straight out of *Amours de Voyage*. Finally, Hayward's letters show that *East Coker* was written at high speed. Letter XI, dated February 1940, reports that Eliot has 'drafted the first two out of five sections'; the completed poem must have been sent to Hayward well before the end of the month. His letter to Eliot with comments and criticisms is not extant, but Eliot's reply to it is dated 27 February. It must have been little more than a fortnight that elapsed between Eliot's telling Hayward he had drafted the first two parts and his sending him the completed draft.

[8] See *The Importance of Recognition* (Tromso, 1973), 34. Eliot wrote to the same effect to Professor William Matchett, at that time writing a senior undergraduate thesis at Swarthmore: 'The idea of the whole sequence emerged gradually. I should say during the composition of *East Coker*. Certainly by the time that poem was finished I envisaged the whole work as having four parts which gradually began to assume, perhaps only for convenience sake, a relation to the four seasons and the four elements. But certainly *Burnt Norton* at the time of writing was a solitary experiment, and I had nothing in mind for the next step.' (Letter of 19 January 1949 in the possession of Professor Matchett, who kindly sent me a copy.)

The Dry Salvages was similarly written at high speed. The first reference to it in Hayward's letters to Morley is in Letter XXVII, January 1941:

> The best possible beginning of another year was marked by the arrival on January 1st of the typescript of the first draft of the third poem of Tom's trilogy. No warning that it was even begun—which confirms what I said about the Master's ability to strike quickly once the iron is hot. It is a superb piece—finer, I think, than its predecessors. I attribute its excellence to the beauty of the marine imagery, which provides a haunting background to the recurrent 'Time Past—Time Present' theme. And you know, probably better than I do, with what nostalgic longing the sea affects Tom's sensibility. (Some of the great passages in his poetry—the end of 'Gerontion', the Phoenician sailor, 'Marina' &c. are evocations of the coast of New England and of white sails flying.)

Hayward then quotes the passage beginning 'The sea is the land's edge also' and the first and last verses of Part IV, going on:

> These small pieces may give you a foretaste of the whole.—(Perhaps you should keep them to yourself, for I don't know if Tom wishes to be quoted just yet; but I think you should know.) The tentative title is 'Dry Salvages'—which I don't care about overmuch. I think the title should be a proper name and complete the pattern begun by the titles of the two previous poems. I've suggested this with due deference.[9] I've urged him to complete the poem as soon as he possibly can, so that you may have the MS. without delay.

Hayward read the poem very quickly, for Eliot's reply to the sheet of queries Hayward sent him[10] is dated 4 January 1941. The first proof of the poem for its publication in the *New English Weekly*, which is heavily corrected, is dated by Eliot 'Jan. 29'. It was published there on 27 February 1941 and by Faber and Faber in pamphlet form on 4 September of that year. *Burnt Norton* had been published in the same format as *East Coker*, but with a green for its yellow cover, on 20 February 1941, so when *The Dry Salvages* was published, with its pale blue cover, in September the first three of the four poems were available in pamphlet form.

The history of the writing of *Little Gidding* is very different. One reason for the difficulty Eliot found in writing the fourth and concluding poem of his series was physical exhaustion brought about by the discomforts of life in wartime England and bombed London, and the varied activities he felt it his duty to undertake. There are many references in Hayward's letters to Morley and in Eliot's own letters to repeated feverish colds and bronchitis.

---

[9] For Hayward's amusing misunderstanding of the title and Eliot's explanation of it, see pp. 120-1.

[10] The sheet was found by Dr. Munby in the Eliot–Hayward Correspondence and placed by him in Hayward's bound volume containing the draft of *The Dry Salvages*.

In addition to these he was enduring one of the most painful and depressing features of late middle-age: teeth-extractions and the consequent struggle with dental plates. His conscience drove him, to Hayward's dismay, to involve himself in numberless time-consuming engagements. 'I think', wrote Hayward to Morley in February 1940, 'his good nature involves him too easily in unending social engagements—too many lunches, dinners, week-ends,—and in increasing committee work *viz.* vestry intrigues, Christian News-Letter conferences, Jordans Jamborees[11] &c. &c., all of which, combined with a somewhat unsettled domestic life . . . tend to leave him with too little time for his own work.' Early in the war Eliot joined J. H. Oldham in editing *The Christian News-Letter* and as 'joint-editor' wrote many whole numbers.[12] He was also involved in Archbishop Temple's Malvern Conference in January 1941. In addition to these specifically Christian activities, he worked for the British Council and for the Overseas Service of the BBC. In April 1942 he went for five weeks to Sweden with Bishop Bell, where, according to Hayward, he lectured for the British Council. It was on this visit, whose purpose was ostensibly to make contact with the Swedish Church, that Bishop Bell made contact with Hans Schönfeld and Dietrich Bonhoeffer who hoped through him to make approaches on behalf of an organized opposition to Hitler to the British Government. Beside these activities Eliot had accepted various literary engagements. On 4 July 1941 he wrote to Martin Browne, who had suggested a scheme for a new play to him:

> I am at present struggling to get on paper the fourth of my series of poems and that attempt, if successful, is likely to occupy my spare time for several weeks more. After that I have several prose engagements ahead of me: I have to revise my Shakespeare lectures to deliver again in Bristol in the autumn, and I have to prepare for the early spring a lecture in Glasgow and an address to the Classical Association. There is also another literary job, the arrangements of which are not quite settled, but which will take some time and must be finished this season.[13]

The other 'literary job' which had to be 'finished this season' was probably the selection from Kipling. Hayward wrote to Morley, Letter XXXVIII, August 1941: 'As a contribution to what he calls his war effort, he is preparing a selection of Kipling's verse to which he is to write a preface. This seems to me a somewhat queer assignment, though I suppose Kipling's verse must

---

[11] 'Jordans Jamborees' were meetings of the Moot, a group of friends who met two or three times a year from 1938 to 1947. A regular meeting place for their conferences was Old Jordans Hostel near Beaconsfield. An account of the Moot and of Eliot's part in its deliberations can be found in Roger Kojecky's *T. S. Eliot's Social Criticism* (1971). The society came to an end with the death of its leading spirit Karl Mannheim. Mr. Kojecky has a chapter on Eliot's 'War Jobs'.

[12] See Gallup, 459 a, b, c, 471, 479.

[13] See E. Martin Browne, op. cit., 157.

be regarded as a kind of stand-by for certain tastes in time of war—no matter what the time or which the war.' *A Choice of Kipling's Verse* must have been done at high speed. It was published on 11 December 1941. The Glasgow Lecture, 'The Music of Poetry' was delivered on 24 February 1942, and the address to the Classical Association, 'The Classics and the Man of Letters' on 15 April 1942.[14] Immediately after, Eliot left for Sweden with Bishop Bell. Hayward's distress at all these distractions from the completion of *Little Gidding* can well be understood; but anyone who lived through the first years of the war will also understand the compulsions that drove Eliot to exhaust himself in this way. As he wrote to Martin Browne, 20 October 1942, after he had completed *Little Gidding*, to tell him he had had to cancel a trip to Iceland for the British Council on doctor's orders:

> It is one thing to see what was best worth one's while doing, in a distant retrospect: but in the midst of what is going on now, it is hard, when you sit down at a desk, to feel confident that morning after morning spent fiddling with words and rhythms is a justified activity—especially as there is never any certainty that the whole thing won't have to be scrapped. And on the other hand, external or public activity is more of a drug than is this solitary toil which often seems so pointless.[15]

But perhaps the fundamental reason for the difficulty that Eliot found in writing *Little Gidding*, beyond physical exhaustion and the distraction of other duties, was his realization that the three earlier poems that he had written so easily had grown into a unity, and that the fourth and concluding poem was to be more than a fourth poem of the same kind as its predecessors. It had to gather up the earlier ones and be the crown and conclusion of the series. *Little Gidding* asked for more deliberation and conscious purpose than *East Coker*, conceived of as simply another poem on the model of *Burnt Norton*, or even than *The Dry Salvages*.

All the same Eliot seems to have set to work soon after the publication of *The Dry Salvages* and by June 1941 he had made a 'rough, preliminary draft'. Hayward wrote to Morley, Letter XXXV, June 1941:

> Tom has been here for the long week-end of Whitsun. He was in bed again last week with his fourth feverish cold of 1940-1 and I regret to say that he looks with [it] very haggard and washed-out and dispirited. For the last two afternoons he has simply gone to sleep on my bed. . . . Like you, I wish there was more chance than there seems to be of his new book of poems appearing before the late autumn. He says he *has* written to you to explain why you can't have it sooner. He wants if possible to complete the cycle with a fourth poem—Earth, Air, Water, *Fire*—and has got as far as making a rough, preliminary draft. I take it as a good sign that he is

---

[14] See Gallup.   [15] E. Martin Browne, op. cit., 158.

dissatisfied with what he has already done. We discussed all this over the dregs of the inestimable hair-oil,[16] which I had husbanded against his coming.

By the beginning of July Eliot had completed a 'first rough draft'. Hayward wrote to Morley, Letter XXXVII, July 1941:

> Tom has completed the first rough draft of the final poem of the Quadrologue—'Little Gidding'. I received a copy yesterday with the injunction that I was not to make any comments on it in its present un-completed form. But even in this state, unfinished and unpolished, it strikes me no less forcibly than 'The Dry Salvages' did at first sight. I hope to be able to report progress later. Meanwhile Tom is exercised to know whether to print the poem separately and postpone the publication of the quartet until the autumn of 1942, or to publish the poems as a collection this autumn with 'Little Gidding' as the novelty to attract purchasers who already possess the earlier pieces. My own view is that in these times the less delay the better in bringing into the world the kind of work that consolidates one's faith in the continuity of thought and sensibility when heaven is falling and earth's foundations fail.

On the first draft of the poem, which Hayward received 7 July, Eliot wrote 'first draft for consideration. / Not sure.' Eliot's letter accompanying it and expressing his misgivings has not survived. Hayward was busy at an annual task, correcting papers for the Cambridge Local Examinations. Eliot wrote to him on 14 July acknowledging 'a brief epistle or demi-letter' and saying he would not 'in the annual circumstances, expect a proper letter for a fort-night or so'. After some details about his own affairs, including dental extractions, the necessity of writing a preface and 'half a dozen blurbs (this is a slow and painful task)', and work on the selection from Kipling, he went on:

> I have pushed on with Little Gidding, and enclose provisional results. You will observe that I have had to remove 'cancel' from Part I, because I wanted the word further on: I have also had some trouble with the words 'broken' and 'common'. There may be others I have overlooked. My suspicions about the poem are partly due to the fact that as it is written to complete a series, and not solely for itself, it may be too much from the head and may show signs of flagging. That is a dilemma. Anyway, how-ever doubtful of it I have been, I had to finish it somehow or it would have stuck in my crop and prevented me from turning to other tasks. The question is not so much whether it is as good as the others (I am pretty sure it is not) but whether it is good enough to keep company with them

---

[16] At this period almost any form of alcoholic liquid, however nauseating, was priceless.

to complete the shape. If the problem is more than one of improving details, it will have to go into storage for some time to come.[17]

The 'provisional results' that Eliot enclosed would seem to have been merely notes on two passages to be cut and on the words mentioned. Hayward entered corrections on his draft. Having finished marking and reporting on his '700 vile little bodies' Hayward was at last free to give his mind to *Little Gidding* and wrote at length on 1 August 1941:

> I am sure that whatever critical faculty I possess is momentarily distempered by the work it has [had] to do in the past fortnight. So please bear this [in] mind as you read the following observations. . . . I agree with you that the poem, in the *unfinished and unpolished* state in which you have allowed me to see it, is not quite up to the standard of the others in the group. But it does not seem to me to be, potentially, inferior to them; nor do I think that it shows signs of fatigue or that, as you seem to fear, it is merely a mechanical exercise; I am sure that it only requires to be revised and perhaps rewritten in certain passages, to which I shall refer, to be brought to perfection as the culminating poem of the series. I need hardly say that it has given me intense satisfaction and pleasure to read it even in its unfinished condition. As a whole, it has moved me no less than its predecessors. My general impression is that Parts I, II, V and all but the first paragraph of Part III are all right. Part IV seems to me to break down.

Hayward went on to enlarge on the weakness of the opening of Part III and of Part IV as a whole and then proceeded to 'a few niggling details'.[18] He ended:

> These are all my comments. Please let me know if they are helpful in the slightest degree; but more particularly, assure me that you intend to add 'LITTLE GIDDING' to the group. You *must not* discard it just because you have the natural misgivings of a poet bringing a movement to its close—misgivings doubtless exacerbated by the miserable time you have had with your teeth. I sympathize with you most keenly and closely, but hope that your general health will greatly benefit from now on.

The letter is signed with 'Love from y[r.] old creating critick: John'.[19] Eliot, who was away at a conference at Oxford, did not reply at once, and Hayward wrote to Morley, Letter XXXVIII, August 1941:

> I have not yet had an acknowledgement of my observations on the poem 'Little Gidding'. He [Eliot] fears that it is uninspired and mechanically repetitive of the earlier poems in the group, but says that he must get

[17] EHC.
[18] Hayward's detailed criticisms will be found in the commentary on the passages in question.
[19] EHC.

it off his mind before he can turn to other work. I don't accept this view, though there are, I think, weaknesses in sections of the poem which could be remedied without much labour. As a whole it seems to me to [be] a fine confirmation of the old tag—*finis coronat opus*.

Eliot's reply (dated 5 August 1941 by Hayward) expresses gratitude for Hayward's 'sapient and useful, and certainly encouraging letter'. He writes that he had been 'particularly unhappy about Part II' and then replies to various of the 'niggling details'. He summed up his general feeling by saying: 'The defect of the whole poem, I feel, is the lack of some acute personal reminiscence (never to be explicated, of course, but to give power from well below the surface) and I can *perhaps* supply this in Part II. It is whatever is wrong with Part IV that bothers me most.' After a comment on some more 'niggling details', he added 'I think I will leave the thing alone for a week or two longer'.

The 'week or two longer' turned out to be much longer. Eliot seems to have done a little tinkering on receipt of Hayward's letter and in response to comments from Geoffrey Faber, to whom, as his letter to Hayward reveals, he had shown his first draft. But in October 1941 Hayward wrote to Morley (Letter XLIII) 'It was only after repeated reminders, (for I had done sufficient work on the poem to justify them) that I learnt that the final section of the tetralogy—"Little Gidding"—had been shelved until December when he intends to work over it again. I'm afraid it will be a long time—too long—before you get the completed work.' In Letter XLIX, February 1942, he wrote 'no news of *Little Gidding* which was to have been taken in hand again in December'; and, in Letter LII, April 1942: 'He [Tom] assured me that he intended to complete the last of the poems of the tetralogy as soon as he got back from Sweden, where he is now spending three weeks lecturing for the British Council.' In Letter LVII, July 1942, Hayward writes:

> You ask me about Tom's progress with 'Little Gidding'. I have nothing to report. . . . My tactful feelers about the poem's progress have been without effect and, as from past experience I know that he finds the summer an unfruitful time for composition, I fear that he may not get down to it again before the autumn. He was, as I think I told you in an earlier letter, dissatisfied with the first draft, considering it to be generally inferior to the first three poems which, by the way, have been as highly praised over here as anything he has written and have more than rehabilitated his current poetic reputation which was in some danger of becoming temporarily dimmed by the vapourings of the young. I think myself that he underrates the fundamental strength and beauty of the poem in its first crystallization, though I believe he is at any rate half persuaded now that it is better material to work on than he had at first supposed. But I see his point in allowing the material to ferment and mature. His chief fear

was that he was simply repeating himself and so running into the risk of producing an elegant parody of the earlier poems in the group.

On 21 July, Hayward had news, though not very encouraging. Eliot wrote 'I have put Part II of Little Gidding into the melting pot, but nothing has solidified yet'.[20] Five days later he wrote again, mentioning that 'This film titan and Little Gidding are both on my mind'.[21] The 'film titan' was George Hoellering, whose film of *Murder in the Cathedral* was not finally produced until 1951. He was urging Eliot to write extra dialogue for the film version of the play. This seems to have sparked off Eliot's determination to finish *Little Gidding*, for on 17 August he wrote to Hayward:

> My life is being plagued by the Napoleon of Cinematography, Mr. Hoellering, and I shall know no peace until I have written my bits of text for him; but obstinately my mind refuses to do its best at the rechauffé of Murder, until it has eased itself of Little Gidding. So here is a recension[22] of Part II, which seemed to me the centre of weakness. Even if this is better than the first version (which I assume you still have by you) it may not be good enough; and if it is not good enough (minor improvements, of course, apart) then I fear the poem must simply be allowed to disintegrate. If this is fundamentally all right, then an improvement of the other sections does not seem to be beyond the bounds of possibility. I submit it (together with another edition of Part III) with some trepidation.[23]

Having resumed work after his year-long break, while the poem fermented and matured, Eliot proceeded rapidly. Ten days later, 27 August, he wrote to thank Hayward for his letter acknowledging and commenting upon the revision of Parts II and III:

> Your letter of the 20th instant gave me great satisfaction and, I hope, assistance, but I will not burden Miss Melton with a communication of compliments which can be deferred to a later occasion as this letter is merely to send you another revision of Part II and a slightly altered I and V and to answer a few questions implied or expressed. You will find that in several cases I have followed your advice negatively if not positively.

On 2 September he sent to Hayward a second complete draft in which he had solved the problem of the unsatisfactory Part IV of the first draft, as well as meeting some of Hayward's criticisms: 'According to my figures', he wrote, 'I have altered nine passages according to your suggestions, rejected six suggestions and remained uncertain about two others. As for Part IV, which

---

[20] EHC. [21] EHC.
[22] Spelt 'rescension'. Eliot's occasional mis-spellings, such as this and 'moalars' for 'molars' in a letter on his dental troubles, show an odd failure to recognize derivations. [23] EHC.

I now include, I am as yet too close to this new version to be able to tell whether it is fundamentally right or fundamentally wrong.' Next day he wrote again to discuss final publication and the title of the whole volume:

Although the poem, if and when ready, will appear by itself as usual, it is not too early to consider the title of the collection of the four poems, which might be published in the U.S.A. first if Frank wants to do it next year. The title I have always had in mind for it was KENSINGTON QUARTETS. I have had a fancy to have Kensington in it. How great is the resistance to 'quartets'? I am aware of general objections to these musical analogies: there was a period when people were writing long poems and calling them, with no excuse, 'symphonies' (J. Gould Fletcher even did a 'Symphony in Blue' I think, thus achieving a greater *confusion des genres*). But I should like to indicate that these poems are all in a particular set form which I have elaborated, and the word 'quartet' does seem to me to start people on the right tack for understanding them ('sonata' in any case is *too* musical). It suggests to me the notion of making a poem by weaving in together three or four superficially unrelated themes: the 'poem' being the degree of success in making a new whole out of them.

On 7 September Hayward wrote jubilantly to Morley,[24] thanking him for P. G. Wodehouse's *Money in the Bank* and lamenting that the 'Master' is 'losing his old cunning and shows signs of having written himself out'.

It is a relief to turn to one greater than he, to the Noble Possum, who, far from having written himself out, seems to me to be now writing at the height of his powers. The present tense is the bearer of long-awaited good tidings. LITTLE GIDDING is almost completed. After almost exactly a year's delay, Tom took it in hand about three weeks ago and since then I have received three revisions and expect to receive the final text this week.

Hayward goes on to quote Eliot's letter, with its suggestion of 'Kensington Quartets' as the title for the volume. He writes that he is 'inclined to support the use of "quartets"', referring to Eliot's explanation of his reasons for wanting to use the word, but goes on:

I feel very much more doubtful about 'Kensington'. I can understand Tom's wanting to associate the tetralogy with the Gloucester Road Period,[25] as anyone must who knows how thoroughly he took on its protective colouring. But, as you know, very few people are aware of his connection with the district; originally a hide-out, his address was always carefully guarded. I'm afraid that 'Kensington' is too likely to suggest to the uninformed majority of readers a private joke of some kind or an

[24] The letter is not numbered. The commissioned series seems to have come to an end.
[25] For the connexion of the 'Gloucester Road Period' with *Four Quartets*, see pp. 32-3.

allusive jibe at all that 'Kensington' is commonly thought to stand for—
the decaying rentier, frayed respectability and the keeping up of out-
moded conventions. (You remember me in Bina Gardens?)

Hayward relayed his objections to Eliot, who, in a postscript to a letter of
9 September, said laconically: 'I see your objection to KENSINGTON.' Rather
oddly, Morley approved. One wonders what he thought American readers
would make of the name. His reasons for liking 'Kensington' are not clear
from Hayward's reply to a letter from him, 8 November 1942:

> Your remarks, which I shall pass on to Tom, have slightly shaken my
> opinion about the general title—Kensington Quartets. I must brood
> about this. Your plea for its retention, or at least for its reconsideration,
> made from a distance where such problems are more sharply seen in
> perspective, is very persuasive.

In letters of 7 and 9 September Eliot continued to discuss points raised by
Hayward until on 19 September he sent him the 'Final Recension'. 'You
will observe', he writes, 'that I have accepted "waning dusk", and my
observation conducted during the last few days leads me to believe that it
will wear. I cannot find words to express a proper manifestation of my
gratitude for your invaluable assistance.' He went on:

> You will also find that I have made other alterations in the same
> section. . . . I am still unsatisfied. . . . But I think that there is a point
> beyond which one cannot go without sacrifice of meaning to euphony,
> and I think I have nearly reached it. Anyway, I have sent a copy to
> Mairet for the N.E.W., and I propose to give a copy of the enclosed
> to Dick.[26] There will still be the possibility for alterations in proof. But to
> spend much more time over this poem might be dangerous. After a time
> one loses the original feeling of the impulse, and then it is no longer safe
> to alter. It is time to close the chapter.[27]

The copy sent to Mairet for printing in the *New English Weekly* was not
the 'Final Recension'. The text set up by the printer is a text lying between
the 'Second Complete Draft' sent to Hayward on 2 September and the
'Final Recension' of 19 September. Eliot corrected it to the readings of the
latter in proof. But there were still some footnotes to the chapter he had
declared 'closed'. The first proof, corrected by Eliot 28 September, makes
yet further alterations. A note to Hayward of 22 September reports one of
these to him and letters of 2 October and 10 October show that up to the
last moment they were discussing minute details of wording. The poem was

---

[26] Richard de la Mare, a director of Faber and Faber.
[27] Coleridge would have agreed: 'Poetry, like schoolboys, by too frequent and severe corrections,
may be cowed into Dullness' (*Notebooks*, ed. K. Coburn, 1957, i. 28).

published in the *New English Weekly* on 15 October and appeared in pamphlet form on 1 December.

Four Quartets appeared first in America. It was published 11 May 1943. There were two impressions of this book. The first was so badly printed that all but 788 of its 4,165 copies were destroyed. The entire impression would have been destroyed but for the need to meet the publication date in order to keep copyright.[28] The English edition did not appear until 31 October 1944. Its dust-jacket bore a rather misleading statement:

> The four poems which make up this volume have all appeared separately. . . . The author, however, has always intended them to be published as one volume, and to be judged as a single work.[29]

As this story of the writing of the poem has shown, no such scheme was in Eliot's mind when he wrote *Burnt Norton*, nor, the war having made the writing of another play seem futile, when he 'picked up his tablets again' and wrote *East Coker*. In *Four Quartets*, the Greek epigraphs were printed on the reverse of the table of Contents, as if applying to the whole sequence. In the *Collected Poems 1909–1962*, they reverted to being epigraphs to *Burnt Norton* alone. Mrs. Valerie Eliot tells me that Eliot had thought of prefixing as epigraph to the volume as a whole an observation by a modern philosopher, Mr. Roker of the Fleet prison: 'What a rum thing time is, ain't it, Neddy?'[30]

---

[28] Gallup, 72.

[29] The statement on the dust-cover is quoted by Gallup, 73. A confused memory of it led to an error in my *The Art of T. S. Eliot* (1949), 46, corrected in the preface to the sixth impression (1968).

[30] *The Pickwick Papers*, chapter 42.

CHAPTER 3

The Sources of *Four Quartets*

'Autumn weather': I do not get the significance of *autumn*? It struck me as having a greater significance than you may have intended it to have. HAYWARD to ELIOT, on a line in the first draft of *Little Gidding*, 1 August 1941.

'Autumn weather' only because it *was* autumn weather—it is supposed to be an *early* air raid—and to throw back to Figlia che piange (but not having my Poems by me I may be misquoting) but with less point than the children in the appletree meaning to tie up New Hampshire and Burnt Norton (with a touch, as I discovered in the train, of 'They' which I don't think I had read for 30 years, but the quotation from E. B. Browning has always stuck in my head, and that may be due to 'They' rather than to the Bardess herself). ELIOT to HAYWARD, 5 August 1941.

. . . between the usual subjects of poetry and 'devotional' verse there is a very important field still very unexplored by modern poets—the experience of man in search of God, and trying to explain to himself his intenser human feelings in terms of the divine goal . . . ELIOT to WILLIAM FORCE STEAD, 9 August 1930.

The major sources of *Four Quartets* are experiences:—'it *was* autumn.' The experiences are both actual experiences and experiences revived in memory. These last come back with a new power as their meaning is apprehended:

> We had the experience but missed the meaning,
> And approach to the meaning restores the experience
> In a different form, beyond any meaning
> We can assign to happiness.

The experiences, whether actual or remembered, arise from, or are connected with, certain places recreated as they were at certain seasons. The places and seasons give rise to memories of what has been and what might have been: the actualities and the potentialities of the past. Although the egoism of a continual use of the first person singular is avoided, sometimes by a rather uneasy use of 'we' or 'one', there is no attempt to disguise the personal and confessional nature of the poems. They are meditations on the experiences of a lifetime, and any study of their sources must begin with biography. But a poet's biography is much more than the narrative of events in his life. In exploring his past to discover its meaning, Eliot also explored his past as a poet. He deliberately echoed himself, 'throwing back' to '*La Figlia che Piange*', 'meaning to tie up' 'New Hampshire' and *Burnt Norton*, and insisting on retaining a phrase that Hayward queried in *Little Gidding* 'because I was using a line from the Family Reunion'.[1] Since a poet's life is not merely the record of events, or the history of his development as a poet, but also the record of what fed his imagination and stimulated his intelligence in his reading, the poems are soaked in literary reminiscences. Some of these, like the memory of Kipling's story 'They', not read for thirty years, or of Mrs. Browning's poem, read some twenty-five years before and I suspect not re-read, lie buried very deep and were recalled unconsciously.[2]

The poems are poems of experience and are not built upon literary sources. There is a certain amount of direct quotation: the passage from Sir Thomas Elyot, given in archaic spelling, and the passage from St. John of the Cross in *East Coker*; the quotation from the *Bhagavad-Gita* in *The Dry Salvages*, ascribed within the poem—'So Krishna, as when he admonished Arjuna'; the quotations from Julian of Norwich and from *The Cloud of Unknowing*, the first identified as a quotation by the capitalized archaic form 'Behovely' and the second by being set as a separate line. These are quotations and they are not made ironically, as are so many of the quotations in Eliot's earlier poetry. It is, therefore, of little importance to our understanding to look up the original passage. Its sense has not been twisted and there is no clash between the original and the context in which Eliot has set it. But, as with minor reminiscences and echoes, although recognition may not assist understanding, it enriches our reading of the poems. They come to us as the fruit of a lifetime's reading and thinking, carrying memories of events and of persons, and of phrases that echoed and sang in Eliot's mind.[3] Thus, when Eliot substituted 'the spectre of a Rose' for 'the ghost of a Rose' in the third section of *Little Gidding*, he built into his poem a memory of one of the great aesthetic experiences of his early years in London, preferring the recollection of Nijinsky's famous leap in the ballet of that name to an echo of Sir Thomas Browne, which he did not in fact recognize until Hayward drew his attention to it.[4] To know this adds nothing to our appreciation of the force of the repudiation of reactionary sentiment in politics in the poem, and the reference may be regarded as a delightful irrelevance. The echo of *Hamlet*, when the 'familiar compound ghost' in *Little Gidding* 'faded on the blowing of the horn', does not equate this mysterious figure with the

---

[1] See p. 223.

[2] In this chapter only the major sources will be dealt with. Occasional allusions and reminiscences are given in the commentary to the poems.

[3] Whoever indulges in spotting allusions and echoes in Eliot's poems must remember Eliot's own comments on Livingston Lowes's *The Road to Xanadu* and on 'the criticism of explanation by origins'. See 'The Frontiers of Criticism' (University of Minnesota Press, 1956), reprinted in *On Poetry and Poets* (1957), 107–8.   [4] See p. 202.

ghost of Hamlet's father, who 'faded on the crowing of the cock'. This was an allusion that Eliot made deliberately and was unwilling to lose in order to meet an objection by Hayward.[5] It might be said to have propriety, enforcing the purgatorial meaning of an encounter that at the beginning appears infernal. But the first scene of *Hamlet* was a scene that Eliot picked out for special praise and analysis in his lecture on 'Poetry and Drama',[6] and I suspect that it was more the beauty of Shakespeare's phrase than its appropriateness that made him want to echo it in *Little Gidding*. Sometimes the original sense of a passage that Eliot echoes is amusingly at odds with the sense in which he uses it. Thus, in this same Dantean passage he substituted for a line that Hayward queried the line as it stands in the final version: 'Where you must move in measure, like a dancer', writing that he rather liked 'the suggestion of the new line which carries some reminder of a line, I think it is about Mark Antony'. Actually the phrase is used by, and not about, Antony, who says contemptuously of Octavius that he 'at Philippi kept / His sword e'en like a dancer'. Sometimes, though rather rarely, the recognition of a source that Eliot had in mind can guide us to an interpretation. A striking example is the obvious reminiscence of Gide's *Le Prométhée mal enchaîné* in the manuscript notes for Part IV of *East Coker*.[7] But literary echoes and allusions are less fundamental as sources than places, times, and seasons, and, above all, the circumstances in which the Quartets were written.

i. BURNT NORTON

In October 1932 Eliot left England for six months in order to deliver the Charles Eliot Norton lectures at his old university, Harvard, and the Page-Barbour lectures at the University of Virginia. He had not visited the United States since 1915, when he had gone over for a brief visit to tell his parents of his marriage and of his decision to settle in England. He said good-bye to his wife at Southampton, and while he was in America instructed his solicitor to begin proceedings for a legal separation. He returned thus to his native country and to his old university, where, but for the accident of the outbreak of war in 1914, he might have made a career as a Professor of Philosophy, knowing that a whole, long, distressful chapter of his life had come to an end. It was a time of painful reflection on what had been and on what might have been, of memories intertwined with the scenes of his childhood and young manhood. It was a time for taking up old contacts and old friendships. It was also a time when the future was uncertain and had somehow to be built on the failure of the past.

---

[5] See p. 196.

[6] *Poetry and Drama* (Harvard University Press, 1951), reprinted in *On Poetry and Poets* (1957), 72–88. Eliot explained in the preface to *On Poetry and Poets* that the passage analysing the first scene in *Hamlet* was taken from a lecture given at Edinburgh University before the war.   [7] See pp. 43–6.

When Eliot returned to England at the end of June 1933, he was met by Frank Morley, the Morleys having offered him a home in their seventeenth-century farmhouse, Pikes Farm, in the 'angle where Surrey, Kent, Sussex come together'. Having settled him in 'Uncle Tom's Cabin', the Morleys went off for a holiday, leaving him alone. 'There are times', writes Morley,

> when a man may feel as if he had come to pieces, and at the same time is standing in the road inspecting the parts, and wondering what sort of a machine it will make if he can put it together again. It was fourteen years later, and speaking of his own feelings, that Tom used that figure of speech, and I fancy there was a stress upon the pronoun; he had to draw upon *his* sources, for reconstruction, perhaps involving redirection, of the machine he knew about better than any outside mechanic.[8]

By the time that the Morleys returned, on 7 August, Eliot was in touch with other friends and had begun discussing collaboration in the pageant-play *The Rock*. On 22 September Martin Browne offered him the commission. He left Pikes Farm at the end of 1933 and moved to a guest-house in Court-field Gardens, South Kensington, wanting to be in touch with the theatre in London. As soon as he settled there he began to attend St. Stephen's, Gloucester Road, and very soon became Vicar's Warden. After only a few months at Courtfield Gardens he moved into the clergy-house at St. Stephen's, and in 1937 he and the Vicar, the Rev. Eric Cheetham, moved to a flat at 11 Emperor's Gate. He was here when the war broke out and enrolled as a Warden at the local Air-Raid Wardens' Post. Both at the clergy-house and at Emperor's Gate, Eliot led an independent life, living and eating alone and making much use of his club, the Oxford and Cambridge University Club. He was also frequently away, lecturing, or at conferences, or visiting friends in the country. During the Kensington period his main interest was in the theatre, first with the two commissioned plays, *The Rock*, produced in May 1934, and *Murder in the Cathedral*, produced in 1935. Between these and his most ambitious effort in the theatre, *The Family Reunion*, produced in March 1939, he brought out the *Collected Poems 1909–1935*. The volume included the slender stock of poems written since the publication of *Ash Wednesday* in 1930: the two 'Coriolan' poems, the 'Five-finger Exercises', the 'Landscapes', and the 'Lines for an Old Man', adding to these, as the final poem in the volume, *Burnt Norton*. Eliot remained at Emperor's Gate for the first year of the war and was there when he wrote *East Coker*. Hayward, writing to Morley in February 1940, refers to Eliot's 'somewhat unsettled domestic life' at Emperor's Gate 'where the pipes froze and then burst, so that for a week he had to shave and shit at the Club, and consequently caught a cold.'[9] In November 1940 Eliot transferred to the

---

8 Frank Morley, 'A Few Recollections of Eliot'; see Tate, 106.
9 HMC, Letter XI, February 1940. The winter of 1939-40 was extremely severe and there was

country. He joined the household of Mrs. Mirrlees, mother of his friend Hope Mirrlees, at Shamley Green, near Guildford. He would come up to London for two days a week, usually from Tuesday to Thursday, sleeping either at the Fabers' house in Hampstead, or in their flat above the office in Russell Square, or at his club; and he took his share of fire-watching at the firm. It was at Shamley Green that he wrote *The Dry Salvages* and *Little Gidding*. But one can understand why, in spite of this, he thought of calling the four poems 'Kensington Quartets'. Their roots lay in the Kensington period in which having 'come to pieces' he had to 'reconstruct the machine'; and, in solitude, had to live with his memories 'and make them into something new'.[10]

After the publication of *Ash Wednesday*, dedicated 'To my Wife', in 1930, Eliot endured one of his recurrent periods of sterility. It has been reported that, in some prefatory remarks before a recital of some passages from *The Rock*, he said that 'he had doubted during the two or three years before *The Rock* was composed, whether he had any more poetry to write'.[11] Having published 'Triumphal March' as an Ariel Poem in 1931 and 'Difficulties of a Statesman' in *Commerce* (Winter 1931-2), he abandoned the plan of writing a political sequence 'Coriolan'. He fell back on 'Five-finger Exercises', which were published in the *Criterion* in January 1933. These, as has been pointed out, are 'exercises in pure allusiveness and imitation; they give a clue to certain "music" in the *Quartets*'.[12] They are woven out of a tissue of allusions loosely associated in the poet's mind and point forward to one mode of allusion in *Four Quartets*. After his return from America Eliot published two short poems under the title 'Words for Music': 'New Hampshire' and 'Virginia'. They were printed in the *Virginia Quarterly Review* in April 1934 and, privately, for distribution by the author in February 1935. In October 1935 'Rannoch, by Glencoe' appeared in the *New English Weekly*, and two further short landscape poems, 'Usk' and 'Cape Ann', were privately printed in the same month for distribution by the author at Christmas. All five poems appeared in *Collected Poems 1909-1935* under the heading 'Landscapes'.[13]

As the title 'Words for Music', used for the first two, shows, the five 'Landscapes' carry further the musical patterning and musical allusiveness

a fuel crisis. I well remember a pupil of mine at Birmingham University ploughing through February fog and snow with a bucket of coal affectionately inscribed 'Flowers for Teacher'.

[10] cf. Reilly in *The Cocktail Party* (p. 165):

> You will have to live with these memories and make them
> Into something new. Only by acceptance
> Of the past will you alter its meaning.

[11] Herbert Howarth, *Notes on Some Figures behind T. S. Eliot* (1965), 294.

[12] Grover Smith, 250.

[13] An exception to the general critical neglect of the 'Landscapes' is an excellent article by Erik Arne Hansen, 'T. S. Eliot's "Landscapes"', *English Studies*, August 1969.

of the 'Five-finger Exercises'. But here, themes and images, rather than literary echoes, are treated musically, and the musical reverie arises out of the memory of a place and a time. Eliot gave his last Harvard lecture on 31 March 1933, and at the end of April went to lecture at the University of Virginia. By 15 May he was back in Cambridge, 'having just returned from Virginia'. On 12 June, just before he sailed back to England, he was staying at Mountain View House, Randolph, New Hampshire.[14] In November 1933 Frank Morley and Donald Brace took him to Scotland. They were 'met by George Blake at Glasgow to drive over Rannoch Moor and to and from Inverness'.[15] Over eighteen months later, at the end of July 1935, the Morleys picked him up at Chipping Campden, where he was staying, to take him on a trip to Wales. The final poem, 'Cape Ann', however, was not inspired by a recent visit but by much earlier memories. In the Eliot–Hayward Correspondence there is a postcard of a crudely coloured representation of the statue of *Notre Dame de Bon Secours*, with a sailing-boat in place of the infant Saviour carried on her left arm, from Gloucester, Massachusetts. The card is addressed to Ezra Pound in St. Elizabeth Hospital, and is postmarked 14 June 1947. It reads: 'E. P. et famille: Here is my Lady that Possum stole. Best dead Madonna this side Atlantic. . . . Yrs. Olson.' A typewritten note by Eliot is attached to the card:

Mr. Olson or Olsen is in error. I have never returned to Cape Ann or to Gloucester Mass. since 1915. Presumably this statue tops the façade of the R.C. Church in Gloucester. I do not think it was there in my time: anyway I had no knowledge of its existence when I wrote 'The Dry Salvages'. But I thought that there *ought* to be a shrine of the B.V.M. at the harbour mouth of a fishing port. The church on which *this* statue stands is probably in the town itself.[16]

T.S.E. 14.8.47.

The 'Landscapes' strikingly anticipate the themes of *Four Quartets*, beginning with the children's voices in 'New Hampshire' and passing through the stillness and heat of 'Virginia', and the legendary and historical themes of 'Usk' and 'Rannoch, by Glencoe' to the memories of a New England boyhood in 'Cape Ann'. But, as has been said, when Eliot wrote *Burnt Norton* in the autumn of 1935 he had no idea that he was inaugurating a sequence of poems which would, unlike the 'Landscapes', combine to make a single unified work. *Burnt Norton* arose out of what would seem to have been the happiest experiences of the Kensington period: his visits

---

[14] The dates are from letters addressed to Mrs. Perkins, who was to be Eliot's hostess in the following summers at Chipping Campden. Eliot's letters to her are in the possession of Dr. Donald Gallup, who kindly allowed me to see them and to take relevant notes.

[15] Frank Morley, 'A Few Recollections of Eliot'; see Tate, 107.

[16] Eliot's suggestion is correct.

to Dr. and Mrs. Carroll Perkins in the house they rented for three summers at Chipping Campden in Gloucestershire. Dr. Carroll Perkins, Minister of the Unitarian King's Chapel in Boston, was a Doctor of Divinity. His wife was the aunt of one of Eliot's old friends from his Harvard days, Emily Hale.[17] He had first met her through his cousin, Eleanor Hinkley, who was still living in the Hinkley family home in Cambridge when Eliot returned to Harvard. Whether he had known the Perkins as a young man or not, he was made welcome to their home and often dined there.

A year after Eliot's return to England the Perkins came over to spend the summer. On 18 June 1934 Eliot wrote that he rejoiced that Mrs. Perkins had 'found a satisfactory habitation', adding 'Chipping Campden is only a name to me, but I know its reputation; the Cotswolds I only know from the motor route between Oxford and Hereford'. He was soon invited for a week-end and on 30 July wrote to express his gratitude. He was at Campden again early in September and on 4 September wrote 'My weekend, apart from being twice the length, gave me still more happiness than the previous one'. The Perkins did not go home until late in the year, for the Visitors Book at the Deanery of Chichester records the signatures of Dr. and Mrs. Perkins, Miss Emily Hale, who gives her address as Scripps College, California, and T. S. Eliot on 30 November 1934.[18] This suggests that Miss Hale had been staying with her uncle and aunt throughout the summer of 1934. In the following spring the Perkins returned to Campden. Eliot wrote on Easter Sunday 1935 to thank Mrs. Perkins for a happy week-end and his letter makes clear that Miss Hale was there again. He was at Campden once more in May, in July, when the Morleys called to pick him up for the trip to Wales, at the beginning of September, and again at the end of the month. On this last visit he wrote a poem 'A Valedictory/Forbidding Mourning: to the Lady of the House', dated 28 September 1935,[19] and on 30 September he wrote to Mrs. Perkins to express his gratitude: 'I want now to thank you for all your kindness and sweetness to me during the past two summers. . . . I had come to feel "at home" in Campden in a way in which I had not felt at home for some twenty-one years, anywhere.' The Perkins did not come over in 1936, for in a letter, dated 10 July 1936, Eliot wrote to Mrs. Perkins to give her news and commented on the bad weather in England that spring, adding 'The only really lovely day that I remember was a day at the end of May when I motored over from Cambridge to Little Gidding'. By April 1937 they had arrived again at Campden and this seems to have been their last visit. In addition to her other gifts, Mrs. Perkins was a skilled gardener. Eliot's poem to her is largely concerned with her talents

---

[17] Emily Hale was a Lecturer in Drama at various American colleges. She died in 1969.

[18] Information from Mrs. E. E. Duncan-Jones, daughter-in-law of the then Dean of Chichester.

[19] There is a fair copy of the poem in the Bodleian Library and a typed draft is preserved with the letters to Mrs. Perkins.

as a gardener, mentioning, among other flowers she 'trimmed and trained and sprayed' *Clematis jackmanii*. Anyone who has wrestled with this most rampant and lovely of climbing plants can appreciate the precision of Eliot's verbs in the lines

> Will the sunflower turn to us, will the clematis
> Stray down, bend to us; tendril and spray
> Clutch and cling?

In a letter written much later, 11 July 1948, Eliot wrote to tell her the good news that the famous gardens at Hidcote Manor, a few miles north of Campden, were being taken over by the National Trust and preserved. 'I was particularly pleased', he adds, 'because I remember so well your taking me there; and of all the gardens I have visited (mostly with you) that is the one I loved the best.' It was probably by Mrs. Perkins's suggestion that Eliot one afternoon visited the garden at Burnt Norton, although his companion on this occasion was not Mrs. Perkins but her niece, Emily Hale.[20]

The house and garden of Burnt Norton stand on the edge of the Cotswold escarpment overlooking the Vale of Evesham and a distant view of the Malvern and Welsh hills. The name is derived from a sensational and horrible event in the 1740s. Sir William Keyte, a Warwickshire landowner of some standing and fortune, having taken as mistress his wife's maid, abandoned his wife and younger children and, with his mistress and two elder sons, set up house in the large seventeenth-century farmhouse which is the core of the present house. He proceeded to ruin himself by building a grandiose mansion and laying out gardens, and by indulging in reckless hospitality and riotous living. After some years of dissipation his fancy turned to a young dairy-maid. His former mistress left him, as did his sons. After he had for a week drunk himself into a state of frenzy, his new mistress, terrified, deserted him also. Left alone, ruined, and desperate with drink, he set fire to the mansion he had built and was burnt alive. Only some bones, two or three keys, and a gold watch remained of him.[21] No trace remains today of the mansion Keyte built; the name that commemorates the catastrophe is attached to the estate and to the original farmhouse which through the centuries has been expanded into an attractive family house. It came into the possession of the Ryder family, the Earls of Harrowby, some ten years after the disaster. The present Lord Harrowby lived there for many years before moving to the main seat of the family at Sandon Hall

---

[20] I suspect, although I have no evidence, that Emily Hale was with Eliot on his short holiday in New Hampshire just before his return to England in 1933. 'New Hampshire' and *Burnt Norton* are obviously very closely linked in feeling as well as in imagery.

[21] The story caused an immense sensation locally and there are many contemporary accounts. The tale is told by Richard Graves in *The Spiritual Quixote* (1773), Book x, chapters xxvi–xxviii, with many improving comments by Wildgoose.

in Staffordshire; but he tells me that the house was let for a short period in the middle 1930s at the time when Eliot visited the garden.[22]

The sinister history that lies behind the name Burnt Norton has no bearing on Eliot's poem and the story seems to have faded from local memory. I give it only because many people are puzzled by the name. In August 1942 I published an article on 'The Recent Poetry of T. S. Eliot' in *New Writing and Daylight* edited by John Lehmann.[23] The article had been written soon after the appearance of *The Dry Salvages*, when there was no indication that a further poem would follow. As both East Coker and the Dry Salvages were associated with Eliot's personal history, I rashly suggested that he had perhaps some family connexion with Burnt Norton also. Mr. Lehmann sent a copy of the issue of *New Writing and Daylight* to Eliot, who replied to him with some kind words which Mr. Lehmann passed on to me. After the publication of *Little Gidding* I wrote to Eliot, wishing to let him know how much these poems had meant to me, and told him that Mr. Lehmann had passed on his remarks. He replied saying my article had given him 'great pleasure' and went on

> Only two very small points occur to me. The first is that I have no such connection as you suggest with the house at Burnt Norton. It would not be worth while mentioning this except that it seemed to me to make a difference to the feeling that it should be merely a deserted house and garden wandered into without knowing anything whatsoever about the history of the house or who had lived in it. . . . The other point is that I have never read or even heard of the book by Herman Melville.[24] American critics and professors have been so excited about Melville in the last ten years or so that they naturally take for granted that everybody has read all of his books, but I imagine that bell buoys sound very much the same the world over.

Like Milton's Paradise, the garden of Burnt Norton is a place set apart from the rest of the world on a high hill. It is far from easy to find, and is approached by a long private road and over a cattle-grid. Passing behind the house, which like the garden overlooks the valley, one comes into a place where nothing can be heard but bird-song. Leaning over the balustrade,

[22] Of recent years the house has been let to a school. It is now being put into order for residence by the present Lord Sandon and the garden will thus revert to the beauty it had when Eliot and his companion visited it and which it had retained on my first visits there. My account is based on photographs taken on my first visit which was in 1952 and ignores the alterations made by the school.

[23] The article was revised to include *Little Gidding* and appeared as '*Four Quartets*: A Commentary' in *Penguin New Writing* (1946) and in *T. S. Eliot: A Study of his Writings by Several Hands*, edited by B. Rajan (1947). With some further revision it became the last chapter of my book *The Art of T. S. Eliot* (1949).

[24] I had suggested, with acknowledgement to Henry Reed, that a passage from *Redburn* lay behind the close of Part I of *The Dry Salvages*. Eliot mistakenly assumed Henry Reed was an American Professor of that name.

one looks down over a steep wooded slope. Near the house, overlooking the garden, is a huge tree with 'figured leaves' on which, as Eliot did, one can watch the light at play. Passing through the rose-garden, down some steps, one comes upon a clipped hedge surrounding a large expanse of grass. Coming out of this, through a gap in the hedge, one finds oneself standing above a grassy bank and looking down on a big rectangular drained pool, 'dry concrete, brown-edged'. Behind it is a smaller semi-circular drained pool, with a pediment in the middle where perhaps there once stood a statue and from which a fountain may have played.[25] Beyond the grass in which the pools are set there is a path sloping up through trees to a yew alley running the upper length of the garden, chill and cold, where no birds sing. The garden, in its stillness and beauty and strange remoteness from the world, stirred in Eliot profound memories and brought together disparate experiences and literary echoes.

Another actual experience besides the visit to the garden at Burnt Norton came into the poem. In September 1933 Eliot paid the first of many visits to Kelham, the headquarters of the Society of the Sacred Mission, an Anglican religious community dedicated to theological education. He visited Kelham frequently up to the outbreak of war. Mr. George Every, who was at that time a member of the community, became a close personal friend and remained in touch with Eliot through the war and after. Mr. Every tells me that on a hot day in the summer of 1935 when Eliot was staying at Kelham he saw a kingfisher on a stream running into the Trent by Averham Church over the fields from Kelham and that there is a yew in the churchyard there and masses of clematis in the rectory garden next to the churchyard by the same stream. He was not himself with Eliot but two students who were told him how excited Eliot was at seeing the bird. Mr. Every remembers a conversation about *Burnt Norton* in the year after when Eliot spoke of this summer scene. I had always a little wondered at the sudden irruption of a kingfisher into *Burnt Norton*, for the garden is so remote from any water—unlike the garden of Appleton House surrounded by meadows that flood from the river on which

> The modest *Halcyon* comes in sight
> Flying betwixt the Day and Night.

Mr. Every's reminiscence provides another instance of the presence of actual and recent experience in *Four Quartets*. Just as, when asked for the

---

[25] There is a third drained pool in the garden of Burnt Norton, a circular pool among the trees. There was some correspondence in *The Listener* (14 and 28 January 1971), following a BBC. *Omnibus* programme on Eliot, as to which pool it was that was 'filled with water out of sunlight'. The producer of the programme thought the circular pool in the trees best fitted the description of the garden in the poem. But the words 'to look down into the drained pool' exactly fit the surprise of coming through the gap in the hedge and seeing these empty pools at one's feet. My photographs taken in 1952 show that the trees around the pools have grown considerably by now. No doubt when Eliot was there in 1935 the pools were less shaded from sunlight even than they were then.

significance of 'autumn', Eliot replied simply 'it *was* autumn', so here he might answer those who look for mystical meanings in the sunflower, clematis, and kingfisher: 'There *was* a clematis; there *was* a kingfisher.'[26]

In his interview with John Lehmann, Eliot mentioned three sources for *Burnt Norton*: 'Bits left over from *Murder in the Cathedral*', the beginning of *Alice in Wonderland*, and the garden.[27] The opening paragraph of *Burnt Norton*, except for minor alterations in wording, was originally written as a comment by the Second Priest after the exit of the Second Tempter. The second of Thomas's temptations is the temptation to attempt to retrace one's steps, to try to go back to the moment when a choice was made and make a different choice:

> The Chancellorship that you resigned
> When you were made Archbishop—that was a mistake
> On your part—still may be regained.

The temptation is presented to Thomas in political terms. The Priest's comment generalizes on 'what might have been and what has been' but then gives the comment a profoundly personal application, applying it to the most poignant 'might have been' of our lives: the rose-garden at the end of 'the passage which we did not take'. As for *Alice in Wonderland*, it was already there in the bit cut from *Murder in the Cathedral*, where Alice hears the footsteps of the White Rabbit in the passage and cannot get through the door into the rose-garden. In a letter to John Hayward, 5 August 1941, quoted in the heading to this chapter, Eliot mentioned three other sources: his own poem 'New Hampshire'; Kipling's story 'They', which he only recognized as having contributed to his poem when, five years later, he was re-reading Kipling for his anthology *A Choice of Kipling's Verse*; and a 'quotation from E. B. Browning'. Many years ago I suggested that 'the image of laughing hidden children may have been caught from Rudyard Kipling's story "They"', since the children in that story are both "what might have been and what has been", appearing to those who have lost their children in the house of a blind woman who has never borne a child'.[28]

---

[26] We should perhaps be a little chary of giving too defined a symbolic meaning to the 'chill fingers of yew' in *Burnt Norton* and the yew tree at the close of *The Dry Salvages*. There *are* yew trees in the garden as there *is* a yew tree in the churchyard where Eliot hoped to be buried at East Coker. A letter from Eliot to Hayward (27 April 1930, EHC), replying to Hayward's appreciation of *Ash Wednesday*, suggests that even the yews there have more a personal than a deliberately symbolic meaning: 'Perhaps the yew does not mean so much as you suppose. It happened to occur in two or three dreams—one was a dream of "the boarhound between the yew trees"; and that's all I know about it.' This dream gave Eliot the beautiful enigmatic line in *Animula*:

> Pray for Floret, by the boarhound slain between the yew trees.

Of course, the question of what symbolic meaning yew trees had for Eliot at this time to make him dream of them remains a legitimate question.

[27] *New York Times Book Review*, 29 November 1953.

[28] *The Art of T. S. Eliot* (1949), 160. The suggestion was made to me by Henry Reed.

I did not, however, identify the song that the blind woman in the story sings as being a quotation from a poem by Elizabeth Barrett Browning. As Eliot did so, though Kipling does not mention its author, the poem must have been known to him[29] and I think unconsciously it contributed more than Kipling's story to *Burnt Norton*. The poem is a long one, called 'The Lost Bower', and the blind woman sings the first four lines of the opening stanza, the narrator commenting 'She dropped the marring fifth line':

> In the pleasant orchard-closes,
> 'God bless all our gains,' say we,
> But 'May God bless all our losses,'
> Better suits with our degree.

The poem goes on to tell how as a child the poet found in a wood a 'bower', a kind of garden, and

> On a sudden, through the glistening
> Leaves around, a little stirred,
> Came a sound, a sense of music which was rather felt than heard.

The music is more beautiful than any bird's song; but, as she 'rose up in exaltation' the music ceased and a silence followed:

> Heart and head beat through the quiet
> Full and heavily, though slower:
> In the song, I think, and by it,
> Mystic Presences of power
> Had up-snatched me to the Timeless, then returned me to the Hour.

She vowed she would return to the bower but she never found it again. The poem then runs through at some length the many losses she has suffered in growing up and growing older but declares that, though her 'first was of the bower', she knows it remains just as it was:

> Springs the linden-tree as greenly,
> Stroked with light adown its rind;
> And the ivy-leaves serenely
> Each in either intertwined;
> And the rose-trees at the doorway, they have neither grown nor pined.

---

[29] From 1916 to 1919 Eliot gave a three-year tutorial class at Southall on Modern English Literature. Lecture III of the first year was devoted to Elizabeth Barrett Browning, and one of the six poems recommended for study, in addition to the 'Sonnets from the Portuguese', was 'The Lost Bower'. See Ronald Schuchard, 'T. S. Eliot as an Extension Lecturer, 1916–1919', *Review of English Studies*, May 1974.

From those overblown faint roses
Not a leaf appeareth shed,
And that little bud discloses
Not a thorn's-breadth more of red,
For the winters and the summers which have passed me overhead.

And that music overfloweth,
Sudden sweet, the sylvan eaves:
Thrush or nightingale—who knoweth?
Fay or Faunus—who believes?
But my heart still trembles in me to the trembling of the leaves.

Is the bower lost, then? who sayeth
That the bower indeed is lost?
Hark! my spirit in it prayeth
Through the sunshine and the frost,—
And the prayer preserves it greenly, to the last and uttermost.

Till another open for me
In God's Eden-land unknown,
With an angel at the doorway,
White with gazing at His Throne;
And a saint's voice in the palm-trees, singing—'All is lost . . . and *won*!'

Apart from its first four lines which Eliot said had 'always stuck in my head'[30] there are no verbal echoes from this mediocre poem; but the music, the bird's song, the silence, the conjunction of the 'Timeless' and the 'Hour', and the whole conception that what is lost is not lost but exists to be known in prayer and to be finally restored make Mrs. Browning's poem a kind of crude and sentimental version of the underlying themes of *Burnt Norton*. It is an interesting example of the ways of the poetic imagination that Kipling's over-emotional story and Mrs. Browning's lax effusion should have been combined unconsciously to contribute to Eliot's austere and rigorously philosophic poem on time and time's losses and gains.

ii. EAST COKER

East Coker was written on the model of *Burnt Norton* and it bears the marks of its origin. It arises less than the other Quartets out of experiences and memories that came together, and at times seems to follow its model too closely, as in the lyrical opening of the second section. East Coker is a singularly beautiful village in Somerset, not far from Yeovil. Eliot visited

[30] The echo from these is in *The Dry Salvages*: 'It tosses up our losses.'

it for the first and only time in early August 1937, when he was staying with
Sir Matthew Nathan at West Coker.[31] The visit would seem to have been
part of his journey into his own past. In this case it was a journey into a remote
past, beyond personal memory. It was from East Coker that the distant
ancestor of the Eliot family, Andrew Eliot, left England around 1669 in
search of religious freedom in the New World. In its churchyard Eliot saw
'old stones that cannot be deciphered', marking the graves of those who may
have been his long-dead and forgotten ancestors. In a field nearby, as the
Ordnance Survey map shows, there is an ancient dancing circle, a place
where generations of men and women, who for centuries had tilled the
ground and tended their beasts, danced together at midsummer to the 'weak
pipe and the little drum'. Whether Eliot was aware of this or not does not
matter.[32] His imagination reached back into pre-history, to a time before
the time of his seventeenth-century ancestors who lie buried in the churchyard. For *East Coker* is concerned with solar time, the cycle of the seasons;
with biological time, the short span between birth and death; and with
historic time, the passage of the centuries, the long process of the rise and
decay of the works of man. It contrasts with these cycles and ages a single
day; and sets against the inevitabilities of the seasons and of historic change
the erratic movements of psychological and mental time.[33]

The sources of *East Coker* are more obvious than the sources of *Burnt
Norton*, and the poem is remarkable for the amount of direct quotation and
obvious reminiscence it contains. It opens with a translation and inversion
of Mary Stuart's motto '*En ma fin est mon commencement*', reverting to it
in its original form at the close. The passage in the first section from Sir
Thomas Elyot's *The Boke of the Governour* (1531) is distinguished by its
archaic spelling. The copy sent to the printer (D5) is marked 'Printer to
copy the spelling exactly'. The passage adapted from *The Ascent of Mount
Carmel* was quoted by William James in his famous book *The Varieties of
Religious Experience* (1902), which Eliot had read when he was a young
man.[34] James's version is a translation from a French translation in *Saint Jean
de la Croix, Vie et Oeuvres* (Paris, 1893). What edition Eliot was using
when he cited St. John of the Cross in an epigraph to *Sweeney Agonistes*
I do not know. By the time he came to write *Burnt Norton* Allison Peers's
translation of the complete works (3 vols., 1934–5) was available, and in

[31] Information from Mrs. Valerie Eliot.
[32] Mrs. Eliot tells me he never spoke of it to her.
[33] cf. Hardy's poem 'I Look into my Glass':

> But Time, to make me grieve,
> Part steals, lets part abide;
> And shakes this fragile form at eve
> With throbbings of noontide.

[34] This was pointed out to me by Professor J. A. W. Bennett. Mrs. Lyndall Gordon tells me that
Eliot's notes on the book are in the Houghton Library, Harvard University.

East Coker he made use of it. The reminiscence of the opening of the *Divine Comedy*

> In the middle, not only in the middle of the way
> But all the way, in a dark wood—

repeated in the closing section—'So here I am, in the middle way'—and the echo of lines from the opening speech of *Samson Agonistes* at the beginning of Part III are so obvious as not to require annotation. It is very unusual for Eliot to make use of such well-known passages.

In a letter to Professor Häussermann (May 1940) Eliot added a more obscure source to the sources from which he had made direct quotation:

> The title is taken from a village in Somerset where my family lived for some two centuries. The first section contains some phrases in Tudor English taken from 'The Governour' of Sir Thomas Elyot who was a grandson of Simon Elyot or Eliot of that village. The third section contains several lines adapted from 'The Ascent of Mount Carmel'. I think that the imagery of the first section (though taken from the village itself) may have been influenced by recollections of 'Germelshausen', which I have not read for many years.[35]

Germelshausen, by Friedrich Gerstärker, is a story, as Professor Häussermann explained, of a parish under a Papal interdict which can neither live nor die. Once every hundred years 'it resumes for the space of one day its ghostly revelry, and then sinks again under earth'. The stranger in the story wanders into this 'lost village' on its centennial re-appearance. What seems to have remained in Eliot's mind is merely the idea of a man from another age encountering the revelry of the long dead. The implications of the story and the poem are entirely different. The village of East Coker lies under no curse; it is there in its late summer beauty, and the dance around the bonfire on a summer midnight is a vision, available to any who 'do not come too close', of the old midsummer rites of the 'coupling of man and woman'.

Another, and more interesting, obscure source is, I think revealed by Eliot's first notes for the lyric of Part IV,[36] which Eliot said, in a letter to Mrs. Ridler,[37] was 'in a way the heart of the matter'. This is André Gide's *Le Prométhée mal enchaîné*, from which Eliot quoted a famous phrase in his Harvard lectures: 'As André Gide's Prometheus said, in a lecture which he gave before a large audience in Paris: *il faut avoir un aigle*.'[38] In his book *Four Quartets Rehearsed* (1946), Mr. Raymond Preston provided an allegorical interpretation of the lyric, identifying the 'wounded surgeon' with Christ, the 'dying nurse' with the Church Militant, and the 'ruined

---

[35] See H. S. Häussermann, *English Studies*, August 1941; also *Life and Letters* (1945).
[36] The notes are transcribed on pp. 94–5.
[37] The letter is quoted on p. 109.
[38] *The Use of Poetry and the Use of Criticism* (1933), 69.

millionaire' with Adam; and in a footnote reported that he had originally thought 'that the ruined millionaire was the Fallen Angel' and that he was 'indebted to Mr. Eliot for the correction'.[39] In *The Art of T. S. Eliot* (1949) I contested this interpretation, in spite of Mr. Preston giving the author as his authority, on the grounds that to endow a hospital is an act of charity hardly to be compared with endowing the world with Original Sin. I took all three figures, surgeon, nurse, millionaire as types of Christ, who 'emptied himself' that he might suffer for man's sake and with man.[40]

Eliot's rough notes for his lyric show that he planned a poem in four stanzas. He wrote '1. The wounded surgeon— / 2) The dying nurse'. For the third stanza he wrote a cryptic phrase '3) Singing is silence' and for the fourth '4) ill of love— / The Lover'. The capital suggests that the final verse was to be centred on a divine lover. Then he cancelled the suggestion for the third stanza and wrote at the foot of the page '—hospital the earth / bankrupt ~~banker~~ / millionaire'. On another page he roughed out phrases for what became the last two stanzas, and added a little summary 'the surgeon / the nurse / the hospital / & final'.

The collocation of the two words 'banker' and 'millionaire' must strike any reader of Gide's *sottie*,[41] where, at the beginning, the stout gentleman walking down the Avenue de l'Opéra, who drops his handkerchief, asks the thin man who picks it up and returns it to him to write a name and address on an envelope, and then unexpectedly and brutally strikes him on the face, is identified as '*Zeus, le banquier*', and immediately afterwards, by the waiter at the café where Prometheus has sat down, as '*un ami, qui est Miglionnaire*'. The *garçon* says that the *Miglionnaire* was performing '*une action gratuite*'. He sent a 500 franc note in the envelope to someone named at random by the man who had at random picked up his handkerchief, and with equal lack of reason, or motive, struck the well-meaning stranger. Prometheus is joined at his table by the two victims of the divine whim: Damoclès, who is tormented by not knowing whom he is to thank, and Coclès, who accepts that one person's gain is another's loss. The latter's philosophy is further tested by the arrival of Prometheus' eagle, which gouges out his eye. Prometheus, who is then imprisoned '*comme fabricant des allumettes sans brevet*', summons his eagle to him. It becomes, as time passes, increasingly beautiful from feeding on Prometheus' liver, as Prometheus becomes more and more gaunt. At last the eagle is strong enough to carry Prometheus out

[39] See *Four Quartets Rehearsed*, 34.

[40] See *The Art of T. S. Eliot*, 65–7. I have to own that Hayward in *Quatre Quatuors* (1950) gives the same allegorical interpretation as Mr. Preston does, and Grover Smith accepts it. Hayward knew my book well and used it for his notes. I regret that I never summoned up the nerve to ask Eliot whether I was wrong to query at some length the identification of the millionaire with Adam. But he would probably have evaded siding with either of his readers.

[41] For an admirable discussion of Gide's treatment of the Prometheus myth, see Helen Watson-Williams, *André Gide and the Greek Myth* (1967).

of prison and he then delivers his oration of which the theme is: '*Il faut avoir un aigle.*' The effect of the speech on Damoclès and Coclès—the one overcome by the burden of his indebtedness to an unknown, the other seeking all over Paris for another blow which will help some other unknown Damoclès—disturbs Prometheus, who thinks the *Miglionnaire* ought to be informed of their plight. The *garçon* takes him for an interview, in which he acts as 'feed'. The *Interview du Miglionnaire* begins:

Le Garçon: — N'est-ce pas que vous êtes très riche?
Le Miglionnaire: — Je suis riche bien plus que l'on ne peut imaginer. Tu es à moi; il est à moi; tout est à moi. — Vous me croyez banquier; je suis bien autre chose. . . .
Le Garçon: — N'est-ce pas que vos actions sont gratuites?
Le Miglionnaire: — Moi seul, celui-là seul dont la fortune est infinie peut agir avec un désintéressement absolu; l'homme pas. De là vient mon amour du jeu; non pas du gain, comprenez-moi — du jeu; que pourrais-je gagner que je n'aie pas d'avance? . . . Oui, j'ai la passion du jeu. Mon jeu c'est de prêter aux hommes. . . . Je prête, mais c'est à fonds perdus; je prête, mais c'est avec l'air de donner. — J'aime qu'on ne sache pas que je prête. Je joue, mais je cache mon jeu. J'expérimente; je joue comme un Hollandais sème; comme il plante un secret oignon.

The *Miglionnaire* then relates to Prometheus his experiment with Damoclès and Coclès. Prometheus reveals that it is on their account that he has come and pleads with Zeus, as the *Miglionnaire* is now called:

Damoclès vous cherche et vous appelle; il s'inquiète; il est malade; par pitié, montrez-vous à lui.
— Monsieur, brisons là — dit Zeus — je n'ai de conseils à recevoir de personne.

Prometheus turns to go; but he turns back:

Monsieur, pardonnez-moi. Excusez une indiscrète demande. Oh! montrez-le, je vous en prie! j'aimerais tant le voir . . .
— Quoi?
— Votre aigle.
— Mais je n'ai pas d'aigle, Monsieur.
— Pas d'aigle? Il n'a pas d'aigle!! Mais . . .
— Pas plus que dans le creux de ma main. Les aigles (et Zeus riait), les aigles, c'est moi qui les donne.[42]
La stupeur de Prométhée était grande.

---

[42] cf. the first version of line 161:

That will not let us be, but must torment us everywhere.

— Savez-vous ce qu'on dit? demanda le garçon au banquier.
— Qu'est-ce qu'on dit?
— Que vous êtes le bon Dieu!
— Je me le suis laissé dire, fit le banquier.

I find it difficult not to think that the icy Zeus of Gide, who plays with men
for his amusement, giving them the eagles that torment them but having no
eagle himself, and who yet, in spite of this is called by men '*le bon Dieu*', was
in Eliot's mind when he crossed out 'Singing is silence', as the theme of his
third stanza and, reverting to his hospital metaphor, wrote 'banker' and then
cancelled that for 'millionaire'. By adding the adjective 'bankrupt' (later
altered to 'ruined') he transformed Gide's cynically selfish Zeus into a
banker or millionaire who gives away his infinite wealth to endow the
hospital in which a wounded surgeon and a dying nurse minister to men.
And, similarly, the 'punch-line' with which Gide ends the interview would
seem to have suggested to Eliot his final line: 'Again, in spite of that, we call
this Friday good', in which Gideian irony is transformed into Christian
paradox.

iii. THE DRY SALVAGES

East Coker arises much less out of the depths of experience and memory than
Burnt Norton and *The Dry Salvages*. Like *Little Gidding*, it is inspired by
a deliberately willed visit to a place whose associations were historic rather
than personal. *The Dry Salvages* is soaked in memories of childhood and
youth. In the winter of 1959-60 Eliot visited the United States and went to
Boston to receive the Emerson-Thoreau award from the American Academy
of Arts and Sciences. In the speech that he gave on this occasion he took as
his subject 'The Influence of Landscape upon the Poet' and concluded by
a reading of *The Dry Salvages*.[43] He explained the association of ideas by
which he had come to his subject by saying that the Emerson-Thoreau
award brought to mind Concord in particular and New England in general,
and that his predecessor in the award had been Robert Frost, 'distinctly in
the mind of everyone a New England poet'. 'I then asked myself', he went
on, 'whether I had any title to be a New England poet . . . and I think I have.'
Owning to begin with that he came from Missouri and that his father before
him was born in St. Louis, he countered the admission by the fact that he
'came East' at seventeen, and that as far back as he could remember and
before, his family had spent every summer on the New England coast:

So my personal landscape is a composite. In St. Louis, my grandmother
—as was very natural—wanted to live on in the house that my grandfather

---

[43] The speech is printed in the journal of the Academy, *Daedalus*, lxxxix (1960), 420-2.

had built; my father, from filial piety, did not wish to leave the house that he had built only a few steps away; and so it came to be that we lived on in a neighbourhood which had become shabby to a degree approaching slumminess, after all our friends and acquaintances had moved further west. And in my childhood, before the days of motor cars, people who lived in town stayed in town. So it was, that for nine months of the year my scenery was almost exclusively urban, and a good deal of it seedily, drably urban at that. My urban imagery was that of St. Louis, upon which that of Paris and London have been superimposed. It was also, however, the Mississippi, as it passes between St. Louis and East St. Louis in Illinois: the Mississippi was the most powerful feature of Nature in that environment. My country landscape, on the other hand, is that of New England, of coastal New England, and New England from June to October. In St. Louis I never tasted an oyster or a lobster—we were too far from the sea. In Massachusetts, the small boy who was a devoted bird watcher never saw his birds of the season when they were making their nests.

Eliot ended by saying that he hoped his words would shed some light on the poem he was about to read, and 'also substantiate, to some degree, my claim to being, among other things, a New England poet. You will notice, however, that this poem begins where I began, with the Mississippi; and that it ends, where I and my wife expect to end, at the parish church of a tiny village in Somerset.'

Much earlier, in 1928, in a preface he wrote to the Faber and Gwyer edition of Edgar Ansel Mowrer's book, *This American World*, Eliot had in the same way attempted to define his heritage as an American. Mowrer had included in his book a 'brief account of his own origins and beginnings, and the American history of his own family', which Eliot described as 'a typical case of the history of the families of "Anglo-Saxon" origin which have penetrated the Middle West and the West Coast', and he had declared that 'Not to have the frontier in one's blood makes emotional understanding of the United States impossible'. Eliot assented to this; but went on to comment on Mowrer's division of Americans into two groups, 'the older stocks and the new-comers', and his assertion that the latter were strong in the cities so that consequently 'to the "sixth generation American", New York often seems as alien as Vienna or Amsterdam'. Eliot singled out 'the Portuguese in the fishing industry, and the Portuguese and Italians in suburban market-gardening' in New England as exceptions to the general drift of new-comers to the cities, and went on to a 'more important' point: 'that those branches of the early-settling families which have remained in the East, in New York, Boston, Philadelphia and the towns of the southern seaboard, are further removed from the "pioneer" than those whose grandparents moved west.' He was himself, he declared, 'a descendant of pioneers, somewhat like Mr. Mowrer':

> My family did not move so often as his, because we tended to cling to places and associations as long as possible; but with a family tendency to traditions and loyalties, I have a background which Mr. Mowrer would recognize, and which is different from that of the native European and from that of many Americans. My family were New Englanders, who had been settled—my branch of it—for two generations in the South West—which was, in my own time, rapidly becoming merely the Middle West. The family guarded jealously its connexions with New England; but it was not until years of maturity that I perceived that I myself had always been a New Englander in the South West, and a South Westerner in New England; when I was sent to school in New England I lost my southern accent without ever acquiring the accent of the native Bostonian.[44] In New England I missed the long dark river, the ailanthus trees, the flaming cardinal birds, the high limestone bluffs where we searched for fossil shell-fish; in Missouri I missed the fir trees, the bay and goldenrod, the song-sparrows, the red granite and the blue sea of Massachusetts. I remember a friend of my schooldays, whose family had lived in the same house in the same New England seaport for two hundred and fifty years. In some ways his background was as different from mine as that of any European. My grandmother—one of my grandmothers—had shot her own wild turkeys for dinner; his had collected Chinese pottery brought home by the Salem clippers. It was perhaps easier for the grandson of pioneers to migrate eastward than it would have been for my friend to migrate in any direction.

In *The Dry Salvages* man is seen by a 'grandson of pioneers' as a voyager whose destiny is always to 'fare forward'. The images of travel, whether by long-distance train or by liner across the ocean, in the third section, are in strong contrast to the parallel, claustrophobic images in *Burnt Norton* and *East Coker* of the London tube.

Eliot himself provided a commentary on the river of his opening paragraph in a preface he wrote to the Cresset Library edition of *Huckleberry Finn* in 1950, where he declared that while Huck gives the book its style, the 'River gives the book its form'.

> A river, a very big and powerful river, is the only natural force that can wholly determine the course of human peregrination. At sea, the

---

[44] Eliot spoke English very beautifully and deliberately, but he never sounded wholly English. The Harvard undergraduate who 'lost [his] southern accent without ever acquiring the accent of the native Bostonian' similarly lost his American accent without ever developing English speed and English slurring or English speech rhythms.

wanderer may sail or be carried by winds and currents in one direction or
another; a change of wind or tide may determine fortune. In the prairie,
the direction of movement is more or less at the choice of the caravan;
among mountains there will often be an alternative, a guess at the most
likely pass. But the river with its strong, swift current is the dictator to
the raft or to the steamboat. It is a treacherous and capricious dictator.
At one season, it may move sluggishly in a channel so narrow that,
encountering it for the first time at that point, one can hardly believe that
it has travelled already for hundreds of miles, and has yet many hundreds
of miles to go; at another season it may obliterate the low Illinois shore to
a horizon of water, while in its bed it runs with a speed such that no man
or beast can survive in it. At such times, it carries down human bodies,
cattle and houses. At least twice at St. Louis, the western and the eastern
shores have been separated by the fall of bridges, until the designer of the
great Eads bridge devised a structure which could resist the floods. In
my own childhood, it was not unusual for the spring freshet to interrupt
railway travel; and then the traveller to the East had to take steamboat
from the levee up to Alton, at a higher level on the Illinois shore, before
he could begin his rail journey. The river is never wholly chartable; it
changes its pace, it shifts its channel, unaccountably; it may utterly
efface a sandbar, and throw up another bar where before was navigable
water. . . .

Thus the River makes the book a great book. As with Conrad, we are
continually reminded of the power and terror of Nature, and the isolation
and feebleness of Man. Conrad remains always the European observer of
the tropics, the white man's eye contemplating the Congo and its black
gods. But Mark Twain is a native, and the River God is his God. It is
as a native that he accepts the River God, and it is the subjection of Man
that gives to Man his dignity. For without some kind of God, Man is not
even very interesting.[45]

The River begins the poem. Its image recurs with great power towards
the close of the second section in four lines added, in two stages, in manuscript, on the first typed draft.[46]

People change, and smile: but the agony abides.
Time the destroyer is time the preserver,
Like the river with its cargo of dead negroes, cows and chicken coops,
The bitter apple and the bite in the apple.

Eliot wrote the words 'The River?' at the foot of the page before inserting
the third, descriptive line into his addition, seeing suddenly that two symbols
from his childhood came together as symbols of the permanence of past

[45] pp. xii–xiii and xv.   [46] See p. 135.

agonies: the Mississippi and the reef of the Dry Salvages off Cape Ann, the ragged rock that 'is what it always was'.

In the summer, the Eliot family migrated every year from the heat of St. Louis to the Massachusetts or Maine coast, usually to the seaport of Gloucester, Massachusetts. Here, in 1896, on Eastern Point, the spit of land which forms the eastern arm of Gloucester's deep harbour, Eliot's father built a house for the family's summer home. It is within earshot of a 'heaving groaner' which sailors have to round on their homeward journey into port. The Atlantic off the great promontory of Cape Ann is studded with rocks and reefs. It is a dangerous and difficult coast, as well as a supremely beautiful one. Eliot and his older brother, Henry, were taught to sail on its waters by an ancient mariner of Gloucester and became expert at navigating its hazards. Later they sailed in Henry's boat, the *Elsa*; and in his Harvard days Eliot sailed in vacations with a college friend, Harold Peters. In the same year as he wrote the preface to Mowrer's *This American World*, 1928, he wrote an unsigned publishers' preface to James B. Connolly's tales of Gloucester fishermen, *Fishermen of the Banks*, writing with authority as one who knew the seamen and their hard life:

> The town of Gloucester, Massachusetts, lies about forty miles north-east of Boston. As, in the old days, New Bedford to the south of Cape Cod was the centre of the whaling industry, and Salem, between Boston and Gloucester, was the centre for the fast clipper ships which traded with China, so Gloucester has always been the port for the deep-sea fishing of the North Atlantic. It has the most beautiful harbour for small ships on the whole of that coast. In the summer, the Gloucester fishing schooner, laden with its seines and dories, can reach the south Banks or 'Georges'; in the winter the Grand Banks of Newfoundland, where the codfish abound; it may even buy and sell in the harbour of Reykyavik, Iceland. All the year round, and on every day of the week except Friday and Sunday, which are unlucky, schooners are setting out for their cruises of several weeks. There is no harder life, no more uncertain livelihood, and few more dangerous occupations. Since the introduction of the 'knockabout rig'—the schooner with a long bow and no bowsprit—there are fewer losses at sea; but Gloucester has many widows, and no trip is without anxiety for those at home.

Eliot went on to refer to Kipling's *Captains Courageous*, and claimed that these 'true stories of the adventures of Gloucester fishermen or "bankers"' were written by 'one who (with all respect) knows the subject much better than Mr. Kipling':

> Mr. Connolly has himself shipped many times with the fishermen 'out o' Gloucester' and knows their life and their ways intimately. He is the

author of several volumes of short stories of this life . . . which . . . have received the exacting approval of the Gloucestermen themselves. But for a reader who is unfamiliar with that life, the tales in the present volume will serve as the best introduction. They are true narratives: most of them can—or could a few years ago—be learnt by word of mouth from the men between trips, as they lounged at the corner of Main Street and Duncan Street in Gloucester.

The Waste Land in its original form included American as well as European experience. Eliot's memories of the Gloucester fishermen, and their stories, which he had listened to, provided him with the material for the long narrative of a shipwreck that originally opened Part IV. In the final version, the note on the 'evening hour' that 'brings the sailor home from sea' records that Eliot 'had in mind the "longshore" or "dory" fisherman who returns at nightfall'. (I imagine many, as I did, had to go to the dictionary to discover that a 'dory' was not a kind of fish but a kind of boat.[47]) The beautiful image in the final section of the boat that

responded
Gaily, to the hand expert with sail and oar,

is the one purely happy image in the poem, as the images of the white sails 'seaward flying' and of the New England coast in the last section of *Ash Wednesday* appear as poignant memories of a happiness the poet dare not allow himself to long for or to hope to enjoy again. Later, in *Marina*, the making of a boat provides a metaphor for the struggle to remake a life, and memories of sailing through drifting fog among grey rocks and islands towards a granite shore, with bird-song half heard and a whiff from the pine woods as the sailor nears land, is a metaphor of spiritual renewal. These memories, carried through the long years away from the homes of his child-hood and youth, give *The Dry Salvages* the authenticity which has earned for it the same 'exacting approval' that the Gloucestermen gave to James Connolly's stories. Quoting the passage that begins by distinguishing the 'sea howl' and the 'sea yelp', Eliot's 'Cousin Sam', the distinguished historian Rear-Admiral Samuel Eliot Morison, U.S.N. (Ret.), has written 'These lines, and indeed all that follow, ring a bell in any sailor's heart. They are authentic, not synthetic like the great mass of so-called sea poetry.'[48]

The Dry Salvages and the Little Salvages lie about a mile east-north-easterly from Straitsmouth Island off the northern point of Cape Ann. The official *United States Coast Pilot, Atlantic Coast, Section A: St. Croix River*

---

[47] *O.E.D.* cites 'dory: a boat' as 'U.S. and W. Indies'.
[48] 'The Dry Salvages and the Thacher Shipwreck', *The American Neptune*, xxv, 4 (1965), 233–47. I have to thank Professor Harry Levin for bringing this fascinating and very informative article to my notice, and Admiral Morison and the editors of *The American Neptune* for permission to quote extensively from this article in the following pages, and later.

to Cape Cod (4th edn., 1941) describes the Dry Salvages as 'a bare ledge about 15 feet above high water near the middle of a reef about 500 yards long in a northerly direction'. I need hardly say that I owe this recondite reference to Admiral Morison, as well as other facts; but I have myself visited Cape Ann and on a summer evening looked out from Rockport over a calm sea to the seamark of the Dry Salvages. Admiral Morison continues:

> Parallel to, and about 500 yards west of the Dry Salvages, is Little Salvages, a rocky reef bare at low water but covered at high tide, and half a mile to a mile northwesterly from Little Salvages is Flat Ground, a rocky ledge half a mile long with a least depth of two feet at mean low water. The *American Coast Pilot* of 1854 describes this as 'a large spot of flat ground which at low water will take up a small vessel'. It 'took up' a Liberty ship during the last war, and a converted 110-foot subchaser in 1955. Tanker *Lucy* and minesweeper U.S.S. *Grouse* foundered there more recently. When an easterly gale is raging the entire group—Dry Salvages, Little Salvages and Flat Ground—becomes a seething mass of foam, as heavy swells from the Atlantic break and roar over it; and at all times it is a menace to navigators attempting to round Cape Ann.
>
> At the time when T. S. Eliot knew it, Dry Salvages was marked by a wooden tripod; but, owing to the frequent need of replacing or repairing this beacon after a storm, it was removed in 1945, leaving the rock bare as 'it always was'.

South of the Dry Salvages is Thacher's Island, so called from a famous shipwreck in 1635.

> The story was first told in the words of Anthony Thacher's letter to his brother Peter, first printed in Increase Mather's *Remarkable Providences* of 1684. Thacher, with his bosom friend the Reverend Joseph Avery and twenty-one other passengers, was sailing a pinnace . . . when they were overwhelmed by the sudden hurricane of 14–15 August 1635. In attempting to round Cape Ann the vessel struck on a rock a few hundred yards from an island. There 'Parson Avery' delivered his 'Swan-Song' (as paraphrased by John G. Whittier from Cotton Mather's *Magnalia*), and thence the poop of the vessel floated off, carrying Mrs. Thacher, grounding on the island ever since named Thacher's.

Her husband swam to the island, where he found his wife alive; and they existed there for thirty-six hours until rescued. All the other passengers perished. Among them was a certain 'Mr. William Eliot of New Sarum'. Nothing is known of him except that he was a bachelor who had only been in New England for a few months. Over the years Eliot, in memory, confused his known ancestor, Andrew Eliot of East Coker, with this unknown man, who may well have been of the same family. He wrote in 1964 to Admiral Morison, who had queried his note on the derivation of the Dry Salvages: 'Did you know that the Reverend Andrew Eliot was in the company of the Reverend Mr. Thatcher when they went ashore on Thatcher's Island?' As Admiral Morison points out, Andrew Eliot of East Coker did not arrive in New England until around 1669, more than thirty years after the Thacher shipwreck; but this confusion in Eliot's memory no doubt played some part in, or was caused by, his deep personal feeling for the rocks, reefs, and islands off Cape Ann. In the letter he wrote replying to Admiral Morison's correction of his derivation, he recalls that he and Harold Peters were once storm-bound on a neighbouring island for a couple of days 'and lived chiefly on lobster'. Perhaps this experience contributed to his mistakenly making his remote ancestor a sharer in Mr. Thacher's thirty-six-hour ordeal.

In the note prefixed to *The Dry Salvages*, Eliot explained the name as presumably deriving from *les trois sauvages* and said it should be pronounced to rhyme with *assuages*, that is to say with the accent on the penult. Admiral Morison has no difficulty in disposing of the derivation proposed. He points out that 'Dry' is 'a not unusual designation along the Atlantic Coast for ledges bare at high water, to distinguish them from others which, like the Little Salvages, are covered twice daily. . . . Moreover "Dry" appears on no map in connection with the Salvages until 1867, when any derivation from *trois* would be farfetched.' Accepting that 'Salvage' is the old spelling for 'Savage', and owning that local historians are unable to explain the name, he hazards the suggestion that the name may have occurred by 'geographical transfer' from a rock off Cape Neddick, now called Neddick Nubble, but by an early voyager, Gabriel Archer, called 'Savage Rock', 'because the Sauages first shewed themselves there'. Or, he suggests, the name may possibly be owing to Champlain who, in his account of his exploration of 1605, describes Cape Ann (which he called *Cap au Isles*) with its islands and reefs, and tells how near it he caught sight of a canoe in which 'were five or six Indians (*sauuages*)' who came towards his pinnace, but then 'went back to dance on the beach'. Champlain may have called the reef of the Dry Salvages, which he describes, though he does not name it or show it on his map, after these friendly Indians he met off the rocks.

These are speculations. The question of the pronunciation is more easily settled. Eliot wrote in reply to Admiral Morison's query: 'My information about the pronunciation of "Salvages" has nothing authentic about it. It is just the pronunciation I learned from my elder brother.' Admiral Morison reports that the spelling 'Salvages', first appeared in *The English Pilot* of 1689 and is constantly repeated, with one exception, in 1757, where it is *Salvigis*. He thinks it probable it was originally pronounced *Sávages*, as he himself heard the rocks called by sailors early in the present century. He

notes that as more and more mariners used charts, spelling affected pronunciation and 'Modern yachtsmen pronounce it just as it is spelt, *Sálvages*,
with the accent on the antepenult'. But, he adds,

> The Reverend Thomas J. Carroll, who sailed in fishing schooners over
> thirty years ago, always heard the fishermen call it *Salvayges*, with
> the accent on the penult; and Captain John A. Muise, secretary of the
> Gloucester Master Mariners' Association, assures me that this is the
> proper pronunciation. So Mr. Eliot's memory is vindicated. Other
> Gloucester fishermen call it *Salvigis*, with the accent on the penult.

I feel glad that the pronunciation to rhyme with 'assuages' is thus confirmed as authentic, since it is with this pronunciation that the title of the
poem is now known all over the world.

Along with these memories of his childhood in St. Louis and his holidays
as a boy and his vacations as a young man at Cape Ann, Eliot also recalled
the two years he spent at Harvard in Professor Charles Lanman's course in
Indian Philology[49] and, in the second of these years, in James Woods's
course in Indian Philosophy. In his lectures at Virginia, published as *After
Strange Gods* in 1933, Eliot spoke slightingly of this experience:

> Two years spent in the study of Sanskrit under Charles Lanman, and
> a year in the mazes of Patanjali's metaphysics under the guidance of
> James Woods, left me in a state of enlightened mystification. A good half
> of the effort of understanding what the Indian philosophers were after—
> and their subtleties make most of the great European philosophers look
> like schoolboys—lay in trying to erase from my mind all the categories
> and kinds of distinction common to European philosophy from the time
> of the Greeks. My previous and concomitant study of European philo-
> sophy was hardly better than an obstacle. And I came to the conclusion—
> seeing also that the 'influence' of Brahmin and Buddhist thought upon
> Europe, as in Schopenhauer, Hartmann, and Deussen, had largely been
> through romantic misunderstanding—that my only hope of really
> penetrating to the heart of that mystery would lie in forgetting how to
> think and feel as an American or a European: which, for practical as well
> as sentimental reasons, I did not wish to do.[50]

Eliot never re-published *After Strange Gods*, a book that reflects only too
painfully the stresses and strains of the period at which his lectures were

---

[49] Among the books from Eliot's library now in the Hayward Bequest in King's College Library is
'*The Twenty-eight Upanishads* (Isha and Others). By Vasudev Laxman Shastri Phansikar. Printed and
published by Tukaram Javaji, Bombay, 1906. Inscribed on the fly-leaf "Thomas Eliot with C. R.
Lanman's kindest regard and best wishes. Harvard College, May 6, 1912": one page of ms. notes by
C. R. Lanman, 22 May 1912, inserted'; see *Handlist of the Literary Manuscripts in the T. S. Eliot Collection*, printed for King's College, 1973. Harvard records show what an impressive range of texts Eliot
read in his two graduate years and that, apart from one A minus, his grades in Indian studies were all A.
[50] *After Strange Gods* (1933), 40–1.

delivered. Its harshness of tone is that of a man at odds with his own recent past who, in his wretchedness, is hot for certainties.[51] From the poet who had deliberately brought together the Buddha and St. Augustine as representatives of western and eastern asceticism, and had found the resolution of his greatest poem in the voice of the thunder on the banks of the Ganges, this defensive denial of the possibility of fruitful contact between western and eastern culture came oddly. The publication of the drafts for *The Waste Land* shows that he had been willing to go beyond the 'collocation of eastern and western asceticism'. The fragment 'I am the Resurrection and the Life' brings together the words of the Lord Christ from St. John's Gospel and the words of the Lord Krishna from the *Gita*. He spoke very differently fifteen years later in his broadcast talks to Germany, delivered in 1948, on 'The Unity of European Culture'.[52] Here it is true he was not speaking of Indian philosophy but of the literature of Asia.

In the literature of Asia is great poetry. There is also profound wisdom and some very difficult metaphysics; but at the moment I am only concerned with poetry. . . . Long ago I studied the ancient Indian languages and while I was chiefly interested at that time in Philosophy, I read a little poetry too; and I know that my own poetry shows the influence of Indian thought and sensibility.

I have had the advantage of reading recently an unpublished essay by an Indian scholar, which discusses Eliot's 'cultural determinants'[53] and supports Eliot's belief that his reading in Indian poetry had influenced his thought and sensibility. Mr. B. P. N. Sinha, himself an orthodox Hindu, provides many parallels in thought and expression between Eliot's poetry, particularly in *Four Quartets*, and Indian poetry. 'The West', he writes, 'has preoccupied itself almost exclusively with the philosophy and thought of India. One consequence of this has been a total neglect of Indian forms of expression, i.e. of its literature. T. S. Eliot is the one major poet whose work bears evidence of intercourse with this aspect of Indian culture.' He goes so far as to write that certain passages in *Four Quartets*, a large number of them, 'would, if translated adequately, pose no problem of communication to an Indian villager who does not know English. . . . Many turns of expression like "you know and do not know", "world not world, but that which is not world", "In order to arrive there . . . where you are is where you are not"[54]

---

[51] Eliot's treatment of Hardy and Lawrence in his last lecture has always been held against him. With regard to Lawrence, it should be remembered that he was willing to be called for the defence in the Old Bailey case of the Crown *v.* Penguin Books over *Lady Chatterley's Lover*. His brief of evidence, which I saw, made quite clear his repudiation of his attack on Lawrence. He was prepared to say that when he spoke of the author of that book as 'a very sick man indeed', he was very sick himself.

[52] Printed in translation as an Appendix in *Notes Towards a Definition of Culture* (1948).

[53] Mr. Sinha very kindly sent me a copy of his essay and has given me permission to make use of it.

[54] It is interesting that Mr. Sinha is here citing as immediately comprehensible to an Indian villager a passage from St. John of the Cross.

echo familiar chords in memory upon reading.' Mr. Sinha gives examples
of the delicacy with which Eliot discriminates in his reminiscences of his
reading in Indian poetry, the most striking being his handling of Krishna's
advice to Arjuna in *The Dry Salvages*.

The *Bhagavad-Gita*, or Song of the Lord, is an episode in the gigantic
Indian epic, the *Mahabharata*, which tells the story of a war between two
branches of a princely family: the Kauravas and their cousins, the Pandavas.
After making every effort to secure their rights by negotiation, the leader of
the Pandavas, the eldest of five brothers, sent a friend, Krishna, to the leader
of the Kauravas, the eldest of a hundred brothers, to make a final bid for
peace. Krishna was no mere neighbouring princeling. As everyone knew,
he was an incarnation of the God Vishnu who had become man 'for the
protection of the good, for the destruction of evil-doers, for the setting-up
of the law of righteousness'.[55] In rejecting Krishna and relying on his army,
the leader of the Kauravas was defying God. His embassy having failed,
and war being certain, Krishna took service as charioteer to his friend
Arjuna, one of the younger of the Pandava brothers and a great warrior-
hero. At the last moment, with battle imminent, Arjuna cannot bring himself to fight, knowing the appalling slaughter that will follow and that he will
be fighting his own kith and kin, among whom are his benefactors. The *Gita*
begins at this point, Krishna not merely urging on Arjuna his duty as
a member of the warrior-caste but revealing to him the structure of the
universe in which men's actions fulfil the will of the Lord. The relevance of
the whole discourse in 1941 with a fratricidal war raging in Europe does not
need stressing.

As Mr. Sinha points out, Eliot does not accept the metaphysics of the
Gita, particularly its doctrine of the soul as being 'unborn, eternal, ever-
lasting' successively re-incarnated in flesh, or its conception of the material
world as illusion. The fundamental concept that he takes from the *Gita* is
the concept of disinterested action: Karma-Yoga. Action (Karma) is
Arjuna's duty: the fruits of action are not his business. 'To work alone thou
hast the right, but never to the fruits thereof. Be thou neither motivated by
the fruits of action nor be thou attached to in-action.' Success or failure is
not man's concern. He must have 'an even mind in success and failure for
evenness of mind is called yoga'.[56] Eliot applies the concept of 'yoga', the
'even, or equal, mind', or 'sameness-and-indifference', as Zaehner renders
the word, to man's attitude to the future and the past. The 'equal mind'
releases man from servitude to either future hopes or past regrets. The
future, as it exists in our imagination, and the past, as it exists in memory,
are infected with sentiments arising from our desires. In the present moment,

[55] See *The Bhagavad-Gita* translated with a commentary by R. C. Zaehner (1969), 5-7. I am much
indebted to this edition.

[56] *Gita*, 2.47 and 48. Mr. Sinha's rendering.

'between the hither and the farther shore', the past is not finished, the future
is not 'before us'. The present, the actual moment, is the moment in which
past and future exist. Eliot's actual quotation from the *Gita*, put in quotation
marks, is only the first part of the sentence that Krishna delivers. As Eliot
completes the sentence he modifies its original meaning. Krishna declares
'Whatever state (or being) one dwells upon in the end, at the time of leaving
the body, that alone he attains because of his constant thought on that state
of being'.[57] Krishna means that the mind of man as it is at the time of death
is fructified in the next life of that man, i.e. when he is reborn. But Eliot
translates the idea into his own terms. The 'fructification' here is in the lives
of others, and the one 'action' that can fructify in their lives is the dis-
interestedness with which man acts not the actions themselves. Those to
whom 'every moment' is the 'time of death' 'take no thought for the morrow'
and do not 'think of the fruit of action'. Eliot recurs again to the *Gita*,
though not explicitly, in *Little Gidding* where he refines on the conception
of the 'equal mind' by distinguishing 'detachment', the true opposite of
'attachment', from 'indifference'.

Eliot's studies in Indian literature come to the surface in *The Dry Salvages*
with a deliberate and obvious reference. They lie behind *Burnt Norton*,
where the exotic image of the lotos rises 'quietly, quietly' in a Cotswold
garden, and in the first draft for the end of *East Coker* the forest of the
hermit-sages of ancient India was joined to the desert of the Christian
hermits and the sea of the early Irish missionaries.[58] *Burnt Norton* revolves
around the thought of what might have been, the missed opportunity; *East
Coker* moves around the two poles of the past of the human race and the
desolation of the personal present. In the third of the Quartets Eliot came
to meditate on his own personal past to discover its meaning, unity, or
pattern. Beginning with the Mississippi and ending in the churchyard of
East Coker, *The Dry Salvages* includes the terms 'Annunciation' and
'Incarnation' of Eliot's mature Christian faith, and a Christian prayer for
its lyric, along with what he had learned as a young man from his reading of
Indian poetry of the test of 'right action'. Both Christianity and the lessons
of the 'great literature of Asia' are explicitly present. The 'shores of Asia and
the Edgware Road' are brought together as they had been brought together
in *The Waste Land*.

iv. LITTLE GIDDING

The titles of the first three Quartets had a purely personal significance and
the poems were concerned with Eliot's personal history. *Little Gidding*

---

[57] *Gita*, 8.6. Mr. Sinha's rendering. Zaehner translates: 'Whatever state a man may bear in mind
when in the end he casts his mortal frame aside, even to that state he does accede, for ever does that
state make him grow into itself.'   [58] See p. 113.

proclaims by its title that its scope goes beyond the personal and involves the history of a nation and its Church. Having published *The Dry Salvages*, Eliot set to work with hardly a pause to complete his 'quadrilogue' by a poem on 'Fire', which should sum up and complete his meditations on 'what might have been and what has been', placing his personal history within the context of the history of his adopted country. The poem was to be about 'now and England'.

The opening paragraph, the only piece of extended natural description in the four poems, unparalleled in Eliot's poetry, is wholly in the present tense. In place of a passage of discursive meditation, which in the three earlier poems follows the lyric opening of the second part, *Little Gidding* has an episode, handled at length. It is set in a context of recent experiences, experiences shared by many of Eliot's fellow-citizens, the London air raids of the autumn of 1940. But the poem, dealing with choice and action, political and religious, is the fruit of choices and acts of long before: Eliot's baptism 'in a secluded chapel' and his confirmation next day in June 1927, and his taking of British citizenship in the following November. In *Little Gidding* he expressed his sense of identification with England at one of the darkest moments in her history, when it seemed only too possible that her legacy to the world might be the legacy of the defeated, and wrote as a man who had discovered a spiritual home in the Church of England. He found a symbol of the irrelevance of victory or defeat to the divine economy in the shrine of an obscure saint of the Church which had nourished his own life of 'prayer, observance, discipline, thought and action'.

Like East Coker, Little Gidding was a place that Eliot apparently visited only once. He went there, as he wrote to Mrs. Perkins, on a 'really lovely day' at the end of May in 1936. Only a farmhouse now remains of the manor house to which old Mrs. Ferrar retired during the great plague of 1625. She was joined there by her son Nicholas, who in the following year took deacon's orders, and her other children and their children. Under the direction of Nicholas, they formed a Christian community of some thirty-five to forty members, of all ages, which attempted to combine the values of monastic and family life. In his quiet and humble way Nicholas Ferrar stands with famous figures of the religious crisis of the Reformation and Counter-Reformation: Ignatius Loyola, with his revolutionary Society of Jesus, Philip Neri, with his Oratorians, and, in the seventeenth century, St. Vincent de Paul, with his Sisters of Charity. All attempted, in different ways, to translate the dedicated religious life into forms suited to the demands of their age. Compared with them, Nicholas Ferrar is a very minor figure, whose work, unlike theirs, died with him. When the religious life was revived in the Church of England in the nineteenth century, it was revived on the classic monastic pattern. Ferrar's experiment was ignored. At the time of Eliot's visit Little Gidding must have seemed only 'a symbol perfected in death'. Some forty years later, it looks a little different. Ferrar could well be regarded as a man in advance of his time in establishing 'a Christian commune'. A community of both sexes and all ages, which combined regular devotions with intellectual and manual labours, and with social service to its neighbourhood, has a curiously modern look. After Ferrar's death in 1637 the community continued under the care of his brother John; but the rising tide of sectarian bitterness that preceded the Civil War made Little Gidding an obvious target for opponents of Laudianism. In 1641 a pamphlet, based on earlier slanders, called *The Arminian Nunnery*,[59] was addressed to Parliament; and in 1646, after the defeat of the Royalist cause, Parliamentary troops despoiled the house and the church. The community was broken up and dispersed. The family papers, including a life of Nicholas Ferrar by his brother John, of which there appear to have been two or three versions, came by marriage into the hands of Dr. Peter Peckard, Master of Magdalene College, Cambridge, who published his *Memoirs of the Life of Nicholas Ferrar* in 1790.[60]

Outside the circle of those interested in the byways of ecclesiastical history, Ferrar's name lived on as the friend of George Herbert to whom, on his deathbed, Herbert sent his poems and who saw *The Temple* through the press. But Little Gidding remained obscure and forgotten, although the church was made fit again for worship after the Restoration. The present stone front was put up in 1714 by the great-nephew of Nicholas Ferrar, who held the livings of Steeple and Little Gidding, probably to replace the organ gallery built by old Mrs. Ferrar. The thorough restoration of the church was due to William Hopkinson of Stamford, who was inspired by having read Peckard's *Memoirs* as a boy.[61] The work was completed in 1853—the original brass eagle-lectern having been discovered in a near-by pond—and Hopkinson, who describes himself on one of the stained-glass windows with which he embellished the church as 'Lord of the Manor of Little Gidding', has the right to be called the first 'Friend of Little Gidding'. Real fame came to Little Gidding during the eighteen-nineties, as a glance at the

[59] The title-page of this defamatory work was most unsuitably used as the illustration to Eliot's broadcast talk on 'The Devotional Poets of the Seventeenth Century' when it was printed in *The Listener*, 26 March 1930.

[60] Some thirty years earlier, Francis Turner, Bishop of Ely, had published a life of Ferrar in *The Christian Magazine* (vol. ii, 1761). Unfortunately the manuscripts on which Turner and Peckard based their much edited Lives have both disappeared, but it is obvious they took considerable liberties with their material. Both Lives were printed by J. E. B. Mayor, with supplementary material, in *Nicholas Ferrar: Two Lives* (1855). The Life of Ferrar by his brother has been scrupulously edited from the extant manuscript sources by B. Blackstone in *The Ferrar Papers* (1938), along with a Dialogue, 'The Winding Sheet', performed in the Great Chamber, a Collection of Short Moral Histories, and a selection of letters from the vast collection of papers left to Magdalene by Peckard.

[61] Mayor, in the preface to his *Nicholas Ferrar: Two Lives* (1855) thanks Hopkinson for his help, and adds: 'If Gidding church now reflects the image of days which have thrown a saintly halo around it . . . all is owing to the impression made on his boyish sympathies some sixty years ago by a perusal of Ferrar's life.' An account of the restoration of the church can be found in Mayor's introduction.

bibliography to Mandell Creighton's excellent article on Ferrar in the *Dictionary of National Biography* shows; and from 1904 there took place a series of annual pilgrimages.[62] This was undoubtedly due to J. H. Shorthouse, whose novel, *John Inglesant*, privately printed at the author's expense in 1880, had an immense success when it was published in the following year by Macmillan, and became the object of a veritable cult among eminent late-Victorians. Shorthouse described his novel as a 'Philosophical Romance'. Its hero, educated by a Jesuit tutor, vacillates through the book between the Church of England and the Church of Rome, is involved in secret services in the Royalist cause during the Civil War, and travels to Italy, where he is attracted by the doctrines of Molinos and horrified by his condemnation. This finally settles the problem of his religious allegiance and the book ends with Inglesant as an old man delivering a long and fervent defence of the Church of England as 'an agency by which the devotional instincts of human nature are enabled to exist side by side with the rational'. Inglesant visits Little Gidding in the autumn of 1637 two months before Nicholas Ferrar's death, and is invited to stay. He joins in the family's round of devotions and takes the Sacrament with them on Sunday morning, an experience that remains in his mind all his life. He is deeply attracted by Ferrar's niece, Mary Collett, and she is, as he secretly acknowledges to himself, his main reason for returning to Little Gidding in 1642 for another, longer stay. Their romance comes to nothing: he is too involved in the plans of his Jesuit tutor to feel free to marry, and she feels dedicated to her uncle's work. He returns once more to Little Gidding after fighting at Naseby, only to be summoned from the chapel by a messenger from the Jesuit. He is given the dangerous, secret mission of negotiating with the Irish Catholics on behalf of the King. This leads him to prison and to the scaffold, where he is saved at the last moment, and consequently to exile. In Paris he encounters Mary Collett, who is dying in a French convent.

Shorthouse was fourteen years writing *John Inglesant*, and it is the fruit of remarkably wide reading in seventeenth-century sources. As is well known, he inlaid his romantic narrative with passages from his reading, often inserted verbatim.[63] His long description of the way of life at Little Gidding he took from Peckard's *Memoirs*, which he read in the reprint in Christopher

---

[62] These were organized by the Rt. Rev. the Hon. Edward Glyn, Bishop of Peterborough (1897–1916). An account of these aristocratic, and far from ascetic, pious jaunts can be found in an article by the Bishop's daughter in *A Little Gidding Miscellany*, published by the Friends of Little Gidding (January 1966), which also contains an article by Montgomery Belgion on the writing of Eliot's poem.

[63] The fullest treatment of Shorthouse's appropriations is by W. K. Fleming, *Quarterly Review* (July 1925). Acton's criticisms of Shorthouse's historical errors can be found in *Letters of Lord Acton to Mary Gladstone* (1904), 135–48. Acton corresponded on the subject with S. R. Gardiner also. The fact that these two great historians read the book with such care and criticized it with such earnestness is best evidence of its extraordinary vogue.

Wordsworth's *Ecclesiastical Biography*.[64] In a review of A. L. Maycock's *Nicholas Ferrar of Little Gidding* in the *Criterion* (October 1938) Bernard Blackstone, who referred rather superciliously to a recent tercentenary which had 'fluttered the Liberal Catholic world into a pilgrimage and a panegyric', spent most of his review attacking *John Inglesant* for the Victorian sentimentality it had cast over Little Gidding. But a few months later, Canon Charles Smyth, reviewing Blackstone's *The Ferrar Papers* in the *Criterion* (January 1939), defended the novel for its appreciation of the 'genius of the Church of England'.[65] I find it difficult to believe that this book, so famous in its day, was not known to the Eliot family, with their passionate interest in religious discussions, and that Eliot had not read it as a boy. But, even if he had not read it when young, it seems likely he would have done so in later life. It was greatly admired by Paul Elmer More, with whom he had a long correspondence on religious matters, particularly on Anglicanism on which More wrote a distinguished book. And even if More's praise of it as the finest of religious novels had not stimulated his interest, it seems likely that Smyth's praise of it would have done so.[66] In any case, any reader who wishes to know what Eliot had in mind when he wrote 'of a king at nightfall' and declared

> It would be the same at the end of the journey,
> If you came at night like a broken king,

could not do better than to turn to Shorthouse's novel.

King Charles visited Little Gidding first in 1633, and as a result of this visit the community made for Prince Charles a beautifully bound and illustrated Bible. He returned there in 1642 with the young Prince and his nephew Prince Rupert, riding over from Huntingdon. The King shot a hare, and the young Prince ate cheese-cake and apple-pie in the pantry (mundane details that *John Inglesant* omits). He gave the Ferrars five pounds which he had won at cards the night before from his nephew and at leaving said 'Pray, pray for my safe and speedy return'. His return was in

---

[64] See *The Life and Letters of J. H. Shorthouse*, edited by his wife (1905), where Shorthouse says that Mayor's more scholarly work only came into his hands after he had published his novel.

[65] There is a similar defence in Henry Scott Holland's *A Bundle of Memories* (1915). Scott Holland devoted a whole chapter (Chapter XVI) to Shorthouse and having praised *John Inglesant* as having 'a special note of charm and distinction', singled out some 'dramatic moments', and spoke of its atmosphere as 'delicate and subtle, admirably sustained throughout'. He ends:

> We may have been slightly bribed into undue delight by the surprise of finding our familiar Anglicanism lifted up into the throne of the mystical and poetical ideal. That unhappy air of being a Via Media, a half-way house, was gone: it was transfigured into the fine and delicate poise of the free soul, moving, entranced along a secret path, known only to the elect, amid the perilous ambushes that might ensnare it on the right hand or the left, if it ever wavered or swerved.

[66] The edition of *John Inglesant* in Eliot's library is that published by Macmillan in 1927 in 'The Caravan Library'. Mrs. Valerie Eliot tells me she cannot say whether he actually read this copy, as he often borrowed books from the London Library and purchased them much later.

May 1646, when he came at night alone, except for his chaplain, on his way north to give himself up to the Scots. Shorthouse took the story from Peckard's *Memoirs*, which it seems unlikely that Eliot had read. He tells it movingly:

A few days afterwards the news ran like wildfire over England that the King had left Oxford secretly; and that no one knew where he was; and a night or two afterwards Mr. John Ferrar was called up by a gentleman who said he was Dr. Hudson, the King's Chaplain, and that the King was alone, a few paces from the door, and that he would fetch him in.

Mr. Ferrar received His Majesty with all possible respect. But fearing that Gidding from the known loyalty of the family, might be a suspected place, for better concealment he conducted the King to a private house at Coppingford, an obscure village at a small distance from Gidding, and not far from Stilton. It was a very dark night, and but for the lantern Mr. Ferrar carried, they could not have known the way. As it was, they lost their way once, and wandered for some time in a ploughed field. Mr. Ferrar always spoke with the utmost passionate distress of this night, as of a night the incidents of which must have awakened the compassion of every feeling heart, however biassed against the King. As proof of the most affecting distress, the King, he said, was serene and even cheerful, and said he was protected by the King of Kings.[67]

But Eliot's visit to Little Gidding in May 1936 was very probably inspired by the fact that some time early in 1936 his friend, George Every, sent him the draft of a verse play on the subject of King Charles's last visit to Little Gidding. Mr. Every very kindly lent me the first draft of the play and told me of his correspondence with Eliot about it during the year. On 26 February Eliot wrote saying 'I am ashamed not to have got round to studying your play sufficiently to report to you'; and on 13 March he wrote to comment on an altered version he had been sent. Later in the same year, in October, he had again been reading an altered version with an alternative ending, which he thought 'a great improvement'. On and off during the year in which he visited Little Gidding, and both before and after the visit, Eliot was con-

[67] *John Inglesant*, chapter xiii. Peckard's account runs: 'On the 27th April, in that fatal year (1646) the King left Oxford. Being unresolved how to dispose himself, he shifted about from place to place, with his trusty Chaplain, Dr. Hudson, and at length came to Downham in Norfolk. From thence he came on May 2nd very privately and in the night to Gidding. Mr. Nicholas Ferrar had been dead for several years. But the king having an entire confidence in the family made himself known to Mr. John Ferrar, who received his Majesty with all possible duty and respect. But fearing that Gidding, from the known loyalty of the family, might be a suspected place, for better concealment he conducted his Majesty to a private house at Coppingford, an obscure village at a small distance from Gidding, and not far from Stilton.' The passage illustrates well Shorthouse's treatment of his sources. Other details can be found in HMC Portland MSS and Peck, *Desiderata Curiosa*: references are given by Dame Veronica Wedgwood, *The King's War* (1958). One of Hopkinson's windows in Little Gidding church commemorates this visit of the king, but it does not mention night. The window has the arms of King Charles with the inscription 'Insignia Caroli Regis qui latitabat apud Ferrarios 2do Maii A.S. 1646'.

cerned with his friend's play. Having read the first draft, it seems to me that when, four or five years later, he planned to write a fourth poem on 'Fire', it was Mr. Every's play that linked fire with Little Gidding in his mind and that his memory of it coloured the discussion of victory and defeat in Part III.

In the manuscript draft I have seen the play begins with a conversation between John Ferrar, the head of the community, his niece Mary Collett, and Richard Crashaw on what is going to happen and what they should do now that the King's cause has gone down to total defeat at Naseby. Crashaw argues that the 'only succour' is over the channel, where 'the monks chant their plainsong' at St. Omer, leaving behind 'the conflagration of the forest fire' which rages in England. Ferrar takes up the metaphor of fire and asks 'Would you walk away or walk through the fire?', declaring that suffering must be endured 'to find the meaning that God intends in it': 'For God has a meaning in defeat.' To which Crashaw replies: 'A meaning, to show we were wrong.' The conversation is interrupted by a neighbour, with a couple of troopers, who comes to persuade Ferrar to 'obey the powers that be' and take the Covenant. He argues that 'God made our victory'. To this Ferrar assents, but not to his 'interpretation of event'. After he has gone and the friends have prayed together, the fugitive king enters with his chaplain, to ask for refuge. A minor point of interest is that there are two references to Richard III's death in battle in Mr. Every's play, and for a moment, during the revision of Part III, Eliot allowed Richard III to stray into Part III, rather strangely accompanied by the Duke of Wellington.[68]

In *The Dry Salvages* Eliot acknowledged by reference and by direct quotation the debt his poetry owed to Indian literature. In *Little Gidding* he paid tribute, in a long passage of deliberate imitation, to the poet who had, from the beginning, been the greatest single influence upon him, Dante.[69] Substituting an alternation of masculine and feminine endings for the alternating rhymes of *terza rima*, and 'the uncertain hour before the morning', the interval between the departure of the last bomber and the sounding of the All Clear, for the landscapes of hell and purgatory in which Dante spoke with the dead, he attempted to reproduce in English what he felt to be the distinctive quality of Dante's poetic style. The passage was revised again and again, and right up to the last moment Eliot was discussing words and phrases with Hayward. Troubled to find the exact word for the light just before the dawn, he wrote 'I am still however wrestling with the demon of that precise degree of light at that precise time of day' adding 'What is quite interesting is to find that this austere Dantesque style is more difficult, and

---

[68] See pp. 209-10.

[69] The only extended treatment of Eliot's debt to Dante and his relation to him which I know of is 'The Dantean Recognitions' by A. C. Charity in '*The Waste Land' in Different Voices*, edited by A. D. Moody (1974).

offers more pitfalls, than any other'. In a later letter he returned to the
subject:

> This type of verse appears to present the greatest difficulties. Every
> word sticks out, and the tax upon one's vocabulary is immense. Syllables
> and terminations also give one great trouble. If it is as difficult in Italian
> as in English (which I find it hard to credit) then my admiration for Dante
> should have no bounds.

Eliot developed at greater length the difficulties he found in writing his
Dantean imitation in his lecture on 'What Dante Means to Me'[70] where he
discussed the writing of this passage. The drafts and the correspondence
show the pains he took over what many would consider the finest passage in
Four Quartets.

In his preliminary scheme for the poem in the Magdalene manuscript
Eliot began 'Winter scene. May. / Lyric. air earth water end && / daemonic
fire. The Inferno.' In the manuscript draft, and in the first typed draft and
the first draft sent to Hayward the 'dead master' or 'familiar compound
ghost' is greeted with the cry 'Are you here, Ser Brunetto?', translating
Dante's cry on recognizing his old master in hell: '*Siete voi qui, Ser
Brunetto?*'[71] Even without this, 'the brown baked features', rendering '*lo
cotto aspetto*', at once recall this most moving of Dante's encounters with the
lost. When, having laid aside his poem for a year, Eliot sent a first revision
to Hayward (17 August 1942) he had completely re-written the close of the
dead master's speech. From the line 'But, as the passage now presents no
hindrance' to the end of his speech, the 'visionary figure', as Eliot calls him,
proffers totally different counsel.[72] In this first revision, 'Are you here,
Ser Brunetto?' was replaced by 'What! are *you* here?', and, at the close of
the speech a new conception appeared: of restoration

by that refining fire
Where you must learn to swim, and better nature.

Hayward appears to have objected to the removal of 'Ser Brunetto' and also
questioned the propriety of swimming in fire. Eliot wrote to him, sending
him a second revision, on 27 August 1942:

> I think you will recognise that it was necessary to get rid of Brunetto
> for two reasons. The first is that the visionary figure has now become
> somewhat more definite and will no doubt be identified by some readers
> with Yeats though I do not mean anything so precise as that. However,
> I do not wish to take the responsibility of putting Yeats or anybody else
> into Hell and I do not want to impute to him the particular vice which

---

[70] Printed in *To Criticize the Critic* (1965). See particularly pp. 128–9.
[71] *Inferno* XV.
[72] The first version is given in full in Appendix A.

took Brunetto there. Secondly, although the reference to that Canto is intended to be explicit, I wished the effect of the whole to be Purgatorial which is much more appropriate. That brings us to the reference to swimming in fire which you will remember at the end of Purgatorio 26 where the poets are found.[73] The active co-operation is, I think, sound theology and is certainly sound Dante, because the people who talk to him at that point are represented as not wanting to waste time in conversation but wishing to dive back into the fire to accomplish their expiation. However, I have for the moment at least discarded the whole image and rather like the suggestion of the new line which carries some reminder of a line, I think it is about Mark Antony.[74]

The manuscript material at Magdalene preserves Eliot's drafts for the new conclusion to the speech of the 'dead master'. The first is a prose outline, which makes clear that the master had become identified with Yeats. This is even clearer in Eliot's first attempt to versify the prose draft. Eliot had given the first Annual Yeats Lecture in Dublin in June 1940.[75] The lecture concentrated on Yeats's 'extraordinary development' as an artist and found his peculiar greatness to lie in his 'capacity of adaptation to the years'. 'It requires, indeed', Eliot wrote

an exceptional honesty and courage to face the change. Most men either cling to the experiences of youth, so that their writing becomes an insincere mimicry of their earlier work, or they leave their passion behind, and write only from the head, with a hollow and wasted virtuosity. There is another and even worse temptation: that of becoming dignified, of becoming public figures with only a public existence—coat-racks hung with decorations and distinctions, doing, saying, and even thinking and feeling only what they believe the public expects of them.

As an example of the 'honesty with oneself expressed in the poetry' of Yeats, Eliot quoted

> You think it horrible that lust and rage
> Should dance attendance upon my old age;
> They were not such a plague when I was young:
> What else have I to spur me into song?

[73] disparve per lo foco,
come per l'acqua pesce andando al fondo. . . .
and Poi s'ascose nel foco che gli affina
(*Purgatorio*, xxvi. 134–5 and 148).

[74] The 'new line' was 'Where you must move in measure, like a dancer'.

[75] Published in *Purpose*, xiii. 3, 4 (July, December 1940), reprinted in *On Poetry and Poets* (1957), 252–62. The first notes for the lecture are preserved on two leaves from a small writing pad at Magdalene (MS D). They owe their survival to the fact that on the verso of the first Eliot made a first attempt at what became the second stanza of the revised Part IV. Eliot was, like Pope, addicted to economizing with paper; but, of course, it was wartime.

and commented:

> These lines are very impressive and not very pleasant, and the senti-
> ment has recently been criticized by an English critic whom I generally
> respect. But I think he misread them. I do not read them as a personal
> confession of a man who differed from other men, but of a man who was
> essentially the same as most other men; the only difference is in the
> greater clarity, honesty and vigour. To what honest man, old enough, can
> these sentiments be entirely alien? They can be subdued and disciplined
> by religion, but who can say that they are dead? . . .
>
> Similarly, the play *Purgatory* is not very pleasant, either. There are
> aspects of it which I do not like myself. I wish he had not given it this title,
> because I cannot accept a purgatory in which there is no hint, or at least
> no emphasis upon Purgation. But, apart from the extraordinary theatrical
> skill with which he has put so much action within the compass of a very
> short scene of but little movement, the play gives a masterly exposition of
> the emotions of an old man.

In the conclusion of his lecture Eliot reverted to the difficulties Yeats had
to contend with in order to arrive at the 'freedom of speech' of his mature
poetry, and made explicit, as he had not done when discussing Yeats as
a poet of middle age and old age, a parallel with himself. 'There was much
also', he said, 'for Yeats to work out of himself.' Seeing him as more the poet
of 'the pre-Raphaelite twilight' than of the 'Celtic twilight', he declared:

> Yeats was born into the end of a literary movement, and an English
> movement at that: only those who have toiled with language know the
> labour and constancy required to free oneself from such influences—yet,
> on the other hand, once we are familiar with the older voice, we can hear
> its individual tones even in his earliest published verse. In my own time
> of youth there seemed to be no immediate great powers of poetry either
> to help or to hinder, either to learn from or to rebel against, yet I can
> understand the difficulty of the other situation, and the magnitude of
> the task.

In his first prose summary[76] for the new speech Eliot took up the theme
of the 'toil with language' and the theme of Purgatory as 'Purgation'. The
first very rough verse draft expands this. By a reference to the 'political fire',
and a contrast between 'the strength and weakness of the English tongue',
in which the speaker had been 'tutored', and the 'archaic tongue' of his
'alien people' it makes the identification with Yeats clear. The theme of old
age first appears in a rough verse draft which bears a clear relation to 'The
Spur', the quatrain quoted by Eliot in his lecture; but this metaphorical
treatment of the horror of aged 'lust and rage' Eliot discarded. He appears

---

[76] The drafts are transcribed in full in the commentary; see pp. 186-9.

then to have started again, concentrating on the 'gifts of age' and the 'purga-
tive fire' in which the 'enraged spirit' must 'learn to swim, and better nature',
in a prose draft that is an admirable brief summary of the final version of
the speech.

Only twelve lines survive of the first typescript (M7) of the revised speech.
The next page may have been lost, but I suspect that Eliot, having written
these four tercets, abandoned this typescript, for he has crossed through the
first and the last tercet and they are the ones that make specific reference to
Yeats. They do not appear in the next typescript (M8), which devotes, as
in the final version, only one tercet to their common 'concern with speech'
(employing, to confuse the persons, a rendering of a line by Mallarmé to
define their compulsion), and concentrates on 'the gifts reserved for age'.
Eliot was thus justified in telling Hayward that, although some readers
would identify the 'visionary figure' with Yeats, he did not mean 'anything
so precise as that'; but the drafts make it clear that he began with Yeats in
mind and worked towards a greater generality.[77] He removed the biographical hints, except for the burial abroad, and gave his whole mind to
echoing, with characteristic differences, the 'honesty' of Yeats as a poet of
old age.

In his letter written in reply to Hayward's comments on the first draft of
Little Gidding, Eliot wrote that he had been 'particularly unhappy about
Part II', thinking that it needed 'some sharpening of personal poignancy',
and, later in the letter made the same criticism of the whole poem in its
earlier form: 'The defect of the whole poem, I feel, is the lack of some acute
personal reminiscence (never to be explicated, of course, but to give power
from well below the surface) and I can *perhaps* supply this in Part II.' When
he took up the poem again and found the dead master took on the features
of Yeats, he found in Yeats a voice his own echoed with a difference and
with personal poignancy. In his lecture Eliot had spoken of Yeats as 'pre-
eminently the poet of middle age' because of his 'adaptation to the years'.
The Eliot of *East Coker*

> in the middle way, having had twenty years—
> Twenty years largely wasted, the years of *l'entre deux guerres*—
> Trying to learn to use words,

[77] In reply to a written enquiry Eliot told Professor Kristian Smidt that he 'was thinking primarily
of William Yeats, . . . the body on the foreign shore was William Yeats's'. Professor Smidt's article
'T. S. Eliot and W. B. Yeats' appeared in the *Revue des langues vivantes* (Brussels) simultaneously with
Richard Ellmann's 'Yeats and Eliot' in *Encounter* (July 1965). They are reprinted in *The Importance of
Recognition* (Tromsö 1973) and *Eminent Domain* (O.U.P., New York 1967) and nicely complement
each other.

In a letter to Hayward, 20 February 1943 (EHC), Eliot wrote: 'Perhaps your visitor who spotted the
Dante allusions had been reading a painstaking article in the Cambridge Magazine which went into
that very thoroughly. But why the phrase "compound ghost" "Both one and many" should still leave
people convinced that the stranger was one particular person, I don't understand.'

spoke ironically of 'the wisdom of age' and cried

> Do not let me hear
> Of the wisdom of old men, but rather of their folly,
> Their fear of fear and frenzy. . . .

The word 'frenzy' at once recalls a famous poem of Yeats's old age, in which, having owned 'My temptation is quiet', he rejected the temptation for 'frenzy':

> Grant me an old man's frenzy,
> Myself must I remake
> Till I am Timon and Lear
> Or that William Blake
> Who beat upon the wall
> Till Truth obeyed his call;
>
> A mind Michael Angelo knew
> That can pierce the clouds,
> Or inspired by frenzy
> Shake the dead in their shrouds;
> Forgotten else by mankind,
> An old man's eagle mind.[78]

'Old men ought to be explorers.' Yeats was such an old man. The likeness and the difference between Eliot and Yeats is beautifully clear in the contrast between Yeats's desire for a mind that can 'pierce the clouds', an 'old man's eagle mind', and Eliot's image of exploring 'through the dark cold and the empty desolation'. In *Little Gidding*, the middle-aged Eliot, in place of a catalogue of 'essential moments' from the past in his first version, turned to the thought of the future: the reward for a 'lifetime's effort' in old age. A verse that he had some years before quoted from Yeats, a poet whose 'thought and theory' he had criticized, added to the Yeatsian 'cold friction of expiring sense' and the 'conscious impotence of rage', 'the rending pain of re-enactment':

> Things said or done long years ago,
> Or things I did not do or say
> But thought that I might say or do,
> Weigh me down, and not a day
> But something is recalled,
> My conscience or my vanity appalled.[79]

---

[78] 'An Acre of Grass.'

[79] 'Vacillation' V, quoted by Eliot in *After Strange Gods* (1934), 46. Both Smidt and Ellmann note this stanza as a source.

But at the close Eliot combines Yeats with Dante and Christianizes, from his favourite canto of the *Purgatorio*, Yeats's plea to the 'sages standing in God's holy fire':

> Consume my heart away; sick with desire
> And fastened to a dying animal
> It knows not what it is; and gather me
> Into the artifice of eternity.[80]

He returns to Dante again at the end of the poem: this time to the end of the *Paradiso*: to the image of the redeemed gathered together in the form of a pure white rose.

In the first draft sent to Hayward Eliot ended Part III with an adaptation of the first four lines of the prayer '*Anima Christi sanctifica me*'. He wrote to Hayward to cut this before Hayward had had time to comment on the whole poem. Hayward approved the excision. As the second verse of the lyric in Part IV had no equivalent in the first version, the poem as originally drafted contained little that expressed personal devotion or recalled the spiritual works on which Eliot's own piety had been nourished, except for this rather irrelevant and sudden break into a prayer commonly used for Eucharistic devotions.[81] It was in his revision that he turned to the English mystics of the fourteenth century to provide a parallel for the use of St. John of the Cross in *East Coker* and the *Bhagavad-Gita* in *The Dry Salvages*. His mind may have turned to them on account of the death of Evelyn Underhill in June 1941.[82] She had been a pioneer in bringing back these writers into circulation, both as masters of the spiritual life and as neglected masters of English prose, and had herself produced modernized editions of both *The Cloud of Unknowing* and Hilton's *The Scale of Perfection*. Evelyn Underhill reviewed for the *Criterion*; but Eliot knew her also as a director of souls. Possibly he was writing out of his own experience when he broke off his manuscript draft of Part II of *Little Gidding* to write two pages of a letter to some paper or journal to supplement an obituary notice of her:[83]

I should like to supplement your admirable notice of the late E. U. (Mrs. S. M.) ~~on~~ [with, a word about] the side of her activity which is not represented by [preserved in] her published work or known to most of her readers. She concerned herself as much with the practice as with the

---

[80] 'Sailing to Byzantium.'

[81] The '*Anima Christi*' is sometimes ascribed to St. Ignatius Loyola, but its composition antedates the sixteenth century. Eliot probably used the translation in *St. Swithun's Prayer Book*, a very popular Anglo-Catholic devotional manual.

[82] Mrs. Lyndall Gordon tells me that Eliot read her highly influential book, *Mysticism* (1911), when he was an undergraduate at Harvard. He took copious notes, particularly from the chapter 'Voices and Visions'. At that time he was also interesting himself in St. John of the Cross, Dame Julian, and Walter Hilton. So his knowledge of these writers goes back to his youth.

[83] MS A, ff. 90, 91. Pencil draft. Words in square brackets are written above the line.

theory of the devotional life—her studies of the great mystics had the inspiration not primarily of the scholar or the champion of forgotten genius, but of a consciousness of the ~~great need~~ [~~absence~~ grievous need] of the contemplative element in [the] modern ~~life~~ [world]. She gave (with frail health & constant illness) herself to many, in retreats which she conducted and in the intercourse of daily life—she was always at the disposal of all who called upon her. With a lively and humorous interest in human beings [especially the young, with shrewdness and simplicity she helped to support the spiritual life of many more than she could in her humility have been aware of aiding.] She was at the same time withdrawn and sociable.

When Hayward received the draft of Eliot's revision, in which the second section of Part III began with the quotation from Julian of Norwich,

> Sin is behovely, but
> All shall be well, and
> All manner of thing shall be well—

and the last page opened with the line from *The Cloud of Unknowing*,

> With the drawing of this love and the voice of this calling,

he apparently made a puzzled comment, for Eliot wrote to him on sending him 'a new fair copy' (2 September 1942):

I forgot in my previous letter to give an explanation which bears on your query of *behovely*. This line and the two which follow and which occur twice later constitute a quotation from Juliana of Norwich. The beautiful line the presence of which puzzles you toward the end of page 11 comes out of *The Cloud of Unknowing*. My purpose was this: there is so much 17th century in the poem that I was afraid of a certain romantic Bonnie Dundee period effect and I wanted to check this and at the same time give greater historical depth to the poem by allusions to the other great period, i.e. the 14th century. Juliana and *The Cloud of Unknowing* represent pretty well the two mystical extremes or, one might say, the male and female of this literature. I might have dragged in Walter Hilton and Richard Rolle, I daresay, but for one thing I don't know them so well and for another I think that would be overdoing it. Does it seem to you possibly that the passages in question ought to be put in inverted commas?

Hayward appears to have written back suggesting capitalizing the quotations, for Eliot wrote on 7 September:

I'm afraid I don't like capitalising the quotes. Too much like headlines: slightly comic. I thought better of restoring the spelling; but I read the texts in modern versions, and the London Library seems to possess *no* texts with the XIII century spelling: neither of these authors appears to have been done by the E.E. Text Soc.[84] I now incline to put between guillemets

'Sin is behovely,' etc.

on its first appearance, but *not* the two repetitions. This means putting 'With the drawing of this love . . .' in quotes also. *Or not?*

Hayward must have written back rejecting this suggestion, for Eliot wrote again on 9 September 'I accept the more limited capitalisation'. In the final recension, as in the final text, only 'Behovely' was capitalized in the quotation from Julian, and 'Love' and 'Calling' in the quotation from *The Cloud of Unknowing*.

Finally, a major source of *Little Gidding* is the earlier poems of the sequence. In writing it Eliot deliberately gathered up themes and images from his earlier meditations on Time's losses and Time's gains, to make the poem not only complete and beautiful in itself but the crown and completion of the exploration of man in Time he had begun in *Burnt Norton*.

---

[84] In a letter of 2 October, obviously replying to a bibliographical query from Hayward, Eliot wrote: 'My edition of Cloud of Unknowing IS m'Cann's, the most recent. My edition of Juliana is also Cressy, but a reprint published where, do you think? Why, in St. Louis Mo., though sent me by Jones & Evans of Cheapside.' Dom Justin McCann, O.S.B. edited *The Cloud of Unknowing* in a modernized text in the Orchard Series (1924). Julian of Norwich's *Revelations of Divine Love* was first printed in a modernized text in 1670 by Serenus de Cressy, once Fellow of Merton and chaplain to Lord Falkland, later a Benedictine at Douai. Cressy's text was reprinted in 1843 and subsequently. There are other modernized versions, some reading 'behoveful', others rewriting the sentence: 'It behoved that there should be sin. . . .' When Eliot wrote, there were no critical editions for him to use. *The Cloud of Unknowing* was edited from the manuscripts by Dr. Phyllis Hodgson for the Early English Text Society in 1944. Julian of Norwich and Walter Hilton still await an editor.

Hayward has pencilled '?XIV' against Eliot's mistaken 'XIII'.

PART TWO

Textual Note

The text of all four poems is that of the first English edition of *Four Quartets* (1944). The critical apparatus gives readings from all available texts prior to that. The only subsequent editions I have collated are *Collected Poems 1909–1962* (1963), the last to be printed in the poet's lifetime, and the paperback edition of this, for which the text was entirely reset in 1974.

The text is divided into sections to allow, whenever possible, the commentary to be printed below the text or on a facing page. *Sigla* for the texts used in the critical apparatus are given in the introduction to each poem. Drafts given to Hayward are distinguished by the letter D from drafts given to Magdalene College, which are given the letter M. Readings commented on by Eliot and Hayward or discussed in the commentary are distinguished by an asterisk.

Alterations made by Eliot in manuscript are printed in italic type to distinguish them from alterations made by him in typescript. Deletions are indicated by a thin bar through the deleted word or words. I have not distinguished cancellations made thus by Eliot from cancellations he made by overtyping a word by a row of typed crosses. It will be clear from the fact that the correction is in roman type and not in italic that a correction has been made in the typing, either by obliterating the rejected word and going forward on the same line, or by typing the correction above the obliterated word. Such corrections, made with the paper in the machine, will have preceded the italicized manuscript corrections. Corrections and suggestions made in the margins appear to be later than those made between the lines. I have printed them within angled-brackets. Those interested have thus a clue to the order in which alterations and suggestions were made. When Eliot decided to revert to a word that he had cancelled he put a line of dots below the cancelled word. These are reproduced as he made them.

Letters quoted from for which no reference is given should be assumed to have been bound up by Hayward with his drafts.

Burnt Norton

Burnt Norton

There is very little material available for the study of the composition of *Burnt Norton*. Hayward was given only one typed draft, and there are no references to the poem in any correspondence which I have seen.

D (9 pages). On page 1 Eliot has written '"Burnt Norton" / printer's copy. / from the T. S. Eliot bequest / to John Hayward Esq.' Pages 1–8, numbered, contain the text, the Greek quotations being written by Eliot above the typescript. Page 9, unnumbered, contains drafts of lines 156–8.

CP. *Collected Poems, 1909–1935*, published 2 April 1936.

BN. *Burnt Norton*, published 20 February 1941.

The first fourteen lines of *Burnt Norton* are adapted with slight alteration from a speech Eliot supplied for the Second Priest to follow Thomas's speech after the exit of the Second Tempter in *Murder in the Cathedral*. It was cut before the first performance. The typescript of the draft containing this speech is in the McKeldin Library at the University of Maryland; see p. 16 supra.

The first two lines of Part II were originally part of the poem published in CP as 'Lines for an Old Man'. Two drafts for this poem are in the Houghton Library, Harvard University.

The first seven lines of the poem as printed stand in both the extant typed drafts. In the first of these, which is untitled, the poem concludes

> When I lay bare the tooth of wit
> *Garlic*
> ~~Thunder~~ and sapphires in the mud
> Clot the bedded axle-tree.

Eliot has written below, with a line to indicate insertion before the last two lines,

> *My hate is more than hate of hate,*
> *More* ~~And~~ the *of ~~in~~*
> *bitter* ~~More bitter er~~ than ~~the~~ Love ~~of~~ youth
> *selfish*

and, again, below this,

> *The*
> ~~The My~~ *hissing ~~of~~ over the flattened tongue*
> *Is inaccessible to the young.*

The second draft is headed 'WORDS FOR AN OLD MAN.' and is dedicated 'to Stephane Mallarmé.'; but the dedication has been crossed through. The poem as typed concludes

> When I lay bare the tooth of wit
> archèd
> The hissing over the ~~flattened~~ tongue
> Is more affectionate than hate,
> More bitter than the love of youth,
> *by*
> And inaccessible ~~to~~ the young.
> ~~Garlic and sapphires in the mud~~
> ~~Clot the bedded axle-tree.~~

The last two lines having been cancelled, Eliot has written the conclusion of the poem as printed below:

> *Reflected in my golden eye—*
> *The dullard knows that he is mad.*
> *Tell me if I am not glad!*

Eliot's original conclusion was inspired by the tercets of a sonnet by Mallarmé, and, when he cancelled the last two lines, he found a new final line in a direct translation of a line from the same sonnet:

> M'introduire dans ton histoire
> C'est en héros effarouché
> S'il a du talon nu touché
> Quelque gazon de territoire
>
> A des glaciers attentatoire
> Je ne sais le naïf péché
> Que tu n'aurais pas empêché
> De rire très haut sa victoire
>
> Dis si je ne suis pas joyeux
> Tonnerre et rubis aux moyeux
> De voir en l'air que ce feu troue
>
> Avec des royaumes épars
> Comme mourir pourpre la roue
> Du seul vespéral de mes chars.

Proust's narrator quoted the tercets in his farewell letter to Albertine as verses '*que vous disiez ne pouvoir comprendre*'. Valéry suggested that the speaker is making an evening promenade in a carriage with wheels either actually red or reddened by the reflection of the setting sun. The thunder suggests the noise of the chariot and the explosion of the speaker's joy at his triumph over his frigid mistress.

As many readers may well share Albertine's incomprehension, I append a translation from Stéphane Mallarmé, *Poems*, translated by Roger Fry (1936):

> To get myself into your story
> 'Tis as a hero affrighted
> Has his naked foot but touched
> Some lawn of that territory
>
> Violator of glaciers
> I know no sun so naïve be it
> That you will not have prevented
> From laughing's victory aloud
>
> Say if I am not joyous
> Thunder and rubies at the axles
> To see in this fire-pierced air
>
> Amid scattered realms
> As though dying purple the wheel
> Of my sole chariot of evening.

The line '*Tonnerre et rubis aux moyeux*' has combined in Eliot's mind with another phrase from Mallarmé: '*bavant boue et rubis*' from 'Le Tombeau de Charles Baudelaire'. Mysterious and suggestive, the discarded conclusion provided the inspiration for the series of musically evocative lines on the reconciliation of opposites and the pattern underlying temporal change with which Part II of *Burnt Norton* opens.

BURNT NORTON

Text of *Four Quartets* (1944)

(1-17)

I

Time present and time past
Are both perhaps present in time future,
And time future contained in time past.
If all time is eternally present
All time is unredeemable.   5
What might have been is an abstraction
Remaining a perpetual possibility
Only in a world of speculation.
What might have been and what has been
Point to one end, which is always present.   10
Footfalls echo in the memory
Down the passage which we did not take
Towards the door we never opened
Into the rose-garden. My words echo
Thus, in your mind.
                    But to what purpose   15
Disturbing the dust on a bowl of rose-leaves
I do not know.

BURNT NORTON] BURNT NORTON. | τοῦ λόγου δ᾽ἐόντος ξυνοῦ ζώουσιν | οἱ πολλοί ὡς ἰδίαν ἔχοντες | φρόνησιν. | *1. p. 77. Fr. 2.* | ὁδὸς ἄνω κάτω μία καὶ ὠυτή. | *1. p. 89. Fr. 60.* | Diels: Die Fragmente der Vorsokratiker (Herakleitos). D (*Greek written by Eliot beneath the title*); CP (*on reverse of title page to* Burnt Norton)   1-14 Time present . . . Into the rose-garden.

> Time present and time past
> Are both perhaps present in the future.
> Time future is contained in time past. . . .
> What might have been is a conjecture
> Remaining a permanent possibility
> Only in a world of speculation. . . .
> Footfalls echo in the memory
> Down the passage which we did not take
> Into the rose-garden.   (Draft of *Murder in the Cathedral*)

The Greek epigraphs were omitted when *Burnt Norton* was published in pamphlet form. In *Four Quartets* they appear on the reverse of the table of Contents, as if they were epigraphs to all four poems. In *The Complete Poems and Plays* (New York, 1952) and *Collected Poems 1909-1962* they appear, as in the draft, below the title of *Burnt Norton*.

(17-46)

Other echoes
Inhabit the garden. Shall we follow?
Quick, said the bird, find them, find them,
Round the corner. Through the first gate,   20
Into our first world, shall we follow
The deception of the thrush? Into our first world.
There they were, dignified, invisible,
Moving without pressure, over the dead leaves,
In the autumn heat, through the vibrant air,   25
And the bird called, in response to
The unheard music hidden in the shrubbery,
And the unseen eyebeam crossed, for the roses
Had the look of flowers that are looked at.
There they were as our guests, accepted and accepting.   30
So we moved, and they, in a formal pattern,
Along the empty alley, into the box circle,
To look down into the drained pool.
Dry the pool, dry concrete, brown edged,
And the pool was filled with water out of sunlight,   35
And the lotos rose, quietly, quietly,
The surface glittered out of heart of light,
And they were behind us, reflected in the pool.
Then a cloud passed, and the pool was empty.
Go, said the bird, for the leaves were full of children,   40
Hidden excitedly, containing laughter.
Go, go, go, said the bird: human kind
Cannot bear very much reality.
Time past and time future
What might have been and what has been   45
Point to one end, which is always present.

Eliot's letter to Hayward, quoted as chapter-heading on page 29, suggests we should take 'our first world' simply, as the world of childhood, and not import into the phrase theological conceptions from the later *Quartets*. The 'dignified, invisible' presences are then the grown-ups, who create for happy children a world of security and love in which they play.

For line 30, cf. 'Let us then make this so accepted a time in itself twice acceptable by our accepting, which He will acceptably take at our hands', quoted by Eliot from Andrewes's Sermon V, 'Of the Nativity' in *For Lancelot Andrewes* (1928), 28.

'Human kind cannot bear very much reality' is said by Thomas to the Chorus at the close of his last speech to them before the martyrdom (*Murder in the Cathedral*, 1935, p. 67).

(47–61)

II

Garlic and sapphires in the mud
Clot the bedded axle-tree.
The trilling wire in the blood
Sings below inveterate scars   50
Appeasing long forgotten wars.
The dance along the artery
The circulation of the lymph
Are figured in the drift of stars
Ascend to summer in the tree   55
We move above the moving tree
In light upon the figured leaf
And hear upon the sodden floor
Below, the boarhound and the boar
Pursue their pattern as before   60
But reconciled among the stars.

51* Appeasing long forgotten] And reconciles forgotten D, BN

I used to think that the change from 'Appeasing long forgotten wars', the reading in CP, to 'And reconciles forgotten wars', the reading of BN, published in 1941, showed a sensitiveness to the political overtones of the word 'appeasement' in the period just after the Munich Agreement, and that the reversion to the reading of CP in *Four Quartets*, published in 1944, indicated that Eliot felt that by then the word had become less loaded. The draft makes clear that 'And reconciles forgotten wars' was the original reading, and that the alteration to 'Appeasing long forgotten wars' must have taken place in the correction of the proof of CP, presumably to avoid anticipating the word 'reconciled' in the last line. The agreement of the draft with BN here and also in lines 64 and 70 shows that Eliot must have sent to the printer of BN a copy of the same corrected draft as he had supplied for CP, forgetting that he had made some further corrections in proof.

(62–82)

At the still point of the turning world. Neither flesh nor fleshless;
Neither from nor towards; at the still point, there the dance is,
But neither arrest nor movement. And do not call it fixity,
Where past and future are gathered. Neither movement from nor towards,   65
Neither ascent nor decline. Except for the point, the still point,
There would be no dance, and there is only the dance.
I can only say, *there* we have been: but I cannot say where.
And I cannot say, how long, for that is to place it in time.
The inner freedom from the practical desire,   70
The release from action and suffering, release from the inner
And the outer compulsion, yet surrounded
By a grace of sense, a white light still and moving,
Erhebung without motion, concentration
Without elimination, both a new world   75
And the old made explicit, understood
In the completion of its partial ecstasy,
The resolution of its partial horror.
Yet the enchainment of past and future
Woven in the weakness of the changing body,   80
Protects mankind from heaven and damnation
Which flesh cannot endure.

64 fixity,] fixity. D, BN   68 where] where ⟨*not ital*⟩ D   69–70 *Break, new paragraph*
at 70 D, BN   79 Yet the] The ⟨*Yet t*⟩ D   81 Protects] Protect⌃ˢ D

'At the still point of the turning world' is quoted from *Coriolan* I. *Triumphal March*, published in 1931. Charles Williams told me, and Eliot confirmed, that the image of the dance around the 'still point' was suggested by Williams's novel *The Greater Trumps*, where in a magical model of the universe the figures of the Tarot pack dance around the Fool at the still centre. Only Sybil, the wise woman of the novel, sees the Fool as moving and completing all the movements of the dancers.

In line 68 Eliot underlined 'where' as well as 'there' for italicization, but corrected by writing 'not ital' in the margin and cancelling the underlining.

(82–107)

                        Time past and time future
Allow but a little consciousness.
To be conscious is not to be in time
But only in time can the moment in the rose-garden,   85
The moment in the arbour where the rain beat,
The moment in the draughty church at smokefall
Be remembered; involved with past and future.
Only through time time is conquered.

III

Here is a place of disaffection   90
Time before and time after
In a dim light: neither daylight
Investing form with lucid stillness
Turning shadow into transient beauty
With slow rotation suggesting permanence   95
Nor darkness to purify the soul
Emptying the sensual with deprivation
Cleansing affection from the temporal.
Neither plenitude nor vacancy. Only a flicker
Over the strained time-ridden faces   100
Distracted from distraction by distraction
Filled with fancies and empty of meaning
Tumid apathy with no concentration
Men and bits of paper, whirled by the cold wind
That blows before and after time,   105
Wind in and out of unwholesome lungs
Time before and time after.

        But only   can
85–8 Yet it is in time that . . .
        Can only bBe remembered;   D

The setting of section III is the London Tube. Eliot travelled daily from
Gloucester Road Station, whose two means of descent, by the stairs or by
the lift, suggested to him the movement down and the 'abstention from
movement', while being carried down, of the next paragraph. He gave this
information in a letter to his brother. Julia in *The Cocktail Party* said 'In
a lift I can meditate' (p. 32).

(108–136)

Eructation of unhealthy souls
Into the faded air, the torpid
Driven on the wind that sweeps the gloomy hills of London,   110
Hampstead and Clerkenwell, Campden and Putney,
Highgate, Primrose and Ludgate. Not here
Not here the darkness, in this twittering world.

Descend lower, descend only
Into the world of perpetual solitude,   115
World not world, but that which is not world,
Internal darkness, deprivation
And destitution of all property,
Desiccation of the world of sense,
Evacuation of the world of fancy,   120
Inoperancy of the world of spirit;
This is the one way, and the other
Is the same, not in movement
But abstention from movement; while the world moves
In appetency, on its metalled ways   125
Of time past and time future.

IV

Time and the bell have buried the day,
The black cloud carries the sun away.
Will the sunflower turn to us, will the clematis
Stray down, bend to us; tendril and spray   130
Clutch and cling?
Chill
Fingers of yew be curled
Down on us? After the kingfisher's wing
Has answered light to light, and is silent, the light is still   135
At the still point of the turning world.

109-10 Into the faded air, the torpid
        Fuddled with images of picture papers,
        Driven on the wind. . . .   D

Line 114, like line 159, is indented in *Collected Poems 1909–1962* (1963 and 1974). None of Eliot's drafts thus marks new paragraphs, which are sufficiently signalized by spaces. This erratic indentation, found to a greater extent in *East Coker* and *The Dry Salvages*, would seem to be a printing-house error.

(137–158)

V

Words move, music moves
Only in time; but that which is only living
Can only die. Words, after speech, reach
Into the silence. Only by the form, the pattern,   140
Can words or music reach
The stillness, as a Chinese jar still
Moves perpetually in its stillness.
Not the stillness of the violin, while the note lasts,
Not that only, but the co-existence,   145
Or say that the end precedes the beginning,
And the end and the beginning were always there
Before the beginning and after the end.
And all is always now. Words strain,
Crack and sometimes break, under the burden,   150
Under the tension, slip, slide, perish,
Decay with imprecision, will not stay in place,
Will not stay still. Shrieking voices
Scolding, mocking, or merely chattering,
Always assail them. The Word in the desert   155
Is most attacked by voices of temptation,
The crying shadow in the funeral dance,
The loud lament of the disconsolate chimera.

156–8 An unnumbered page given to Hayward with the final draft contains four versions of these lines,
the last being the text as printed:

> Is most attacked by voices of temptation,
> The circling fury and the funeral dance,
> The loud lament, the sweet disconsolate chimera.

> Is most attacked by voices of temptation,
> Crying shadows, and disconsolate chimeras.

> Is most attacked by voices of temptation,
> The crying shadow and the funeral dance,
> The loud lament of the disconsolate chimera.

(159-175)

The detail of the pattern is movement,
As in the figure of the ten stairs.   160
Desire itself is movement
Not in itself desirable;
Love is itself unmoving,
Only the cause and end of movement,
Timeless, and undesiring   165
Except in the aspect of time
Caught in the form of limitation
Between un-being and being.
Sudden in a shaft of sunlight
Even while the dust moves   170
There rises the hidden laughter
Of children in the foliage
Quick now, here, now, always—
Ridiculous the waste sad time
Stretching before and after.   175

161-75 *Indented in* CP   166-7 Except in the aspect of time
                            ~~Under which all things are relative~~
                            Caught in the form of limitation   D

The 'figure of the ten stairs' refers to the ten steps of the ladder of love described by St. John of the Cross in *The Dark Night of the Soul* (Book II, chapter 19). St. John calls his 'secret wisdom' a ladder because a ladder is used for ascent and descent, and communications from God simultaneously exalt and humble the soul: 'For on this road, to descend is to ascend, and to ascend is to descend, since he who humbles himself is exalted, and he who exalts himself is humbled' (II. 18). The word 'figure' suggests Eliot has confused in memory the description of the 'ladder of love' with the famous drawing prefixed to *The Ascent of Mount Carmel*, which also shows ascent and descent but does not have ten steps or stairs. *The Ascent of Mount Carmel* treats of the 'active purgation' of the senses and spirit. Its teaching is briefly summarized in lines 114-21 of *Burnt Norton*. *The Dark Night of the Soul* treats of 'passive purgation' in which God works upon the soul.

Lines 161-75 are not indented in D, so directions to indent must have been given to the printer on the proof of CP. In both BN and *Four Quartets* lines 159-60 occur at the foot of a page, so that it is impossible to judge whether, if this were not so, the following lines should be indented. In *Collected Poems 1909-1962* line 159 is indented, an error perpetuated in the reset edition of 1974.

East Coker

East Coker

The five typed drafts that Hayward had bound up are marked in pencil by him as 1, 2, 3, 4, 5. Whether the error was Eliot's, putting the drafts together, or Hayward's, or the binder's, the first pages of D2 and D3 have been interchanged.

D1 (8 pages). This contains only the first four sections. Apart from its first page, which is a carbon of D3, it is a carbon of pages 2–8 of D2. It contains only one verbal alteration and one correction of punctuation by Eliot.

D2 (10 pages). If we substitute for its first page the first page of D3, this is the top copy of which D1 is the carbon, with two further pages, containing Part V, added. Eliot has made the same two corrections as he made in D1, added a considerable number of further alterations, and supplied line numbering. On the back of pages 5 and 7 Eliot has scrawled the first jottings for Part V. Page 9 contains the larger part of Part V, ending with line 199: '(The evening with the photograph album).' It has only two alterations and one short insertion in pencil, and a rather longer insertion—the end of one line and the beginning of the next—typed between two lines. Page 10, containing the last ten lines of the poem, begins with a draft that has been cancelled, followed by a second draft with manuscript alterations and additions. D2 is the draft that went to Herbert Read and has pencilled comments by him.

D3 (9 pages). This is a fresh typing from D2. It incorporates manuscript corrections made in D2 into its typescript,[1] along with some further alterations. It has, in addition, manuscript alterations of its own. D3 is the copy that went to John Hayward. His own letter to Eliot with objections and suggestions is not extant; but Eliot's letter to him of 27 February 1940,[2] thanking him for his 'prompt comment' makes clear what they were. All the points that Eliot replies to are marked in D3 in pencil by a light underlining and a pencil cross in the margin, and the words 'arras' (supplied in the margin against line 13 with its archaic spelling 'aresse') and 'sickness' (similarly suggested against line 156) are in Hayward's hand. Hayward must have returned the draft to Eliot as some of the manuscript alterations are made in response to Hayward's criticisms.

---

[1] Three manuscript corrections in D2 do not appear in the typescript of D3; two are added in manuscript, but on the third occasion a different correction is made (see apparatus to ll. 151, 161, 200). Eliot went back to niggle with D2 after typing D3 from it.

[2] Hayward did not bind up this letter with the drafts. It is preserved in the Eliot–Hayward Correspondence.

D4 (9 pages). This is a carbon of D3. It has only five manuscript alterations: three are corrections found also in D2 and D3, the fourth is a minor alteration, and the fifth—more important—is the transference of a line.

D5 (9 pages). This is the final draft that was sent to the printer and has been marked with directions in the printing-house. The typescript has adopted corrections from D3 and D4 and has made some further alterations, including the addition of two and a half lines (133–5). It has also some manuscript corrections.

Hayward bound up with the drafts the proof sent to Eliot by Philip Mairet, corrected by Eliot; and the first appearance of the poem in the *New English Weekly*, Easter 1940 (Supplement).

NEW proof. Mairet has written on it 'Shocking bad proofs. I've asked them to send you better ones; as these show breaks in the lines owing to faulty bedding. But these would do for corrections.' Eliot has corrected a reading of D5 back to the reading of D1–D4, corrected one misprint, and made an important correction in the first stanza of Part IV. He also made a suggestion in the same stanza in the margin, but he must have rejected it in a second proof as it does not appear in the text in NEW.

NEW. *New English Weekly*, Easter Number 1940 (Supplement). The text is well printed. There is one reading which differs from the reading in all drafts and the proof, which may be due to a correction by Eliot in the second ('better') proof that Mairet promised, or may be an error in the final text (l. 15).

EC. *East Coker*, published 12 September 1940.

Apart from the jottings for Part V and the cancelled first version of the conclusion in D2, the typescripts of *East Coker* represent a late stage in the poem's composition. By the time the first four parts were typed out in D2 and its carbon D1 they were virtually in their final form and Eliot's refinements in wording can be sufficiently studied by means of a critical apparatus. It is only with Part IV that the survival of Eliot's first jottings allows us to see the poet's initial conception.

MS (4 leaves from a ruled pad), written in pencil. This was given by Eliot to Hugh Walpole to sell in aid of the Red Cross. It is now in the possession of Dr. Donald Gallup, Yale University. Eliot began by indicating at the top of two pages the content of the first two stanzas:

f. 1.   *1.   The wounded surgeon—*

f. 2.   *Our only health is the disease*
           2)   The dying nurse

On the third page he has written a note for a third stanza at the top of the page and a note for the fourth halfway down. He then put a query against the first phrase, cancelled it by a slanting line, and at the foot of the page wrote slantwise a new suggestion for stanza three:

f. 3.   3)   ~~*Singing is silence*~~   ?

                4)   *ill of love —*
                     The Lover

            —   *hospital the earth*
                 bankrupt ~~*banker*~~
                     millionaire

On the fourth page Eliot wrote four lines, perhaps as a suggestion for a conclusion, and below, slantwise, some words, the first attempt at the concluding line of the first stanza, and a summary of the poem to be written:

f. 4.   *I am cold*
              —must be consumed in fire
                 I faint with heat
          —must be frozen in the lonely North,

                  the chill
                  the fever   *freeze*

            sharp Enigma of our fever chart

                         the surgeon
                         the nurse
                         the hospital
                         & final

EAST COKER

Text of *Four Quartets* (1944)

(1–23)

I

In my beginning is my end. In succession
Houses rise and fall, crumble, are extended,
Are removed, destroyed, restored, or in their place
Is an open field, or a factory, or a by-pass.
Old stone to new building, old timber to new fires,   5
Old fires to ashes, and ashes to the earth
Which is already flesh, fur and faeces,
Bone of man and beast, cornstalk and leaf.
Houses live and die: there is a time for building
And a time for living and for generation   10
And a time for the wind to break the loosened\pane
And to shake the wainscot where the field-mouse trots
And to shake the tattered arras woven with a silent motto.

In my beginning is my end. Now the light falls
Across the open field, leaving the deep lane   15
Shuttered with branches, dark in the afternoon,
Where you lean against a bank while a van passes,
And the deep lane insists on the direction
Into the village, in the electric heat
Hypnotised. In a warm haze the sultry light   20
Is absorbed, not refracted, by grey stone.
The dahlias sleep in the empty silence.
Wait for the early owl.

2* extended] rebuilt D1–4; rebuilt ⟨extended⟩ D3   3* restored] replaced D1–4; replaced
⟨restored/supplied⟩ D3   12 wainscot] wainscoat D1–4   13* arras] aresse D1–5, NEW
15* field] fields D1–5, NEW proof   deep] dark D5; dark ⟨deep⟩ NEW proof

---

On both D2 and D3 the line 'Are removed, destroyed, replaced, or in
their place' (l. 3) is marked by underlining the repetition of 'place' and by
a query or a cross in the margin. Eliot wrote to Hayward: '*Replaced* and
place. It was intentional, but Herbet also objects, so I had better do something about it.' This identifies the reader of D2 as 'Herbet', presumably
Herbert Read. Eliot did do something about it, first making two suggestions
in the margin of D3. A line drawn from 'restored' to the cancelled 'replaced'

indicates this was his choice between them, and having made this choice he
no doubt felt the same objection might be felt to the repeated prefix in
'rebuilt . . . removed . . . restored' and substituted 'extended' for 'rebuilt'.
Hayward also marked 'wainscoat' to call attention to the spelling and 'field'
in 'field-mouse' (l. 12), making no doubt some objection to their presence
in a house. Eliot replied:

> *Fieldmice.* They *did* get into our country house in New England, and very
> pretty little creatures too: we always restored them to the Land, and only slew
> the housemice. But the particular point here is that the house is supposed to
> have been long deserted or empty. Do housemice go on living in an unoccupied
> house? If so, I had better alter this; because I admit that in a tenanted house the
> fieldmouse is an *exception.*

Hayward also underlined 'aresse' (l. 13), putting 'arras?' in the margin.
Eliot replied here laconically: '*Aresse.* This early Tudor spelling is O.K.',
and retained it stubbornly up to the first printing in NEW.[1] This piece of
pointless archaism went when he came to print *East Coker* in pamphlet
form. Hayward also marked the word 'electric' in line 19, and Eliot commented: '*Electric.* I will think about alternatives.' The reading 'dark' for
'deep' (l. 15) is plainly a typing error in D5 reproduced, but caught by Eliot,
in the proof; but the reading 'field' in the same line may be an error for
'fields', the reading of all drafts and the proof, made and not noticed in the
printing of the poem in NEW. It has been perpetuated in all subsequent
printings.

Lines 1, 14, 47, 68 are indented in *Collected Poems 1909-1962* (1963 and
1974); but after Part II there is no indentation. The same phenomenon is
found in *The Dry Salvages*, where the opening lines of the two paragraphs
of Part I and the second section of Part II are indented, and the first lines
of the stanzas of the lyrics in Part II and Part IV, but not the opening lines of
Parts III and V. This erratic indentation is not found in *Little Gidding*.

---

[1] Frank Morley, who was responsible for arranging the American publication of the poem, reports:
'Tom wished the poem to appear first in some unexpected place: I suggested *Partisan Review*. Tom
cabled his approval and told me to keep his spelling of *aresse* for *arras* (line 13). The reason? The spelling *aresse* is out of *The Governour*, by Sir Thomas Elyot. T. Elyot was a grandson of Simon E. of East
Coker. At Harcourt, Brace we had a standing order to follow, exactly, the Faber spelling. The Faber
spelling, and therefore the "H, B" spelling (in 1943), was *arras*. I gathered there had been a row about
it. Geoffrey Faber wanted all old spelling modernized: Bruce Richmond, when consulted, didn't want
that: Faber "compromised" by chucking Sir Thomas Elyot out. Tom yielded, but it rankled. "You
may say all this doesn't matter; but it does to me. (ob. 1546 . . . ob. 1946? beginning & end of A epoch)."'
(Frank Morley in 'A Few Recollections of Eliot', Tate, 111.)

(23–50)

In that open field
If you do not come too close, if you do not come too close,
On a summer midnight, you can hear the music   25
Of the weak pipe and the little drum
And see them dancing around the bonfire
The association of man and woman
In daunsinge, signifying matrimonie—
A dignified and commodious sacrament.   30
Two and two, necessarye coniunction,
Holding eche other by the hand or the arm
Whiche betokeneth concorde. Round and round the fire
Leaping through the flames, or joined in circles,
Rustically solemn or in rustic laughter   35
Lifting heavy feet in clumsy shoes,
Earth feet, loam feet, lifted in country mirth
Mirth of those long since under earth
Nourishing the corn. Keeping time,
Keeping the rhythm in their dancing   40
As in their living in the living seasons
The time of the seasons and the constellations
The time of milking and the time of harvest
The time of the coupling of man and woman
And that of beasts. Feet rising and falling.   45
Eating and drinking. Dung and death.

Dawn points, and another day
Prepares for heat and silence. Out at sea the dawn wind
Wrinkles and slides. I am here
Or there, or elsewhere. In my beginning.   50

                              summer
25* summer] May D1–4; ~~May~~   D5   30* A dignified and commodious sacrament] D1–4 *omit
and have* 'A most dignified . . .' *at the close of the paragraph, after l. 46*; D4 *cancels* 'most' *and transfers*
                              rustic   *rustic*
the line to l. 30   35 rustic] ~~solemn~~ D3, 4; ~~solemn~~ D5   44 man and woman] men and
women D1, 2   45–6 Feet rising and falling./Eating and drinking. Dung and death.] Eating
and drinking./Dung and death. Feet rising and falling. D1–4; D4 *transposes to read with text*
47* Dawn points, and another day] Dawn points and the star fades, and another day D1–4; Dawn
points. ~~and the star fades, and a~~ *A*nother day D3   48–9* Out at sea the dawn wind/Wrinkles
and slides.] Out at sea the little/Dawn wind slides. D1–4;
                    Out at sea ~~the little~~
                    wrinkles   〈*And the dawn wind*
          〈*The*〉 Dawn wind slides.   *Wrinkles the sea*〉 D3
50 my beginning] the beginning D1–4

The month of May, from 'Gerontion', through *Ash Wednesday* to *Little Gidding*, is always to Eliot the time of 'the awakened senses'.[1] It is here 'The time of the coupling of man and woman'. He did not alter 'May' to 'summer' (l. 25) until the final draft. Possibly the alliteration in 'a May midnight' seemed too strong, or possibly the three stressed syllables coming together seemed too heavy. It is difficult to see quite why Eliot ever thought of rounding off his paragraph by a phrase adapted from his earlier quotation from Sir Thomas Elyot's *The Governour*. Hayward has marked the word 'most' and put a cross against it in the margin and must have made some comment on 'dignified', while 'Herbet' in D2 has put a bracket against the line with a queried deletion mark in the margin. Eliot wrote at some length:

> *Dignified*. Herbet also objects. I think this line is out of its place, and I can't think why I put *most*. It looks as if *daunsinge* and not *matrimonie* was the sacrament. I will deal with this. The text goes:

>> 'And for as moche as by the association of a man and a woman in daunsinge may be signified matrimonie, I could in declarynge the dignitie and commoditie of that sacrament make intiere volumes, if it were nat so commonly knowen to all men, that almoste euery frere lymitour carieth it writen in his bosome' etc.

> The public intention is to give an early Tudor setting, the private, that the author of The Governour sprang from E. Coker (apparently born in Wilts. but his father was the son of Simon E. of E.C.).

Eliot 'dealt with this', not, as with most of Hayward's criticisms, in D3 but in D4, where he transferred the line to the place it occupies in the final text and also altered the order of the preceding phrases, putting 'Feet rising and falling' first, and ending with the sombre reminder of mortality in 'Dung and death' (ll. 45-6). The deletion of 'and the star fades' (l. 47) was also in response to an objection by Hayward. Eliot simply writes: '*Star fades*. You are right.' Probably Hayward pointed out that the morning star does not fade at dawn. The most interesting alteration in the drafts is the suggested alternative in the margin of D3 to 'Out at sea the little / Dawn wind slides' (ll. 48-9): 'And the dawn wind / Wrinkles the sea.' The next stage would seem to have been the deletion of 'the little', the insertion of 'The' at the beginning of the next line, and the writing of 'wrinkles' above 'slides', as if he could not choose between them. In the final version in D5 he preserved both.

---

[1] See drafts of *Little Gidding*, p. 162.

II

What is the late November doing
With the disturbance of the spring
And creatures of the summer heat,
And snowdrops writhing under feet
And hollyhocks that aim too high   55
Red into grey and tumble down
Late roses filled with early snow?
Thunder rolled by rolling stars
Simulates triumphal cars
Deployed in constellated wars   60
Scorpion fights against the Sun
Until the Sun and Moon go down
Comets weep and Leonids fly
Hunt the heavens and the plains
Whirled in a vortex that shall bring   65
The world to that destructive fire
Which burns before the ice-cap reigns.

That was a way of putting it—not very satisfactory:
A periphrastic study in a worn-out poetical fashion,
Leaving one still with the intolerable wrestle   70
With words and meanings. The poetry does not matter.
It was not (to start again) what one had expected.
What was to be the value of the long looked forward to,
Long hoped for calm, the autumnal serenity
And the wisdom of age? Had they deceived us   75
Or deceived themselves, the quiet-voiced elders,
Bequeathing us merely a receipt for deceit?
The serenity only a deliberate hebetude,
The wisdom only the knowledge of dead secrets
Useless in the darkness into which they peered   80
Or from which they turned their eyes. There is, it seems to us,
At best, only a limited value
In the knowledge derived from experience.

                  the
56 and 57 down, . . . snow. D1, 2   66 that] ~~that~~ D3   67 Which burns before the ice-cap reigns]
                                                                      At best
Before the patient ice-cap reigns D1-4   82 At best, only] None, or only D1, 2; *(*None, or*)*
                                          that is merely
only D2   83 knowledge derived] knowledge ‸ derived D2

The opening paragraph of Part II is obviously modelled on the beginning of the second part of *Burnt Norton*. The lines

> Thunder rolled by rolling stars
> Simulates triumphal cars

recall the sonnet of Mallarmé which gave Eliot his cryptic first two lines there. Here he has combined the 'Thunder' of

> Tonnerre et rubis aux moyeux

with the 'chariots' of Mallarmé's last line:

> Du seul vespéral de mes chars.[1]

The denigration of this way of writing in lines 68–9 is a rejection of symbolism in favour of a poetry that wrestles with meanings.

The line which Eliot told Hayward he had 'got rid of', but which 'did not look quite so silly as all that in its context'—

> The Archer's bow and Taurus ire—[2]

must have occurred in a first drafting of this passage. It suggests that Eliot originally tried to develop further the disturbances in heaven paralleling the disturbance on earth. The sun is in Scorpio from 24 October to 20 November, when it has begun its declination, which continues while it is in the next sign, Sagittarius, the Archer. Taurus is the zodiacal opposite of Scorpio. The sun enters it in April when it is moving to its exaltation.

The passage provoked no comment from Hayward. The reader of D2 bracketed line 56, cancelling its comma, supplied a question mark for line 57, and bracketed lines 58–9 with the comment 'reminiscent of something'. Below, in a different pencil, he identified the reminiscence with the note 'Burnt Norton II, 4–5'. He also queried 'that' in line 66 and suggested 'its' in the margin. The suggestion, which would have improved the last two lines of the paragraph as they stood in the first four drafts, probably suggested to Eliot his rewriting of the last line in his final draft.

Hayward has marked with a cross in the margin the word 'receipt' in line 77. Eliot was puzzled as to what his objection was and wrote: '*Receipt*. I mean of course in the sense of *recipe* or formula. Is there any objection to bequeathing a formula? You can bequeath a copyright or a patent. I don't quite see your point.' Hayward's objection may have been to the rhyming of 'receipt' and 'deceit', a similar objection to his querying of 'replaced' and 'place' in line 3 and his objections to 'jingles' in *Little Gidding*.[3] More probably, he was unfamiliar with the use of 'receipt' for 'recipe', which is old-fashioned in England.

---

[1] See p. 80.   [2] See the letter from Hayward to Morley quoted on p. 17.   [3] See pp. 163, 165.

(84-111)

The knowledge imposes a pattern, and falsifies,
For the pattern is new in every moment   85
And every moment is a new and shocking
Valuation of all we have been. We are only undeceived
Of that which, deceiving, could no longer harm.
In the middle, not only in the middle of the way
But all the way, in a dark wood, in a bramble,   90
On the edge of a grimpen, where is no secure foothold,
And menaced by monsters, fancy lights,
Risking enchantment. Do not let me hear
Of the wisdom of old men, but rather of their folly,
Their fear of fear and frenzy, their fear of possession,   95
Of belonging to another, or to others, or to God.
The only wisdom we can hope to acquire
Is the wisdom of humility: humility is endless.

The houses are all gone under the sea.

The dancers are all gone under the hill.   100

III

O dark dark dark. They all go into the dark,
The vacant interstellar spaces, the vacant into the vacant,
The captains, merchant bankers, eminent men of letters,
The generous patrons of art, the statesmen and the rulers,
Distinguished civil servants, chairmen of many committees,   105
Industrial lords and petty contractors, all go into the dark,
And dark the Sun and Moon, and the Almanach de Gotha
And the Stock Exchange Gazette, the Directory of Directors,
And cold the sense and lost the motive of action.
And we all go with them, into the silent funeral,   110
Nobody's funeral, for there is no one to bury.

85 every moment] every movement D1, 2

Hayward notes in *Quatre Quatuors* the adaptation of the opening of Dante's *Divine Comedy*—

> Nel mezzo del cammin di nostra vita
> mi ritrovai per una selva oscura—

in line 89 and the adaptation of lines from Samson's opening speech in *Samson Agonistes*—

> O dark, dark, dark, amid the blaze of noon . . .
> The Sun to me is dark
> And silent as the moon
> When she deserts the night
> Hid in her vacant interlunar cave—

in lines 101-2. *East Coker*, when compared with *Burnt Norton*, is marked by a large amount of direct quotation and adaptation.

It seems strange, at first sight, that Hayward did not call Eliot's attention to the word 'grimpen' in line 91, which was not, at this time, in any dictionary and puzzled many of the poem's first readers. The *Supplement to the Oxford English Dictionary*, *A–G* (1972) gives 'grimpen. [Etym. uncertain] ?A marshy area'. It cites as the first use Conan Doyle, *The Hound of the Basker-villes* (1902): 'Life has become like that great Grimpen Mire, with little green patches everywhere into which one may sink and with no guide to point the track.' The second citation is from *East Coker*. The third from W. S. Baring-Gould, *Annotated Sherlock Holmes* (1968): 'As is well known, Watson's "Great Grimpen Mire" is *Grimspound Bog*, three miles to the north and west of Widecombe in the Moor.' Presumably Hayward and Eliot, who were addicted to the Holmes cycle, being familiar with the story, did not recognize that 'grimpen' was a nonce-word.

Professor Roy Fuller has called my attention to what seems an odd slip in line 108, which one would also have expected Hayward to have queried, where 'the Stock Exchange Gazette' appears between 'the Almanach de Gotha' and 'the Directory of Directors'. 'The *Stock Exchange Gazette* is', he writes, '(or was—it has now been absorbed by the *Investors Chronicle*) simply a weekly paper.' He wondered whether Eliot really meant to refer to *The Stock Exchange Official Yearbook*, which contains particulars of public companies and so forth and is more comparable with the Almanach and the Directory than a weekly bulletin of financial news.

(112-133)

I said to my soul, be still, and let the dark come upon you
Which shall be the darkness of God. As, in a theatre,
The lights are extinguished, for the scene to be changed
With a hollow rumble of wings, with a movement of darkness on darkness,   115
And we know that the hills and the trees, the distant panorama
And the bold imposing façade are all being rolled away—
Or as, when an underground train, in the tube, stops too long between stations
And the conversation rises and slowly fades into silence
And you see behind every face the mental emptiness deepen   120
Leaving only the growing terror of nothing to think about;
Or when, under ether, the mind is conscious but conscious of nothing—
I said to my soul, be still, and wait without hope
For hope would be hope for the wrong thing; wait without love
For love would be love of the wrong thing; there is yet faith   125
But the faith and the love and the hope are all in the waiting.
Wait without thought, for you are not ready for thought:
So the darkness shall be the light, and the stillness the dancing.
Whisper of running streams, and winter lightning.
The wild thyme unseen and the wild strawberry,   130
The laughter in the garden, echoed ecstasy
Not lost, but requiring, pointing to the agony
Of death and birth.

116 trees, the distant] trees, and the distant D1-4; trees, and . . . D3   117* rolled away] taken
     rolled   into silence
away D1, 2; taken . . . D2   119* fades into silence] fades away D1, 2   120* the mental
                                              image
emptiness deepen] the mental activity fail D1-4; . . . activity fail D3   126* faith and the love
and the hope are all in] faith and the hope and the love are in D1, 2   128 So the darkness]
So that the darkness D1, 2; But the darkness D3, 4   129 Whisper] Whispers D1-4   *lightning.]
                                                                                    echoed
lightning, D1-5, NEW, EC   131 echoed ecstasy] shadowed ecstasy D1, 2; shadowed . . . D2
133* death and birth.] death and birth D1-5, NEW

Comparison with the drafts of the later Quartets shows that Eliot found that the writing of relaxed passages in the long line came easily. He profited here from his experience in writing for the theatre. Although there is more revision here than on the previous pages, the revisions are not very interesting. The alteration made in D1, 2 of 'fades away' into 'fades into silence' (l. 119) was plainly made to avoid echoing the 'away' at the end of a line only two lines before. 'Rolled away' for 'taken away' (l. 117) immensely improves the scene-changing simile; it echoes the 'hollow rumble of wings' (l. 115). It may, as Grover Smith suggests, be a reminiscence of Eliot's old friend Conrad Aiken's poem 'The Jig of Forslin' (V. 7):

> Darkness descends, more walls are rolled away . . .
> Sudden, they lower the curtain on the play. . . .

In line 120 the original reading, 'the mental activity fail', though weak, is better sense than the alternatives. In D3 'activity' is crossed through and 'image' written above. Hayward has put a cross in the margin and must have made a query, for Eliot wrote, rather puzzlingly, '*Mental image* is right: I crossed out the wrong word'. Possibly, when Hayward had returned him the draft Eliot corrected it by crossing through 'activity' and rubbing out and rewriting the wrongly deleted 'image'. The reading of the final text, arrived at in D5, is not very satisfactory, as it is difficult to see how 'emptiness', whether mental or not, can 'deepen'. The alteration of 'the faith and the hope and the love', the Scriptural order, to 'the faith and the love and the hope' (l. 126) makes the summary correspond with the previous lines, in which 'love' is central, while retaining the emphasis on 'faith'.

In all the drafts and in the first printing in NEW there is a space left between lines 128 and 129, the stop after 'lightning' (l. 129) is a comma, and there is no stop after the half line 'Of death and birth' (l. 133). In EC and in *Four Quartets* line 128 comes at the foot of the page and consequently no break appears. Whether Eliot accepted this accident of printing as an improvement or did not notice it cannot be decided. There is something very striking in the drafts and first printing in the isolation of these four and a half lines with no final stop after 'birth'. They have no main verbs and make a kind of whispered parenthesis that trails off into silence. The instruction to the printer on D5 is 'Please keep exactly to spaces shown'. The comma after 'lightning' was replaced by a full stop in *Four Quartets*, which has remained ever since. The comma of the drafts, NEW, EC is obviously right and should be restored.

(133-151)

           You say I am repeating
Something I have said before. I shall say it again.
Shall I say it again? In order to arrive there,   135
To arrive where you are, to get from where you are not,
     You must go by a way wherein there is no ecstasy.
In order to arrive at what you do not know
     You must go by a way which is the way of ignorance.
In order to possess what you do not possess   140
     You must go by the way of dispossession.
In order to arrive at what you are not
     You must go through the way in which you are not.
And what you do not know is the only thing you know
And what you own is what you do not own   145
And where you are is where you are not.

                    IV

The wounded surgeon plies the steel
That questions the distempered part;
Beneath the bleeding hands we feel
The sharp compassion of the healer's art   150
Resolving the enigma of the fever chart.

133-5* You say ... say it again?] *Not in* D1-4   135 Shall I say it again?] Shall I say it
here and now?
~~again?~~   D5; ... it here and now? NEW   142 at what you are not] at where you are not
     what   ~~Under~~   Under
D1, 2; at ~~where~~ ... D3, 4   149* Beneath] Beneath D2; ~~Beneath~~ D3; Under D5; ~~Under~~
⟨*Beneath*⟩ NEW proof   150* compassion] ⟨compassion⟩ ⟨*Compunction??*⟩ NEW proof
                                                                                        beneath
151* Resolving the enigma] And faint below the strict enigma D1-4; ~~And faint b~~Below the strict
enigma D2; ~~And faint b~~Below the strict ... D3, 4; Below the strict ... D5; ~~Below the strict~~ ...
⟨*Resolving the*⟩ NEW proof

     For a transcript of Eliot's notes for Part IV, see pp. 94-5, and for a dis-
cussion of his possible debt to André Gide's *Le Prométhée mal enchaîné*, see
pp. 43-6.

The insertion in the final draft of lines 133-5 is a regrettably defensive response to possible criticism. It is unfortunate that Eliot did not find a less self-conscious way of introducing the passage adapted from St. John of the Cross.[1] It is clear from reading the first drafts that some kind of bridge is necessary, after the series of images, to introduce the riddling, hortatory passage that closes the third part of the poem. In D3 Eliot has put a caret mark sideways in the space after the first half of line 133, as if to indicate to himself 'Something wanted here'.

Eliot's rough notes for his lyric show that the 'wounded surgeon' and the 'dying nurse' were the subjects of the first two stanzas in his original conception. In his first draft Eliot extended the last line of the first and third stanzas from twelve to fourteen syllables. In D2, 3, and 4 he corrected this and reduced them by deleting two syllables. His alteration of the last line of the first stanza (l. 151) led to difficulties with the third line (l. 149). He obviously preferred his first thought, 'Beneath' to 'Under', but felt 'Beneath' could not stand if the fifth line began with 'Below'. He solved the problem in correcting the proof for NEW by discarding the remains of his original line 'And faint below the strict enigma...' for the much more powerful 'Resolving the enigma...'. This allowed him to return to 'Beneath' in line 149. Also in proof, he boxed in the word 'compassion' and wrote 'compunction' with two queries in the margin. Either the printer ignored this, or Eliot decided not to make the correction in the copy of the proof he sent to the printer. I imagine he thought of 'compunction' as giving a pun on 'puncture'; but he was surely right to reject it. It suggests reluctance, pricking of conscience, or scruples in the 'wounded surgeon', where 'compassion' implies the surgeon suffering with the sufferer.

---

[1] Eliot has very freely adapted the maxims St. John wrote below his 'figure'. The translation by Allison Peers, from which I quote, was in Eliot's library:

> In order to arrive at having pleasure in everything,
> Desire to have pleasure in nothing.
> In order to arrive at possessing everything,
> Desire to possess nothing.
> In order to arrive at being everything,
> Desire to be nothing.
> In order to arrive at knowing everything,
> Desire to know nothing.
> In order to arrive at that wherein thou hast no pleasure,
> Thou must go by a way wherein thou hast no pleasure.
> In order to arrive at that which thou knowest not,
> Thou must go by a way that thou knowest not.
> In order to arrive at that which thou possessest not,
> Thou must go by a way that thou possessest not.
> In order to arrive at that which thou art not,
> Thou must go through that which thou art not.
>
> (*Ascent of Mount Carmel*, I. xiii)

(152–171)

Our only health is the disease
If we obey the dying nurse
Whose constant care is not to please
But to remind of our, and Adam's curse,   155
And that, to be restored, our sickness must grow worse.

The whole earth is our hospital
Endowed by the ruined millionaire,
Wherein, if we do well, we shall
Die of the absolute paternal care   160
That will not leave us, but prevents us everywhere.

The chill ascends from feet to knees,
The fever sings in mental wires.
If to be warmed, then I must freeze
And quake in frigid purgatorial fires   165
Of which the flame is roses, and the smoke is briars.

The dripping blood our only drink,
The bloody flesh our only food:
In spite of which we like to think
That we are sound, substantial flesh and blood—   170
Again, in spite of that, we call this Friday good.

                              ailment
156* sickness] suffering D1, 2; malady D3, 4; ~~malady~~ D3   158* ruined] bankrupt D1, 2;
                              sickness
ruined
~~bankrupt~~ D2   161* That will not leave us, but prevents us everywhere] That will not let us be,
                                                                              leave
but must torment us everywhere D1–4; That will not ~~let~~ us ~~be~~, but ~~must~~ torments us everywhere
D2–4; . . . not leave us, but torments . . . D5, NEW

Hayward in *Quatre Quatuors* has a note to line 157: 'cf. Sir Thomas
Browne, *Religio Medici* II 12: "For the world, I count it not an Inn, but an
Hospital, and a place, not to live, but die in."' Eliot may have been as
unconscious of this as of his echo of Browne in *Little Gidding*, and, if
Hayward had pointed this echo out to him, might well have replied as he
did later: 'Damn Sir T. Browne, a writer I never got much kick from: I
suppose it *is* a reminiscence. . . .'; see p. 202.

Although the original reading 'suffering' in line 156 seems too general, the alteration to 'malady' in the typescript of D3, 4, and the pencilled correction to 'ailment' in D3 in different ways weaken the line. 'Malady' is too affected, and 'ailment' suggests a not very serious condition. Hayward suggested 'sickness' with a query and Eliot wrote back simply '*Sickness. I will make this alteration*', and did so.

In his first notes for the poem Eliot jotted down for his third verse '3) Singing is silence' with a query. He cancelled this and at the foot of the page reverted to the hospital metaphor of his first two stanzas, writing 'hospital the earth / bankrupt banker'. He then cancelled 'banker' and wrote 'millionaire'. The change in D2 from 'bankrupt' to 'ruined' removes the commercial implications of 'bankrupt' and the possible suggestions of misfortune, incompetence, or even shady dealings. The general word 'ruined' allows us to regard the millionaire as suffering from a Timon-like generosity. The original reading 'torments us', like the image of the 'banker / millionaire', recalls the Zeus of Gide who 'gives eagles' to torment men. The change to 'prevents us' (l. 161) was not made until the appearance of *East Coker* in pamphlet form. It softens the harsh paradox of an 'absolute paternal care' that 'torments'; but the meaning of 'prevents' may escape those not familiar with its use in a collect in *The Book of Common Prayer*: 'Prevent us, O Lord, in all our doings with thy most gracious favour, and further us with thy continual help.' For many readers, the word must suggest 'thwarting'. It is possible that Eliot intended the word to carry both meanings: of God's 'prevenient care' and of paternal thwarting of a child's wilfulness and folly.

In a letter to Anne Ridler, dated 10 March 1941, replying to a letter from her on *The Dry Salvages*, Eliot wrote:

I don't think the ordinary reader will like it so much as E Coker—in fact, the success of that poem is a little disconcerting: I find it hard to believe that a poem of mine which sells nearly 12,000 copies can be really good. (I am glad, by the way, that you like part IV [of *East Coker*], which is in a way the heart of the matter. My intention was to avoid a pastiche of George Herbert or Crashaw—it would be folly to try—and to do something in the style of Cleveland or Benlowes, only better; and I liked the use of this so English XVII form with a content so very un-English—which George Every calls Jansenist. But the poem as a whole—this five part form—is an attempt to weave several quite unrelated strands together in an emotional whole, so that really there isn't any heart of the matter).[1]

---

[1] I have to thank Mrs. Ridler for showing me this letter.

(172-199)

V

So here I am, in the middle way, having had twenty years—
Twenty years largely wasted, the years of *l'entre deux guerres*—
Trying to learn to use words, and every attempt
Is a wholly new start, and a different kind of failure   175
Because one has only learnt to get the better of words
For the thing one no longer has to say, or the way in which
One is no longer disposed to say it. And so each venture
Is a new beginning, a raid on the inarticulate
With shabby equipment always deteriorating   180
In the general mess of imprecision of feeling,
Undisciplined squads of emotion. And what there is to conquer
By strength and submission, has already been discovered
Once or twice, or several times, by men whom one cannot hope
To emulate—but there is no competition—   185
There is only the fight to recover what has been lost
And found and lost again and again: and now, under conditions
That seem unpropitious. But perhaps neither gain nor loss.
For us, there is only the trying. The rest is not our business.

Home is where one starts from. As we grow older   190
The world becomes stranger, the pattern more complicated
Of dead and living. Not the intense moment
Isolated, with no before and after,
But a lifetime burning in every moment
And not the lifetime of one man only   195
But of old stones that cannot be deciphered.
There is a time for the evening under starlight,
A time for the evening under lamplight
(The evening with the photograph album).

---

                                                                                  the years of
172-209 *Not in* D1   172 So here] Here D2   173 wasted, the years of] wasted,/   D2
175 a different kind of failure] a wholly fresh failure D2   177 the thing] the things D2
177-8 say, or the way in which/One is no longer disposed to say it. And so each venture] say, ~~so each~~
~~venture~~ D2 *with* or the way in which/One is no longer disposed to say it, and so each venture *typed*
                                                                         shabby
between the lines   180 shabby equipment] worn-out equipment D2-5; ~~worn-out~~ D5   186 the
                                                                      trying
fight] the task D2; the urge D3, 4 (urge *is ringed by Eliot in* D4)   189 trying] ~~effort~~ D2
                     our business.
189 our business] ~~ours.~~   D2   190 As we grow] As one grows D2   193 Isolated, with]
Isolated in a lifetime, with D2   194 moment] moment, D2-4   198 A time
      And a
for] A . . . D4   199 (The . . . album)] The . . . album D2

D1 does not contain Part V. The first eight pages of D2 are the typescript of which D1 is a carbon. Eliot has scrawled on the back of pages 5 and 7 his first jottings for this part. A typescript has been added on two fresh pages (9 and 10). The jottings on the back of page 5 are the first notes for the conclusion:

> *Alone—the ice cap*
> *Separated from*
> *the surfaces of*
> *human beings*
> *To be reunited and*
> *the Communion*

On the back of page 7 are the first notes for the opening passage:

> *20 yrs*
> *l'entre 2 guerres*
> *20 yrs. or 600 upwards*[1]
> *Home is where we start from.*

It is impossible to be certain which jotting was made first; but it seems likely that Eliot first thought of his ending and then turned to consider a passage to introduce it.

Page 9 of D2, containing the first section of Part V, ending with line 199 '(The evening with the photograph album)', is a very clean typescript with few manuscript alterations. In the next draft (D3), sent to Hayward, there were only minor changes. The opening was made more conversational by prefixing 'So' to the abrupt 'Here' (l. 172), and the change from 'a wholly fresh failure' to 'a different kind of failure' (l. 175) avoids both repetition and a hint of exaggeration. In line 186 'the task to recover' (D2) has become 'the urge . . .', the less intimate 'As one grows older' has become 'As we . . .', and the words 'in a lifetime' have been dropped to leave the word 'Isolated' (l. 193) more isolated. Hayward made no comment in criticism of this passage which he singled out for special praise in his letter to Frank Morley.[2] In the final draft (D5) Eliot typed 'fight' to replace 'urge' (l. 186) and over 'worn-out' wrote 'shabby' (l. 180). The whole passage plainly came effortlessly.

Hayward in *Quatre Quatuors* has a note on line 196: 'There is a particular allusion in this line to the village churchyard at East Coker, where the old gravestones are now indecipherable.'

---

[1] Presumably Eliot is thinking of the centuries of English poetry since its first great master, Chaucer.
[2] See p. 17.

(200–209)

Love is most nearly itself   200
When here and now cease to matter.
Old men ought to be explorers
Here and there does not matter
We must be still and still moving
Into another intensity   205
For a further union, a deeper communion
Through the dark cold and the empty desolation,
The wave cry, the wind cry, the vast waters
Of the petrel and the porpoise. In my end is my beginning.

200 Love is most nearly itself] Love is itself unmoving/But love is most nearly itself D2–4;
    And   *And*
. . . But . . . D2; Love is itself unmoving/But lLove . . . D3; Love is itself unmoving/But lLove . . . D4
201 here and now] now and now D2   202 Old men ought to be explorers] *Inserted in pencil in*
margin of D2   203* here and there] . . . or . . . D2–5, NEW, EC   207 Through the dark
                                         dark   *and*   *empty*
cold and the empty desolation] Through the empty cold with the ˄ desolation D2   209 In my
end is my beginning.] *Added in pencil by Eliot in* D2

Page 10 of D2 contains a typed draft of the conclusion, which has been heavily scored through. This is followed by a second attempt with manuscript alterations. Eliot first typed

Here or there does not matter. We must be still
And be still moving. The mind must venture
Where it has not been, be separated
For a further union, a deeper communion,
Aranyaka, the forest or the sea
The empty cold with the desolation
The wave cry, the wind cry
With the knowledge understanding and the consolation
Of the petrel and the porpoise. In my end is my beginning.

The typescript is in double spacing, and the line 'The wave cry, the wind cry' has been typed between two lines.

Having crossed through this draft, Eliot began again:

Love is itself unmoving
And
~~But~~ love is most nearly itself
When now and now cease to matter.
                          Old men ought to be explorers
Here or there does not matter.
We must be still and still moving
Into another intensity
For a further union, a deeper communion,
          dark   and   empty
Through the ~~empty~~ cold ~~with~~ the ˄ desolation,
The wave cry, the wind cry, the vast waters
Of the petrel and the porpoise.   *In my end is my beginning.*

In this second attempt at a conclusion Eliot began with a line from the conclusion of *Burnt Norton*. He cancelled it in D3 and D4. He wisely dropped the reference to 'Aranyaka, the forest'. The Aranyakas are sacred books whose name can be interpreted as meaning either that they were written in the forests by forest hermits, or that they were written for those who, after a life of action, had retired to the forests. The 'collocation of eastern and western mysticism', to which Eliot drew attention in his notes to *The Waste Land*, and which is explicit in *The Dry Salvages*, is hinted at here, but not effectively. The word 'Aranyaka' would have required a gloss to make it intelligible; and the 'forest or the sea' are not imaginatively equal alternatives in this context. The forest is to eastern asceticism what the desert is to western; but Eliot's sea-image is personal, with no historic or cultural associations. It speaks directly to the imagination of the journey of the alone to the alone, whether undertaken in the forest or the desert. Whether Eliot already had in mind his next poem, *The Dry Salvages*, and intended by the close of *East Coker* to lead into his third Quartet is uncertain; but the close of *East Coker*, while recalling 'Cape Ann', also points forward to Eliot's greatest poem of the sea.

The reading 'Here and there does not matter' appears first in *Four Quartets* and is an error overlooked in the correction of the proofs. Mr. Hermann Peschmann called Eliot's attention to the false concord and kindly sent me a copy of Eliot's reply: 'How very odd. Thanks for calling my attention to it. What I prefer is *Here or there does not matter* (Here-or-there—i.e. an abbreviation of "whether here or there") is the subject of the singular *does*.' The error remained in *Collected Poems 1909–1962* (1963), but was corrected in the edition of 1974.

The Dry Salvages

The Dry Salvages

Eliot gave Hayward only one typed draft of *The Dry Salvages*. He had this bound up with a letter from Eliot dated 4 January 1941. Eliot writes:

> My dear John
> Thank you very much for your helpful letter, and for its promptitude: I was surprised at hearing from you so soon.[1]
> There are some, perhaps most, of your suggestions which I accept at once; some which I must think about; some which my first impulse is to reject. That is the normal and proper mixture.

Four other typed drafts Eliot gave to Magdalene College, Cambridge, labelling them '1st Draft, 2nd Draft, 3rd Draft, 4th Draft'.[2] The first three drafts (M1–3) are top copies. The fourth draft (M4) is a carbon copy of a professional typist's retyping of M3, the top copy being presumably the one sent to the printer. Eliot also gave to Magdalene the first proof for the publication of the poem in the *New English Weekly*, dated 'Jan 29'.

M1 (11 pages). This is a very untidy typescript with a great many corrections and additions, some made in typing by cancellation and typing above the line, others in pencil above the line and in the margin.

M2 (10 pages). Line references are added in pencil. M2 is neatly typed. It shares five manuscript corrections with its carbon copy (D), the draft sent to Hayward. But it has further corrections, less neatly made, many of which are in response to Hayward's criticisms.

M3 (10 pages). This is a fresh typing made from M2, incorporating its corrections and additions, and making a few others.

M4 (10 pages). This is a carbon copy of a professional retyping of M3, incorporating all but one of its corrections and alterations. It is heavily annotated by Geoffrey Faber. On getting it back from Faber Eliot made some alterations to meet his objections. M4 is the final recension and its text, before Eliot made his alterations, was the text sent to the printer of NEW.

D (10 pages). This is a carbon copy of M2 and is the draft sent to Hayward. It has five neatly written manuscript corrections, which are also found in

---

[1] Hayward must have replied with his queries almost by return, since he reported to Morley that the poem arrived on his desk on New Year's Day.
[2] He first, mistakenly, labelled the fourth draft as the third.

M2. Hayward has put lightly pencilled crosses in the margin to indicate some of the words and phrases he wished to query. A sheet containing his queries was found in the Eliot–Hayward Correspondence and placed by Dr. Munby in the volume bound up by Hayward. Dr. Munby also extracted from EHC and put in the bound volume a postcard from Charles Olson to Ezra Pound, to which is attached a typed note by Eliot, and a photograph of the Dry Salvages sent to Eliot by his brother and sister-in-law.

T (University of Texas: 10 pages). This is a carbon copy of M3 now in the Humanities Research Center of the University of Texas at Austin. There is no record of its provenance. It has some of the manuscript alterations made in M3, but Eliot continued to work on his top copy after sending away the carbon. Someone has underlined and queried the word 'rote'.

NEW proof. This has been dated 'Jan. 29'. It is very heavily corrected, many of the corrections being in response to queries from Faber. It also shows Eliot struggling to the last with the final lines.

NEW. *New English Weekly*, 27 February 1941.

DS. *The Dry Salvages*, published 4 September 1941. The only correction made from the text in NEW is the dropping of a final sentence from the prefatory note.

MS (Magdalene College Library). On five leaves torn out of a scribbling pad Eliot jotted down a scheme for the poem, possible rhymes for the sestina in Part II, and verse drafts of the beginning of Part III and of the three stanzas of Part IV. The scheme runs:

Notes

1. Sea picture   —general
2.   —particular
   problem of permanence
   of past pain
3. Past error can only be reconciled
   in eternity. Arjuna & Krishna.
4. Invocation to the B.V.M.
   meaning of 'mother' & 'father'.
5. Generalisation: Liberation from
   the past is liberation from the
   future. To get beyond time &
   at the same time deeper into
   time. the Spirit & the Earth

It is interesting that the River does not appear in Eliot's first notes for the poem. Also, one wonders how the 'meaning of "mother" and "father"' was to have been handled in the 'Invocation to the B.V.M.' The 'father' is so much a missing image in Eliot's poetry that his appearance in the notes is striking and his disappearance from the poem, though understandable, is disappointing. Many years later Eliot explored the meaning of 'mother' and 'father' in *The Confidential Clerk*.

THE DRY SALVAGES

Text of *Four Quartets* (1944)

(The Dry Salvages—presumably *les trois sauvages*—is a small group of rocks, with a beacon, off the N.E. coast of Cape Ann, Massachusetts. *Salvages* is pronounced to rhyme with *assuages*. *Groaner*: a whistling buoy.)

(The Dry . . . buoy.)] *Not in* M1–3, D, T   *assuages*] *rampages* M4; ~~rampages~~ ⟨*assuages*⟩ NEW proof buoy.)] buoy. The Gloucester fishing fleet of schooners, manned by Yankees, Irish or Portuguese, has been superseded by the motor trawlers.) M4, NEW *omitting* the *which is deleted in proof*

This note, which first appears in M4, was a response to difficulties raised by Hayward, whose first query is '1) Title. (Dry Salvages in a quotation?)' He also queried 'rote' (l. 30), though he scratched this out but went on '—groaner?? grainer??'. Eliot replied to both queries:[1]

1. 'The Dry Salvages' *is* a place name (rhymes with 'rampages'). It is ('Les trois sauvages') the name of a group of three rocks off the eastern corner of Cape Ann, Massachusetts, with a beacon: convenient for laying a course to the eastward, Maine or Nova Scotia. It happens to have just the right denotation and association for my purpose; and therefore I am the more disturbed by your comment. It doesn't matter that it should be obscure, but if it is going to lead people quite on the wrong track, then something must be done. I don't like the idea of a note of explanation. Please advise.
2. 'Groaner'. Yes, I was waiting to see what you would make of this. It is the New England word for a 'whistling buoy', which by some arrangement of valves, makes a groaning noise as it rises and falls on the swell. There must be some English equivalent, but that would give the wrong effect. I noted absence from O.E.D. This is a pretty problem too.

[1] Eliot's first response to Hayward's query over the name of the poem was to type '(Les trois sauvages)', underlined for italicization, beneath the title on M3/T. On M3 he pencilled quotation marks round the title, as Hayward advised in his letter. Then, having had second thoughts, he crossed through the bracketed addition beneath the title.
For Samuel Eliot Morison's correction of Eliot's misconception about the name and his family's connexion with the reefs, see p. 53.

Hayward replied promptly and wittily:

I deplore my ignorance of 'The Dry Salvages', for it was just such a title (now that I understand its significance) that I hoped for—my imagination, as I read, having fixed nostalgically on the coast of New England—in the region of Martha's Vineyard—known to me only through books and in dreams of ten years ago when someone to whom I was greatly attached spent her honeymoon sailing there—as the setting of the poem. *My* setting—for this is a good example of the kind of sea-change—the expression seems apt—that a poem suffers and must necessarily suffer in the mind of each reader. I remember Valéry saying how baffled he was when he tried to imagine one of his poems making a different impression on everyone who read it. But I took Dry Salvages—for you omitted the inverted commas that might have suggested to me that it was a place-name—to be in some sense a reference to what the sea gives up—the torn seine and the dead, and, by extension, memories of a dead life and so on; supporting this interpretation with a vague conviction (unchecked by the dictionary) that insurance companies recognize 'dry' salvage and 'wet' salvage, the former being more valuable than the latter. I think the least you can do is to place single quotation marks round the title. This, I think, should at once suggest a proper name—and one that, perhaps, requires to be defined in this way (like, say, 'The Casquets') because it is not, like East Coker, a place-name so much as a name of a place, if the distinction is not too subtle. (Cf. 'The Hard' Lyme Regis: 'Fastnet', &c.) You could, alternatively add Cape Ann, viz. 'The Dry Salvages' Cape Ann. For irrelevantly personal reasons I should like this because Cape Ann has similar romantic associations for me as Cape Wrath and Bloody Foreland. I do think there is a danger of some people making my mistake about wet & dry salvage, so I hope you will consider adopting one or other of my suggestions if none better occurs to you.

My first reaction to 'groaner' was that it was a buoy of some kind. Then O.E.D. shook me and I assumed it must be a type of vessel (though still with a local name) on account of the following words: rounded homewards—which I then took to refer to the creaking, groaning play of the ship's timbers as, turning the headland, she set a course for home; the springing of timber being a characteristic sea-voice. This is a bit of a problem. At the moment I can only suggest changing the qualifying adjective to one that would, by implication, suggest that 'groaner' is a navigational signal and not a vessel. What about 'warning groaner'? ('moaning' would be a good word but for the repetition of the broad 'o' sound). The trouble is that 'heaving' is too good to lose. But something may occur to you along the line of my suggestion that 'groaner' should be explained by its epithet.[1]

[1] Letter of 7 January 1941, EHC.

(1-14)

I

I do not know much about gods; but I think that the river
Is a strong brown god—sullen, untamed and intractable,
Patient to some degree, at first recognised as a frontier;
Useful, untrustworthy, as a conveyor of commerce;
Then only a problem confronting the builder of bridges.   5
The problem once solved, the brown god is almost forgotten
By the dwellers in cities—ever, however, implacable,
Keeping his seasons and rages, destroyer, reminder
Of what men choose to forget. Unhonoured, unpropitiated
By worshippers of the machine, but waiting, watching and waiting.   10
His rhythm was present in the nursery bedroom,
In the rank ailanthus of the April dooryard,
In the smell of grapes on the autumn table,
And the evening circle in the winter gaslight.

                                                    to some   *degree*   *recognised*
3 Patient to some degree, at first recognised as a frontier] Patient/ to all appearance, known for a time
                                                                              at first
as a frontier M1; . . . degree, recognised for a time as . . . D; . . ., ‸ recognised for a time as . . . M2
6* solved, the brown god is almost forgotten] solved, then the brown god is forgotten M1-3, D, T;
solved, then a ⟨the⟩ brown god is forgotten M4; solved, then the brown god is ⟨almost⟩ forgotten NEW
                                    underneath
proof   11 was present in] was present/ is present/ in M1   12* In the rank ailanthus of
                                    rank ailanthus   garden
the April dooryard] In the efflorescence of the April suburbs ⟨dooryard. backyard?⟩ M1; . . . ailantus . . .
M2-4, D, T; . . . ailantus ⟨ailanthus⟩ . . . NEW proof   13 In the smell] ⟨In⟩ Tthe smell M1

For the river as 'a strong brown god', see Eliot's introduction to *Huckle-berry Finn* quoted on pp. 48–9.

The alteration in line 12 shows Eliot replacing a general image of April's 'efflorescence' with the 'rank ailanthus'[1] of his childhood memories, and 'suburbs' first by 'garden' and then by the Americanisms 'dooryard' and 'backyard'. He rightly chose of these a word which lacks the dreary associations for English readers of 'backyard' and has instead an American flavour. He probably intended to echo Whitman's famous poem 'When lilacs last in the dooryard bloomed'. Hayward queried 'for a time' (l. 3), writing 'for a *while* (time confusing)'. Faber also made a comment against line 3: '"to some degree". possibly not the finally satisfactory expression?' He also queried the repetition 'Then . . . then' in lines 5–6, writing 'Perhaps the repetition might be considered further—but I don't know. I think it is needed.' Being sensitive, like Hayward, to Eliot's trick of internal rhyming he queried 'ever, however' (l. 7): 'is this intentional? Yes, it must be. Not quite sure I get the exact significance of "however" in that case. One reads it at first as "Always, nevertheless". Does it then mean, rather "Always, whatever happens"?' Eliot did consider 'Then . . . then' further, and made an alteration in proof. 'Ever, however' he left, perhaps not minding an ambiguity. Faber also wrote against 'ailantus' (l. 12), whose spelling Eliot finally got right in proof, 'one of the words I don't know! tho' I feel I ought to'.

---

[1] Although Eliot spelt it correctly in typing, he cancelled the 'h' in pencil.

(15–26)

The river is within us, the sea is all about us;   15
The sea is the land's edge also, the granite
Into which it reaches, the beaches where it tosses
Its hints of earlier and other creation:
The starfish, the horseshoe crab, the whale's backbone;
The pools where it offers to our curiosity   20
The more delicate algae and the sea anemone.
It tosses up our losses, the torn seine,
The shattered lobsterpot, the broken oar
And the gear of foreign dead men. The sea has many voices,
Many gods and many voices.
                              The salt is on the briar rose,   25
The fog is in the fir trees.

15 us;] us, M1   18* creation] existence M1–4, D, T; existence ⟨creation⟩ NEW proof
19* horseshoe crab *Four Quartets*, third impression, 1945; hermit crab M1–*Four Quartets*, second
                                        offers to
impression   20 offers to] nourishes for M1; nourishes for M2, D   22 tosses up] tosses
up   torn   *seine*   *on*
us M1   torn seine] broken fishnet M1   25 salt is on] . . . is in M1

'Seine' for 'fishnet' (l. 22) is another change to a word that holds up an
English reader but would be familiar to a New Englander. Hayward
queried the jingle of 'tosses up our losses' (l. 22), 'Tosses—losses—flotsam,
jetsam, wrack.—spintthrift' and, against 'Tosses', put 'X five lines earlier'.
Faber queried 'Its hints of earlier and other existence' (l. 18), writing
'ITS INTS SIST NB ?onomatopeia but if so isn't the effect possibly too much
muffled by the middle part of the line?' Eliot put a heavy cross against the
line in the margin of M4 and made the alteration of 'existence' to 'creation'
in proof.

Eliot did not discover his error over 'hermit crab' (l. 19) until 1945, when
he wrote to Hayward on 12 January:

My dear John,

At the bottom of the first page of The Dry Salvages in the four Quartets please alter *hermit* crab to *horse-shoe* crab. I do not know how I came to make such a blunder (though obviously the wrong crab scans better). I have written a letter to the New English Weekly to point this out, and I shall have it altered in the next printing, whenever that is,[1] and send you a copy. How could one find the remains of a hermit crab on a beach? All there could be would be the shell of some other crustacean. I am surprised that neither you nor anyone else has spotted this.[2]

The letter to NEW appeared on 25 January 1945:

Sir,

. . . There is, however, one error in the text which has escaped the observation of any of my friends or critics, and of which I have only just myself become aware. In the first section of 'The Dry Salvages', 'hermit crab' should be 'horse-shoe crab'. It was, of course, the horse-shoe crab that I had in mind: the slip must have been due to the fact that I did not want a spondee in that place. What is more curious is that the term 'hermit crab' should have continued to do duty for 'horse-shoe crab' in my mind, in this context, from the date of original publication of the poem until last week. I shall be grateful to any of your readers who may possess the poem, if they will kindly make the alteration.

T. S. Eliot

The hermit crab is a creature that finds a home for itself in the shell of another crustacean, and so no traces of it could be found to hint at 'earlier and other creation'; but the horseshoe crab is 'a crab-like animal of the genus *Limulus*, so called from the shape of its shell' (*O.E.D.*). I am told that finding shells of horseshoe crabs on the beaches of Massachusetts and Maine is as much a sport for New England children as hunting for fossils near Lyme Regis is for English children.

The sea-anemone found a place in Eliot's Harvard dissertation on F. H. Bradley, where he wrote: 'The sea-anemone which accepts or rejects a proffered morsel is thereby relating an idea to the sea-anemone's world.' And he returned to it pertinently later when discussing the roots of poetry in experiences not themselves very remarkable:

There might be the experience of a child of ten, a small boy peering through sea-water in a rock-pool, and finding a sea-anemone for the first time: the simple experience (not so simple, for an exceptional child, as it looks) might lie dormant in his mind for twenty years, and re-appear transformed in some verse-context charged with great imaginative pressure.[3]

---

[1] The next impression, the third, was in August 1945.
[2] EHC.
[3] *The Use of Poetry and the Use of Criticism* (1933), 78–9.

(26-48)

The sea howl
And the sea yelp, are different voices
Often together heard: the whine in the rigging,
The menace and caress of wave that breaks on water,
The distant rote in the granite teeth,   30
And the wailing warning from the approaching headland
Are all sea voices, and the heaving groaner
Rounded homewards, and the seagull:
And under the oppression of the silent fog
The tolling bell   35
Measures time not our time, rung by the unhurried
Ground swell, a time
Older than the time of chronometers, older
Than time counted by anxious worried women
Lying awake, calculating the future,   40
Trying to unweave, unwind, unravel
And piece together the past and the future,
Between midnight and dawn, when the past is all deception,
The future futureless, before the morning watch
When time stops and time is never ending;   45
And the ground swell, that is and was from the beginning,
Clangs
The bell.

28 heard:] heard; M1-NEW   29* menace and caress] soothing menace M1-4, D, T;
soothing menace ⟨menace and caress and⟩ NEW proof   34* And under the oppression of the
                                                                        under the oppression
silent fog] And heard in the stillness of the silent fog M1-4, D, T; . . . heard in the stillness . . . M4;
. . . heard in the stillness ⟨calmness⟩ ⟨under the oppression⟩ . . . NEW proof   36 rung by the
                                                                        rung by the unhurried
unhurried] ringing to   M1   41 unweave] penetrate M1   43 when the past]
                                                                        unweave
and the past M1   44-5* before the morning watch/When time stops] and at the same
                                while in the night watch ⟨morning⟩
time/Time stops M1, D; and at the same time/Time stops M2   46* And the ground swell,
that is and was from the beginning,] And through the fog the pretemporal ground swell M1-4, D, T;
And through the fog the pretemporal ground swell ⟨the ground swell, that is and was from the beginning,⟩
NEW proof   47 Clangs] Rings Clangs M1

Both Hayward and Faber queried the inversion in line 28: 'Often together heard', Faber writing 'I don't much like this order of the words.' His next two criticisms were responsible for two of the finest descriptive lines in the poem. Against lines 28–32 he wrote 'rather a lot of -ing terminations', and marked them. In proof Eliot improved 'soothing menace' to 'menace and caress'. Against line 34 Faber wrote 'does "silent" add enough to "stillness"?' In proof Eliot crossed through 'stillness' and wrote 'calmness' in the right-hand margin. In M4 he made a different suggestion. Without cancelling 'heard in the stillness', he wrote above it 'under the oppression'. These words appear in the proof in the left-hand margin in pencil in a hand that is certainly not Eliot's and Eliot's own correction 'calmness' and the words 'heard in the' are cancelled, also in pencil. It would seem that Eliot thought of 'under the oppression' after he had returned the proof and sent a further correction, which was made in the printing-house.[1] Faber's similar query in line 39, 'does "worried" add enough to "anxious"?', was ignored. Hayward objected to 'And at the same time / Time stops' (l. 44), commenting 'at the same *time* (tricky pun)'. In M2 Eliot first substituted 'While in the night watch', and then struck out 'night' for 'morning'. The final text, taking its phrase from the *De Profundis*, was arrived at in M3. The first version of line 46, 'And through the fog the pretemporal ground swell' made Faber uneasy. He wrote 'A difficult image—not *quite* sure I get its implication, or rather the implication of the prefix "pre"'. It's all right if *you* are sure of it. On the sound aspect, I confess I don't like the "-al" ending, with its (to my ear) weakening anticipation of the sound which concludes the line.' Eliot substituted in proof the phrase from the doxology; but Hayward, in a letter congratulating him on the poem's appearance in the *New English Weekly* expressed some regret: 'I'm slightly sorry that in the final version "the bell" (last words of section I.) has become an object from being a subject; I liked the sonorous emphasis of "bell" coming after the intransitive "clangs". Clang as a transitive verb seems to me to be weaker.'[2] The comment is rather odd, since in either version 'the ground swell' is surely the subject and 'bell' the object of 'Clangs'.

Faber was puzzled by the word 'rote', writing 'This meaning of "rote" is new to me—which isn't to say anything against it'. Presumably he had looked it up in *O.E.D.*, which has both 'rote' and 'rut' with the note 'now U.S.' Hayward originally queried it, but crossed out his query. It is rather surprising that he did not suggest that it, like 'groaner', should be glossed, since it does not appear in this sense in dictionaries available to the ordinary English reader. *O.E.D.* cites Thoreau, *Cape Cod* v (1894) 115: 'The old

---

[1] Another example of a pencilled correction on the proof that is not in Eliot's hand is 'union' (l. 216); but it is also not in the same hand as has written 'under the oppression'.

[2] Letter of 5 March 1941, EHC.

man said that this was what they called the "rut", a peculiar roar of the sea before the wind changes.'

The best commentary on these lines is provided by Admiral Morison in the article already quoted from.[1] He writes:

Tom was not only steeped in the lore of Cape Ann; he became familiar with the encompassing ocean. Cruising in college days with his friend Harold Peters, the Dry Salvages was the last seamark they passed outward bound, and the first they picked up homeward bound. Approaching or departing in a fog, they listened for the mournful moans of the 'groaner', the whistling buoy east of Thacher island, and the 'wailing warning' of the diaphone [fog-signal] on Thacher's itself. They doubtless learned to allow an extra quarter point for the set of current when sailing from the Maine coast to Cape Ann, as insurance against running on the Salvages. . . .

Tom remembered the music of Cape Ann—'the sea howl and the sea yelp,'

> . . . the whine in the rigging
> The menace and caress of wave that breaks on water,
> The distant rote in the granite teeth,
> And the wailing warning from the approaching headland

And the 'tolling bell' off Flat Ground. . . .

These lines, and indeed all that follow, ring a bell in any sailor's heart. They are authentic, not synthetic like the great mass of so-called sea poetry. Take, for instance, 'the menace and caress of wave that breaks on water', which Eliot could have observed at Flat Ground or Milk Island Bar. When a moderate wave from the ocean strikes a shoal, it suddenly lifts—a warning to an approaching mariner—and then breaks, with a susurration that may be rendered as a hissing menace or a wooing caress. Notice also 'the distant rote'. *Rote* or *Rut* is an old English word now seldom heard outside New England. It means a distant, continuous roar made by waves dashing on a long rocky coast.[2] Often have I heard a Maine man say, 'Sea's making up. Hear that rote!' It may be ten miles distant, but you can distinguish it from traffic noises, jet planes or any other sound. T. S. Eliot doubtless listened to the rote from his parents' house, during the windless calm after a storm, or on a 'weather-breeder' day when swells from the eastward begin crashing on the 'granite teeth' of Cape Ann before a storm breaks.

---

[1] See pp. 51–4.
[2] In Robert Juet's account of Henry Hudson's voyage of 1609, 'We heard a great Rut, like the Rut of the shoare'.

Part II

After the leaf of the manuscript pad that contains the notes for *The Dry Salvages* two leaves are missing. They possibly contained rough verse drafts of portions of Part I and an opening stanza or two of Part II, for on the next leaf that survives Eliot jotted down possible rhymes for the lyric opening of Part II. They suggest that he had written at least his first verse, and perhaps made an attempt at one or two others and was becoming anxious as to whether he could find sufficient rhyme words. It is interesting that two he has cancelled found a place in the text.

	sailing
	lowers
	oceanless
	wastage
unflyable	*liable*
	destination[1]
scaling	~~*hailing*~~
	ours
	~~*devotionless*~~
dockage	*trackage*
	~~*reliable*~~
	consummation

[1] With the exception of 'lowers' for 'cowers' these are the rhymes of the fourth stanza.

(49-84)

II

Where is there an end of it, the soundless wailing,
The silent withering of autumn flowers   50
Dropping their petals and remaining motionless;
Where is there an end to the drifting wreckage,
The prayer of the bone on the beach, the unprayable
Prayer at the calamitous annunciation?

There is no end, but addition: the trailing   55
Consequence of further days and hours,
While emotion takes to itself the emotionless
Years of living among the breakage
Of what was believed in as the most reliable—
And therefore the fittest for renunciation.   60

There is the final addition, the failing
Pride or resentment at failing powers,
The unattached devotion which might pass for devotionless,
In a drifting boat with a slow leakage,
The silent listening to the undeniable   65
Clamour of the bell of the last annunciation.

Where is the end of them, the fishermen sailing
Into the wind's tail, where the fog cowers?
We cannot think of a time that is oceanless
Or of an ocean not littered with wastage   70
Or of a future that is not liable
Like the past, to have no destination.

---

                                                    had
52 to] for M1   59 Of what was believed in as] Of that which ˄ persisted as M1; Of that which
                                                    what
had persisted as M2, D; Of that which was believed in as M3, T; Of ~~that which~~ . . . M4; Of ~~that which~~
⟨what⟩ . . . NEW proof   reliable—] reliable M1, 2, D   62 Pride or resentment at]
Pride or   at
~~Lack of~~ resentment ~~of~~ M1   67 Where] What M1   68 cowers?] cowers— M1
        in

We have to think of them as forever bailing,
Setting and hauling, while the North East lowers
Over shallow banks unchanging and erosionless   75
Or drawing their money, drying sails at dockage;
Not as making a trip that will be unpayable
For a haul that will not bear examination.

There is no end of it, the voiceless wailing,
No end to the withering of withered flowers,   80
To the movement of pain that is painless and motionless,
To the drift of the sea and the drifting wreckage,
The bone's prayer to Death its God. Only the hardly, barely prayable
Prayer of the one Annunciation.

                            as
73 them as forever] them ∧ forever M1   75 unchanging] unshifting M1, 2, D   76 Or
                                   money   *as*
drawing their money] ⟨Or⟩ Drawing their p̶a̶y̶ M1   77 Not as making] Not ∧ making M1
                the
79 the] t̶h̶a̶t̶ M4   73, 76 (:), 79, 80, 81 *Final stops supplied in pencil* M1   82 wreckage,]
wreckage M1

.

Like many of Eliot's lyrical passages, this lyric received little revision in
the drafts. Hayward made no comments. Faber raised a few mild objections.
Next to the first verse he wrote approvingly: 'the run of participles seems
right here.' But against line 59 he wrote 'I feel that this is a little short of its
context—I mean in the form of expression'. Eliot marked the line with
a heavy cross and in proof made a minor alteration of 'that which was' to
'what was'. Against line 63 Faber wrote 'I stick a little over this line, somehow
—only over the elliptical grammar, not the sense or sound. But not seriously.'
He also queried the word 'bear' (l. 78), asking: 'Do you mean this in the
usual sense of not repaying exam[n]? or do you mean "that never will undergo
exam[n]"? The latter sense seems to be suggested—if so is "bear" the right
word?' Since Eliot left this we can assume he intended the usual sense: that
the cargo is too poor to merit consideration. At line 83 Faber asked: 'Is the
extra tension of the 2nd adverb so much needed as to warrant the sudden
lengthening of the line? (That is a question, not a criticism.)'

(85–103)

It seems, as one becomes older,   85
That the past has another pattern, and ceases to be a mere sequence—
Or even development: the latter a partial fallacy
Encouraged by superficial notions of evolution,
Which becomes, in the popular mind, a means of disowning the past.
The moments of happiness—not the sense of well-being,   90
Fruition, fulfilment, security or affection,
Or even a very good dinner, but the sudden illumination—
We had the experience but missed the meaning,
And approach to the meaning restores the experience
In a different form, beyond any meaning   95
We can assign to happiness. I have said before
That the past experience revived in the meaning
Is not the experience of one life only
But of many generations—not forgetting
Something that is probably quite ineffable: 100
The backward look behind the assurance
Of recorded history, the backward half-look
Over the shoulder, towards the primitive terror.

85* It seems, as one becomes older] One has to repeat the same thing in a different way/And risk being
tedious: ⟨np?⟩ it seems . . . older M1; One has to repeat the same thing in various ways/And risk being
tedious./(space) It seems, . . . older M2, D; M2 cancels One . . . tedious.   86 pattern, and
                          and
ceases] pattern/ It ceases M1   87* development] a mere "development" M1; a "development"
M2, D; "development" M3, T; "development" M4, NEW proof   partial] cheerful M1-4, D, T;
cheerful ⟨partial⟩ NEW proof   88* evolution] Evolution M1-4, D, T; Evolution ⟨l.c.⟩ NEW proof
89* Which becomes, in the popular mind, a means of disowning the past] Which is but, in the popular
                                     Regarded Thought of   as a sort of
view, cremation of the past M1, D; Which is but, in the popular view, cremation of the past M2
                                                                          not
90 not the sense] I don't mean the sense M1, D; I don't mean . . . M2   93 We had] One had
        We
M1, D; One had M2   96* assign to happiness] attach to "happiness" M1-3, D, T; assign to
"happiness" M4, NEW proof   I have said before] I have suggested also M1-4, D, T; . . . suggested also
⟨said before⟩ NEW proof   100 that] which M1   ineffable:] ineffable, M1   101 behind]
beyond M1-3, D, T   102 recorded] recordable M1, 2, D

Eliot had considerable difficulty with the tone here. Hayward drew his attention with a query to the line and a half that originally opened this passage, with its embarrassing defensiveness, and Eliot accepted the criticism and struck it out. He also suggested the transposing of 'but' (l. 89) to make it read 'in the popular view, but cremation'. Eliot, after some fiddling, rewrote the line, replacing the exaggeration of 'cremation' by the exactitude of 'disowning'. Hayward suggested 'not merely' for 'I don't mean' (l. 90), and drew Eliot's attention to the uneasy alternation of pronouns throughout this and the following section by writing '*I—One—We*', and he queried 'I have suggested also' (l. 96).

The most cogent criticism of this passage is Faber's in the margins of M4. It may well be felt that Eliot did not go far enough in meeting his comments. A simple suggestion, which Eliot accepted, was for a break between the lyric and the discursive passage. In all the drafts the space between the lyric and the following lines is the same as that between the stanzas of the lyric. Faber wrote 'Why do you not make a formal break here? It would ease the reader's acceptance of the sudden change of tone.' Eliot gave direction to the printer on the proof: 'double this space.' Faber summarized his general uneasiness over the tone at the top of the page that began with the line 'The moments of happiness—not the sense of well-being' (l. 90), writing 'I find all this passage very impressive: and all the more, for that reason, I dislike the "lecture-stigmata" you (as it seems to me) wilfully give to it! The *Xs* mark my points of resentment!' He has underscored, with an X in the margin, 'I have suggested also' (l. 96), and two similar phrases in the section that follows: 'Now, the point is' (l. 104), which Eliot altered in proof, and 'We appreciate this better' (l. 108), which Eliot left. Faber also disliked the inverted commas around 'development' (l. 87) and 'happiness' (l. 96) and Eliot removed them in proof. He queried lines 99–100: 'not forgetting / Something that is probably quite ineffable', commenting 'is the grammatical structure right here? Who does the "not forgetting"? I don't like "probably".' The inverted commas around 'development' and the capital given to 'evolution' (l. 88), which Eliot removed in proof, suggested a certain element of disdain for popular subservience to scientific ideas, as did the adjective 'cheerful' applied to 'fallacy' (l. 87), which was replaced by the more scrupulous and less contemptuous word 'partial'.

(104–123)

Now, we come to discover that the moments of agony
(Whether, or not, due to misunderstanding,　　　　　　　　　　　105
Having hoped for the wrong things or dreaded the wrong things,
Is not in question) are likewise permanent
With such permanence as time has. We appreciate this better
In the agony of others, nearly experienced,
Involving ourselves, than in our own.　　　　　　　　　　　110
For our own past is covered by the currents of action,
But the torment of others remains an experience
Unqualified, unworn by subsequent attrition.
People change, and smile: but the agony abides.
Time the destroyer is time the preserver,　　　　　　　　　　115
Like the river with its cargo of dead negroes, cows and chicken coops,
The bitter apple and the bite in the apple.
And the ragged rock in the restless waters,
Waves wash over it, fogs conceal it;
On a halcyon day it is merely a monument,　　　　　　　　　120
In navigable weather it is always a seamark
To lay a course by: but in the sombre season
Or the sudden fury, is what it always was.

　　　　　　　　　　　　　　　　　　　　　　　　　　the point is
104 Now, we come to discover] Now I would say, M1, D; Now I ~~would say,~~ M2; Now the point is,
M3, T; Now, the point is M4; Now, ~~the point is~~ ⟨*we come to discover*⟩ NEW proof　　　107 Is not
in question] Is beside the point M1, 2, D　　　permanent] ~~eternal~~ permanent M1　　　　　108 We
　　　　　　　　　　　　　　　　　　　We
appreciate] One appreciates M1, D; ~~One~~ appreciates M2　　　110 ourselves . . . our own] oneself
　　　　　　　　　　　　　our　　　　　　　　　　　　　　*our*
. . . one's own M1, D; oneself . . . ~~one's~~ M2　　　111 our] one's M1, D; ~~one's~~ M2　　currents of
　　　compulsion of
　　　sea　　　　　　　　　　　　　　*remains*
action] ~~tides~~ of action ⟨*currents*⟩ M1　　　112 remains] is　　M1　　　114–17 *These four lines*
　　　waters
are not in the typescript of M1, *but are added in manuscript at the foot of the page; see opposite*
118 restless] moving M1, 2, D　　　121 seamark] sea-mark M1–3, D, T　　　122 by↑, ⟨:⟩ M1
122 sombre] sullen M1, 2, D; ~~sullen~~ ⟨*sombre*⟩ M3, T　　　123* always was.] always was./(*space*)
Now about the future M1; always was./Now about the future M2, D; M2 *cancels* Now . . . future.

The four lines Eliot added to his first typed draft in M1 were added in stages. The text as typed ran

> But the torment of others is an experience
> Unqualified, unworn by subsequent attrition;
> And the ragged rock in the moving waters,
> Waves wash over it, fogs conceal it; . . .

Eliot substituted a full stop for a semi-colon after 'attrition', and then wrote at the foot of the page, with a line drawn to show that the insertion was to be made after 'attrition':

> *abides*
> *People change, & smile: but the agony* ~~remains:~~
> *Time the destroyer is time the preserver,*
>
> *bitter*
> *bitten*
> *The ‸ fruit and the bite in the fruit*

He then wrote below this:

> *The River?*

and drew a line to show that he needed a line on the river to come between the second and third lines of his addition. Then, below, he supplied it in parentheses:

> *stiff*
> *(Like the river with its cargo of dead negroes, ‸ cows*
> *and chicken coops)*

Having deleted 'remains' for 'abides', he was able to strengthen line 112 by substituting 'remains' for the weak 'is'.

Hayward's only comment on this passage was 'Abrupt end to sect. II?', which caused Eliot to delete the final sentence. It more than deserves Faber's criticism of 'lecture-stigmata' in this part, but was removed before he saw the poem. The substitution of 'sombre' for 'sullen' (l. 122) in M3 and T was possibly made to avoid the near-echo of 'sullen'/'sudden'. Faber wrote against the last line 'I admit I want the "it" again here' and put a caret mark before 'is'. Eliot rightly ignored this.

(124–145)

III

I sometimes wonder if that is what Krishna meant—
Among other things—or one way of putting the same thing: 125
That the future is a faded song, a Royal Rose or a lavender spray
Of wistful regret for those who are not yet here to regret,
Pressed between yellow leaves of a book that has never been opened.
And the way up is the way down, the way forward is the way back.
You cannot face it steadily, but this thing is sure,   130
That time is no healer: the patient is no longer here.
When the train starts, and the passengers are settled
To fruit, periodicals and business letters
(And those who saw them off have left the platform)
Their faces relax from grief into relief,   135
To the sleepy rhythm of a hundred hours.
Fare forward, travellers! not escaping from the past
Into different lives, or into any future;
You are not the same people who left that station
Or who will arrive at any terminus,   140
While the narrowing rails slide together behind you;
And on the deck of the drumming liner
Watching the furrow that widens behind you,
You shall not think 'the past is finished'
Or 'the future is before us'.   145

                     opened
128 opened.] read/ M1   130 You cannot face it steadily, but this thing is sure] . . . for long at a
                                                          steadily
time, but one thing . . . M1; . . . for long at a time . . . D; . . . for long at a time . . . M2   134 And]
And M2   135 Their faces] And their faces M1, D; And tTheir faces M2   136 the sleepy
        sleepy
rhythm] the ∧monotone ⟨rhythm⟩ M1   . hours.] hours- M1, 2, D   138 future;] future: M1
        that   *And on*
139 that station] one station M1   141 narrowing] narrow(ing) M1   142 And on] Or from M1
142 liner] liner, M1–3, D, T

The rough first draft of these lines in the manuscript at Magdalene reads:

> *I sometimes wonder. I wonder if that*
> *was what Krishna meant,*
> *Among other things or one way of*
> *putting the same thing*
> *That the future is a faded song, a*
> *Royal Rose or a lavender spray*
> *Pressed* in the *between leaves of a*
> *forgotten book which has not yet been read*[1]
> *Keepsake, and that the past*
> *Is a pit for us still to explore: and*
> *the way up is the way down*
> *The way forward is the way back.*
> *You cannot think long at a time,*
> *but one thing is sure*
> *That time is no healer. Time can*
> *only distract*
> *And not even time can show*
>
> *and the light is the darkness, the*
> *darkness is light.*[2]

>   (*new leaf*)
> *the right judgement or else the mistaken*
> *For what alters the past to fit the*
> *present, can alter the present to fit*
> *the past.*

The alteration in line 130 was in response to a suggestion made by Hayward: 'this is certain (too many monosyllables at present?)' Hayward also pointed out that lines 134 and 135 both began with 'And'. Faber made no comments on Parts III and IV.

For Eliot's use of the *Bhagavad-Gita*, see pp. 56–7. Bonamy Dobrée reported that, after reading the first draft of *Little Gidding*, he asked Eliot about the significance of the rose in his poems, and Eliot replied:

> There are really three roses in the set of poems; the sensuous rose, the socio-political Rose (always appearing with a capital letter) and the spiritual rose: and the three have got to be in some way identified as one.

Dobrée commented: 'I must confess I was not much illuminated.'[3]

---

[1] Inserted as a second thought between two lines.
[2] A line has been drawn to indicate this should come after 'The way forward is the way back'.
[3] Tate, 86.

(146-168)

At nightfall, in the rigging and the aerial,
Is a voice descanting (though not to the ear,
The murmuring shell of time, and not in any language)
'Fare forward, you who think that you are voyaging;
You are not those who saw the harbour   150
Receding, or those who will disembark.
Here between the hither and the farther shore
While time is withdrawn, consider the future
And the past with an equal mind.
At the moment which is not of action or inaction   155
You can receive this: "on whatever sphere of being
The mind of a man may be intent
At the time of death"—that is the one action
(And the time of death is every moment)
Which shall fructify in the lives of others: 160
And do not think of the fruit of action.
Fare forward.
                    O voyagers, O seamen,
You who come to port, and you whose bodies
Will suffer the trial and judgement of the sea,
Or whatever event, this is your real destination.'   165
So Krishna, as when he admonished Arjuna
On the field of battle.
                    Not fare well,
But fare forward, voyagers.

Is   a   descanting

147 Is a voice descanting] ~~Are the~~ voices singing M1   149 that] M1 *omits*   151 who
                                   will
will disembark] who ‸ disembark M1   152 farther] further M1-DS   160 shall]
                                                                          Or
should DS   lives] souls M1, 2, D   165 Or whatever event, this is] ~~And~~ whatever
    this
event, ‸ is M1   167 battle./Not fare well,/But fare forward, voyagers] battle. *Not farewell,/*
But fare forward, voyagers./~~The way up etc.~~ M1

Hayward commented 'Fare forward? Browning—'. Eliot replied:
'"Fare Forward". I had quite forgotten the Browning, and I don't even
remember it now. I was thinking of the words of the sibyl to Alaric (wasn't
it?) on his way to Rome: "not fare well, but fare forward". This point bothers
me.' Hayward was in error, as he owned:

As to the Browning 'canard' (as it turns out to be) I hasten to put your mind at ease. It's the old story of a half-remembered and unchecked tag floating in and out of one's memory. The hortatory phrase 'Fare Forward' struck, as they say, a chord—or what I took to be a chord. I recalled at once the familiar 'Epilogue to Asolando', but recalled it inaccurately, thinking the last words were: 'Cry "Speed,—fight on, fare forward / There as here."' Browning in fact wrote 'Fare ever'. So, there has been some ado about nothing. I apologize. I didn't know about the Sybil and Alaric.[1]

Hayward's ignorance about 'the Sybil and Alaric' is shared by me and all I have consulted. It seems highly improbable that sibyls would be allowed to have any dealings with Alaric when he was marching on Rome, and difficult to see how 'not fare well, but fare forward' could be rendered in Latin. Mr. Peter Brown of All Souls whom I consulted thinks Eliot was remembering 'a more precise and epigrammatic re-working of a vaguer rumour—that Alaric did give out that he was "driven" to sack Rome by some divine force'. Mr. Brown referred me to Claudian's poem on the Gothic war, which describes a Gothic chieftain attempting to dissuade Alaric from the sacrilege of attempting to sack Rome, and gives Alaric's reply:

> The gods, too, urge me on. Not for me are dreams or birds but the clear cry uttered openly from the sacred grove: 'Away with delay, Alaric; boldly cross the Italian Alps this year and thou shalt reach the city.'[2]

A similar story is told by two ecclesiastical historians writing in Constantinople in the mid-fifth century, where the dissuader is a pious monk. My own belief is that Eliot was remembering some obscure historical novel read in his youth.

The original version of the phrase 'Is a voice descanting' (l. 147), 'Are the voices singing', makes closer the reminiscence of lines in the shipwreck passage that Eliot cut from Part IV of *The Waste Land*:

> One night
> On watch, I thought I saw in the fore-cross trees
> Three women leaning forward, with white hair
> Streaming behind, who sang above the wind
> A song that charmed my senses. . . .

Eliot has added the last half-line and line (ll. 167–8) to the typescript in M1, and written below the words 'the way up etc.' with a line to show the words were to be inserted before line 165; but he changed his mind and crossed through the words and the directing line.

---

[1] Letter of 7 January 1941, EHC.
[2] Ed. M. Platnauer, *De Bello Gothico* (1922), ii. 164, ll. 544–7.

(169–183)

IV

Lady, whose shrine stands on the promontory,
Pray for all those who are in ships, those   170
Whose business has to do with fish, and
Those concerned with every lawful traffic
And those who conduct them.

Repeat a prayer also on behalf of
Women who have seen their sons or husbands   175
Setting forth, and not returning:
Figlia del tuo figlio,
Queen of Heaven.

Also pray for those who were in ships, and
Ended their voyage on the sand, in the sea's lips   180
Or in the dark throat which will not reject them
Or wherever cannot reach them the sound of the sea bell's
Perpetual angelus.

                                                                          who are
169 stands] *is* MS   170 all those who are in ships] *those in the ships* MS; all those ᴧ in the
ships M1; . . . in the . . . NEW proof   172 Those concerned with every lawful traffic] *Those*
        affairs   *every*
about their lawful traffic, and MS; Those about their . . . M1   173 conduct] *defend* MS
                                Compose a
174 Repeat a prayer] *Accept this intercession* MS; Transmit our prayer M1; Compose a prayer M2, D
175 Women who have seen their sons or husbands] *Women waiting on the hither shore/Those who see their*
                              or
sons & husbands MS; . . . sons and . . . M1   177 Figlia] *Tu, figlia* MS   *tuo] suo* MS; suo M1–DS
                              Queen
178 Queen] *Bride* MS; Bride M1   179 Also pray for those] *Also for those* MS; Also we
                                        Find their
                                        Cease   *Ended*
pray . . . M1   in] *in the* MS   180 Ended] *End* MS; End M1   181 which]
that   *Where*
which M1   182 Or wherever] *Where* MS; And wherever M1
                              Or

The first extant draft, in the Magdalene manuscript, is written without any alterations in the first two stanzas, except for 'affairs' written above the uncancelled 'traffic' and a deletion of 'and' at the close of the same line when Eliot accidentally ran on into the next line. The second stanza is extended by an extra line:

> *Accept this intercession also on behalf of*
> *Women waiting on the hither shore*
> *Those who see their sons & husbands*
> *Setting forth, and not returning:*
> *Tu, figlia del suo figlio,*
> *Bride of Heaven.*

In the third stanza Eliot made two shots at a beginning of the second line before hitting on 'End'.

Neither Hayward nor Faber made any comment on Part IV. It is odd that neither of them noted the misquotation from Dante (l. 177), which survived up to the appearance of the poem in pamphlet form. One of its first readers suggested to me that the whole poem was addressed not to the Virgin but to her mother St. Anne, who could be regarded as 'daughter of *her* Son, (who is) Queen of Heaven'. It was a relief to find such contortions of sense and syntax were unnecessary and 'suo' a mere mistake for 'tuo'.

When, in 1961, the Rev. William T. Levy mentioned to Eliot his admiration for the church of Notre Dame de la Gard, high up overlooking the Mediterranean at Marseilles, Eliot told him that this was the 'shrine' he had in mind. He reports Eliot as saying, in response to his expressing surprise at not having realized this:

> You accepted it as a class of churches, and were not thinking of a particular church. And that is the right way to think of it. It is fortuitous in our case that I as writer and you as reader of these lines happened to know and react identically to the same place—and then we had to know each other for me to affirm it.[1]

---

[1] William Turner Levy and Victor Scherle, *Affectionately, T. S. Eliot* (J. P. Lippincott Co., New York, 1968), 121.

(184-198)

V

To communicate with Mars, converse with spirits,
To report the behaviour of the sea monster,   185
Describe the horoscope, haruspicate or scry,
Observe disease in signatures, evoke
Biography from the wrinkles of the palm
And tragedy from fingers; release omens
By sortilege, or tea leaves, riddle the inevitable   190
With playing cards, fiddle with pentagrams
Or barbituric acids, or dissect
The recurrent image into pre-conscious terrors—
To explore the womb, or tomb, or dreams; all these are usual
Pastimes and drugs, and features of the press: 195
And always will be, some of them especially
When there is distress of nations and perplexity
Whether on the shores of Asia, or in the Edgware Road.

                                                    report   behaviour
185 To report the behaviour] To report the appearance M1, 2, D; to ~~verify~~ the ~~convolutions~~ M3;
report   *haruspicate*
To ~~verify~~ the convolutions T   186* haruspicate or scry] ~~divine~~ in sand M1; haruspicate with
or scry
sand D; . . . ~~with sand~~ M2   187 Observe] Define M1, 2, D   188 from] in M1, 2, D
in   *release*
189 from] ~~from~~ M1; in M2, D   189-90* release omens/By sortilege, or tea leaves] ~~realise~~
                                                    use sortilege or peer/⟨At⟩ From the
omens/By crystal gazing M1; release omens/By crystal gazing D; release omens/   ~~By crystal~~
bottom of [a] tea cups,
~~gazing~~   M2   191 With playing cards] By laying cards M1, 2, D   *pentagrams]
                                                    acids
pentagons M1, 2, D, T; ~~pentagons~~ ⟨*pentagrams*⟩ M3   192 acids] forces M1   193 The
                                                    image   *or dreams*
recurrent image] ⟨*The*⟩ Recurrent ~~dreams~~ M1   194 or tomb, or dreams] or tomb ‸ : M1
195 press:] press. *corr. to* press: M1   196 And always will be, some of them especially] Have
                                                    some of them
been and always will be, and especially M1; ~~Have been a~~ And always will be, ‸ ~~and~~ especially M2, D
198 or in the Edgware Road] or the Edgware Road M1.

Eliot obviously enjoyed writing this return to the world of Madame Sosostris, Doris, and Dusty, and composing a fantasia on fortune-telling. In his congratulatory letter on the appearance in print of the poem Hayward, commenting on line 185, wrote: 'I prefer the original "appearance" to "behaviour". It is always the appearance of the Loch Ness monster and its fellows that excites the vulgar mobile.'[1] In his notes on the draft in D, he noted the error in 'haruspicate with sand' (l. 186),[2] and supplied the correct term 'coscinomancy' for riddling with sand in a sieve held on a pair of shears. Mercifully Eliot did not accept this learned term. He apologized meekly: '"Haruspicate". Gross carelessness on my part. I wonder whether haruspicate with guts would do. I don't think it would.' Hayward did not think so either and wrote:

> No. I don't think 'with guts' is quite nice! Isn't it a pleonasm anyhow? I should not like to lose the conjunction of horoscope-haruspicate: on the other hand (speaking as a coscinomancer) I should like to keep 'sand' (or sieves). I think you should be able to find a solution without great difficulty. But let me know if the change raises more trouble than I envisage.[3]

Eliot did not wholly abandon 'sand' and 'sieves' when in M2, where he made corrections to meet Hayward's criticisms, he hit on 'scry'. The current sense of the word is 'to gaze into a crystal to foretell the future'; but there is an obsolete sense, 'to sift', and a noun, also obsolete, meaning 'a sieve'. The word puzzled Faber who underlined it and wrote in the margin: 'I didn't know this word either. But the *C.O.D.* (which failed me over ailantus) does.' Having hit on 'scry' in line 186, Eliot had to abandon 'By crystal gazing' four lines further on. He first wrote 'From the bottom of tea cups'; then he went back and in the line above, without cancelling 'release omens', wrote 'use sortilege or peer', altered 'From the bottom' to 'At the bottom' and 'tea cups' to 'a tea cup'. In M3, T he condensed this to 'By sortilege, or tea leaves'. It is surprising that Hayward did not catch the error in line 191 where the harmless geometrical figure 'pentagon' was mistakenly written for the magical five-pointed star or pentagram. Eliot ignored Faber's dry comment against the statement that 'all these are usual . . . and always will be' (ll. 194–6): 'It's perhaps an unfair comment to say that psycho-analysis is a very *new* addition to the list.'

[1] Letter of 5 March 1941, EHC.
[2] Haruspication is 'divination by inspection of entrails'.
[3] Letter of 7 January 1941, EHC.

(199–215)

Men's curiosity searches past and future
And clings to that dimension. But to apprehend   200
The point of intersection of the timeless
With time, is an occupation for the saint—
No occupation either, but something given
And taken, in a lifetime's death in love,
Ardour and selflessness and self-surrender.   205
For most of us, there is only the unattended
Moment, the moment in and out of time,
The distraction fit, lost in a shaft of sunlight,
The wild thyme unseen, or the winter lightning
Or the waterfall, or music heard so deeply   210
That it is not heard at all, but you are the music
While the music lasts. These are only hints and guesses,
Hints followed by guesses; and the rest
Is prayer, observance, discipline, thought and action.
The hint half guessed, the gift half understood, is Incarnation. 215

199 past and future] the past and future M1; the past and the future M2, D   200 that] this M1
200 *to apprehend] to attend to M1, 2, D; to attend to ⟨be aware of⟩ M3, T; to be aware of M4; to be
aware of ⟨apprehend⟩ NEW proof   201 point of intersection] unheeded intersection M1, 2, D
202 saint—] saint, M1, 2, D   203 No occupation either] And not an occupation M1
203–5* given . . . self-surrender] given. M1, 2, D   207 Moment] Rare moment M1, D;
Rare mMoment M2   209* The wild thyme unseen, or the winter lightning] The wild thyme
unseen, or winter lightning (insertion) M1   212* While the music lasts. These are only hints
and guesses,] . . . lasts, the spell lasts. Hints and guesses; M1, 2, D (M2 brackets the spell lasts)
213–15* guesses; and the rest/Is prayer, observance, discipline, thought and action./The hint half
guessed, the gift half understood, is Incarnation] guesses: but our ultimate term/And ultimate gift, is
Incarnation M1, 2, D; . . . hint unguessed . . . gift not understood . . . M3, 4, T; . . . hint unguessed
⟨half guessed⟩ . . . not understood ⟨half understood⟩ NEW proof

The change in proof of 'be aware of' to 'apprehend' (l. 200) was in response to a comment by Faber on this and the following line, 'too many "ofs"'. The expansion of the idea of 'something given' in lines 204-5 appears in the typescript of M3, T. Hayward had commented on the last five lines of page 9 of his draft 'weakly expressed', and they certainly are rather bleak in the first two drafts:

> And clings to that dimension. But to attend to
> The unheeded intersection of the timeless
> With time, is an occupation for the saint,
> No occupation either, but something given.
> For most of us there is only the unattended . . .

The echo from *East Coker*—'The wild thyme unseen, or winter lightning' —was written by Eliot at the foot of the page in M1. Hayward queried the jingle of 'the music lasts, the spell lasts' (l. 212) and Eliot, who, in his letter replying to Hayward's suggestions wrote 'One or two ("spell lasts") I had discovered for myself in the meantime', bracketed the words in M2 and omitted them in M3, T. Faber underlined 'distraction fit' (l. 208) and put a query in the margin. He also queried 'hint unguessed' and 'gift not understood' (l. 215) in Eliot's expansion of the over abrupt 'but our ultimate term/And ultimate gift, is Incarnation', writing: 'Isn't this in want of *some* qualification? *You* must guess and understand, or you couldn't say it; and you wouldn't claim to be the only percipient, would you?' Eliot met this objection by correcting to 'half guessed' and 'half understood' in proof; but he did not respond to another query by Faber: 'Does Incarnation mean "The Incarnation" (of Christ) or the incarnation of every human spirit?'

The same kind of objection which Faber made to the words 'unguessed' and 'not understood' could also apply to 'the unheeded intersection' (l. 201) in the first two drafts. The concept of the 'point of intersection' is a favourite one with Karl Barth, whose *Commentary on the Epistle to the Romans* was extremely influential in the period just before the war.

(216–233)

Here the impossible union
Of spheres of existence is actual,
Here the past and future
Are conquered, and reconciled,
Where action were otherwise movement   220
Of that which is only moved
And has in it no source of movement—
Driven by dæmonic, chthonic
Powers. And right action is freedom
From past and future also.   225
For most of us, this is the aim
Never here to be realised;
Who are only undefeated
Because we have gone on trying;
We, content at the last   230
If our temporal reversion nourish
(Not too far from the yew-tree)
The life of significant soil.

216 union] meeting M1–4, D, T; meeting ⟨union⟩ NEW proof   217 Of spheres of existence is
existences
actual] Of worlds becomes actual M1   218 the] both M1–4, D, T; both ⟨the⟩ NEW proof
219* and reconciled,] and reconciled,/And here is implied Atonement/And Atonement makes action
possible M1–3, D, T (cancelled in M3); no comma in M2, 3, T   220 Where action were
otherwise movement] When action had been but movement M1; When action had been only movement
M2, D; Where action had been only movement M3, 4, T; . . . had been only . . . ⟨were otherwise⟩
NEW proof   222–4 And . . . movement   Driven . . . Powers.] (And . . . movement,/Driven . . .
Powers). M1, 2, D   227 here to be] to be quite M1, 2, D; here quite M3, 4, T; here
quite ⟨to be⟩ NEW proof   228–33 For the variants in the conclusion, see opposite

In a letter dated, according to Hayward, 12 February 1941 Eliot wrote:

> I forgot to say that I have made a number of alterations to the dry Salvages, incorporating most of your suggestions and some from Geoffrey. I have chiefly altered the last page, which I thought rather too heavily loaded theologically. I now have 'haruspicate or scry'. I have not had a spare copy to send you, and I did a lot more to the proof: you will see the N.E.W. in ten days time. This, however, need not be regarded as the final version (what is periodical publication for?) and I shall be grateful for further comments.[1]

Hayward had not objected to the two lines on 'Atonement'; but Eliot had removed them before Faber saw M4.[2] Hayward made his usual query at 'chthonic', '(sound)', objecting to its chiming with 'dæmonic' (l. 223). The alteration in line 220 of 'had been only' to 'were otherwise' was in response to an objection by Faber:

> I suppose this means that in the material world, without incarnation of spirit, there *would* have been no spontaneous or willed movement? I'm not sure whether 'had been' is factual or hypothetical.

Both Hayward and Faber queried the ellipse in line 230 'We content', Hayward putting a caret mark and query between the two words, whereas Faber spelt out his objection: 'Does the rhythm demand the elliptical "We content"? It is difficult for me to take it without jibbing a bit & searching for a lost auxiliary!!' Eliot merely inserted a comma.

Eliot had great difficulty with his concluding six lines.[3] The only line that remained unaltered from the first draft was the concluding one: 'The life of significant soil.' In M1 the poem ended with four lines:

> We content and should be
> If the temporal aspect of the soul
> Nourish (not too far from the yew-tree)
> The life of significant soil.

---

[1] EHC.

[2] They are cancelled in M3 but not in its carbon copy T.

[3] In the Humanities Research Center of the University of Texas there is, in addition to an autograph copy of the last eighteen lines, a letter from Eliot to Mairet, dated 15 February 1941:

Dear Mairet,

   I am wondering whether you got my corrected proof. I hope so, because I made a number of alterations, and I don't want the poem to appear without them. Also, by the time I had finished the pages had become such a griffonage that they were almost illegible, and I am particularly [anxious] to get the last six lines right: which was why I asked for another pull. In case, here are the last lines again. . . . It is important, because, however I have tried it, it turns out to be something to which people will give a topical allusion—not part of the fundamental intention—and if so, then it must not be a wrong twist which will put the rest of the poem out of joint. . . .

Presumably it was the word 'undefeated' that Eliot feared might in 1941 give a 'topical allusion'.

M2 and D read:

> We content and should be
> If the temporal aspect nourish
> (Not too far from the yew-tree)
> The life of significant soil.

In both 'aspect' is cancelled and 'conclusion' written above it; but in M2 'conclusion' has also been cancelled and 'reversion' written in the margin. In M3, T Eliot typed 'our temporal reversion' for 'the temporal aspect' and in M3 went on to make further suggestions. M3 reads:

      ~~in the~~
We content ~~and should be~~
If our temporal reversion nourish . . . .

and should be
*   ⎧ at last*
We content ⎨ in the end
If we have gone on trying;
We content at last

In M4 the marginal insertion is incorporated into the typescript; but with an unhappy choice of 'and should be', which, unfortunate on one occurrence, is disastrous on two:

> We content and should be
> If we have gone on trying;
> We content and should be
> If our temporal reversion nourish. . . .

This was set up by the printer.

The foot of this page of the proof is covered by drafts by Eliot in pencil and ink. In pencil he has written on the verso of the page

> *We are the undefeated*
> *If we have gone on trying;*
> *We, content*

This has been transferred in ink to the recto at the right-hand foot of the page as

> *We are undefeated*
> *If we have gone on trying*
> *We, content at the last*
> *If our*

Then, in pencil, he supplied 'the' before 'undefeated' and made another attempt in pencil above:

> *We must find the contentment*
> *That is found in going on trying:*
> *We, content at the last,*

For the moment he seems to have been satisfied, for he scrawled through

the last two attempts and wrote in ink a slightly different version of the
second at the foot of the page:

> *find the*
> *We must* ~~*learn*~~ *serenity*
> *the act of*
> *Which is* ~~*to be*~~ *found in* ∧ *trying;*

then cancelled in ink the lines

> We content and should be
> If we have gone on trying

and drew a line to indicate they were to be replaced by the new draft. Then
he had second thoughts, crossed through the new version, and wrote in ink
in the margin

> *Who are only undefeated*
> *Because we have | gone on trying*
> *We, content at the last*

and drew another line to indicate this was to replace the cancelled lines in
the proof. The next line 'We content and should be' is cancelled in pencil,
probably by someone in the printing-house on Eliot's instructions.

I think it has to be conceded that Eliot did not find a fine enough conclusion to his poem and it remains a lame close. The end does not match the
beginning, nor does it lead forward as the end of *East Coker* does to the
theme of the next poem. It is only the last two words 'significant soil' that
have a mysterious suggestiveness and hold layers of meaning.

Little Gidding

Little Gidding

Eliot gave Hayward five typed drafts of *Little Gidding* which he bound up with a title-page designating them and dating them. The dates are those of Eliot's covering letters. He also pencilled the dates on the drafts. This was necessary as he broke up the drafts to bind pages from different drafts to face each other, thus facilitating comparison. Included in the volume are ten letters from Eliot,[1] the first corrected proof, and the text of the poem as published in NEW.

In addition to the five drafts sent to Hayward, there are thirteen typescripts of parts or the whole of the poem which Eliot gave to Magdalene College, Cambridge. These are working copies with a great many alterations and suggestions made on them. Five of them are top or carbon copies of the drafts sent to Hayward. Some are fragments which Eliot put together unsorted with typescripts of the whole poem. I have indented the intermediate Magdalene typescripts to distinguish these working copies from the drafts sent to Hayward whose readings are the subject of Hayward's comments and criticisms and Eliot's replies. In discussion and in the apparatus Hayward's drafts and the corresponding Magdalene typescripts are treated as a single text, e.g. D1/M3.

M1 (3 pages). Part I only. This is inscribed by Eliot 'Draft'. It is the earliest extant version of Part I and has many manuscript alterations.

M2 (14 pages). This is inscribed by Eliot 'Little Gidding/1. Draft 2'. Part I incorporates alterations made by Eliot in M1 and adds some others. There are manuscript alterations throughout Parts II to V and there are two versions of Part IV.

D1 and M3 (12 pages). D1, 'First Complete Draft 7 July 1941', is a carbon copy of M3. It has one manuscript correction, which is also in M3. Eliot has marked stanzas 1 and 2 of Part IV for reversal, with a note 'Perhaps omit 2?' He has also written on a covering sheet 'first draft for consideration./Not sure.' Eliot has made a few manuscript alterations in M3.

M4 (originally 12 pages. Page 10, containing the last stanza of Part IV and the beginning of Part V, is missing). This is a retyping of M3. It has a great many manuscript alterations made at different times. The earliest would seem to belong to the month during which Eliot was waiting for

---

[1] Hayward's letter commenting on the first draft is in EHC and is transcribed with the first draft in Appendix A, pp. 234-6. There are some further letters by Eliot referring to *Little Gidding* in EHC.

Hayward to comment on D1, others were made in response to Hayward's criticism, others were radical, including the cancellation of the close of Part II and the first two stanzas of the original version of Part IV. These last probably belong to the time when Eliot took up the poem again in the summer of 1942.

M5 (11 pages). This is a retyping of M4 incorporating its first corrections. Eliot also pencilled in two suggestions and made an underlining with a cross in the margin in response to comments by Hayward. He appears then to have abandoned M5.

M6 (2 pages). Part III only. This is a retyping of Part III in M4, incorporating some of its revisions and making others.

M7 (2 pages). Part II (second section) only, incomplete at the end. The description of the meeting with the stranger is heavily reworked in manuscript. The last twelve lines on page 2 are the first typed draft of a new version of the counsel of the 'dead master'.

M8 (3 pages). Part II (second section) only. This has a great many alterations made in the typing, as well as a few in manuscript. It is the best example of Eliot composing as he typed.

D2 and M9 (11 pages). Parts I, II, III, V. D2 is designated by Hayward as 'First Revision. Parts I. II. III 17 August 1942' and 'First Revision. Part V. 27 August 1942'. Hayward was in error here; but he has given the dates correctly on the drafts. Eliot in a letter of 17 August writes that he is sending 'a recension of Part II' and submits it with 'another edition of Part III'; his letter of 27 August sends 'another version of Part II and a slightly altered I and V'. Parts II and III of D2 are the typescript of which M9 is a carbon copy on orange flimsy-paper; but Parts I and V are, like the other drafts sent to Hayward, carbon copies, of which M9 is the typescript.

D3 and M10 (5 pages). Part II only. D3, 'Second Revision. Part II. 27 August 1942', is a carbon copy of M10. Eliot did some work on M10 in response to comments by Hayward.

M11 (3 pages). Part III only. This is a retyping of M9 with only one minor difference in a reading and no manuscript alterations.

D4 and M12 (12 pages). D4, 'Second Complete Draft 2 Sep. 1942', is a carbon copy of M12. M12 has a great many manuscript alterations and suggestions, particularly in Part II.

D5 and M13 (11 pages). D5, 'Final Recension. 19 Septem^r. 1942', is a carbon copy of M13. On the top right-hand corner of M13 Eliot has written the name 'John Easton'. John Easton was a member of the firm of

R. MacLehose and Company which printed *Little Gidding* in pamphlet form. The presence of his name and the instructions to the printers—'no space' and 'wide space'—show that M13 was the copy for LG.

NEW proof. In addition to the proof bound up by Hayward, there is another first proof in Magdalene College, Cambridge. On both Eliot has written 'Corrected / T.S.E. / 28.ix.42'. The proof was not set up from the 'Final Recension' (D5/M13) but from a text lying between D4/M12 and D5/M13. I imagine that after he had made a certain number of the corrections in M12 and cancelled others, reverting to his first idea, Eliot either made a retyping, or handed M12 to a professional typist, and sent the text to NEW. The text has been corrected in proof to the readings of D5, except on three occasions, either because Eliot intended a reversion to the reading of D4 or because he did not notice the difference in reading. In addition to its first proof, Magdalene has a second and a final proof. The second merely corrects some misprints and the final proof makes a spelling correction that does not appear in the NEW text.

NEW. *New English Weekly*, 15 October 1942. The text is well printed and Eliot's directions as to spacing have been followed. It differs from the corrected proof in one punctuation variant and in two readings which Eliot refers to in letters to Hayward of 2 and 10 October.

LG. *Little Gidding*, published 1 December 1942. The text, set from M13, differs from the text in NEW on the three occasions referred to above, where it agrees with D5/M13 against D4/M12. On all three occasions *Four Quartets* follows LG.

MS. (Magdalene College, Cambridge.) The manuscript material at Magdalene preserves the earliest drafts of all parts of the poem, with the exception of Part I.[1]

The amount of material available for the study of the composition of *Little Gidding* makes it necessary to vary the method of presentation in the central sections of the poem. Parts I and V were, as Eliot wrote to Hayward, only 'slightly altered' in revision, and provoked little discussion in the correspondence. The same is true of the lyric opening of Part II. Parts I, II(a), and V can therefore be presented in the manner used hitherto, by a critical apparatus to the final text with a commentary at the foot or on facing pages.[2] But Parts II(b), III, and IV demand narrative treatment with successive drafts and reworkings set out in order along with the correspondence each stage of the rewriting stimulated.

---

[1] For a description of the manuscript material at Magdalene, see Appendix B, pp. 237–9.

[2] I have not attempted to record punctuation variants in the typescripts as distinct from the drafts. The drafts sent to Hayward were carefully punctuated but in the manuscript and working copies Eliot obviously did not punctuate consistently or completely.

Eliot jotted down on a page that has been torn out of his scribbling pad his first notes for *Little Gidding*. They are only a preliminary scheme, showing that he had come to see the seasons and the four elements as an organizing element in the sequence of four poems, and that the underlying theme of the last poem was to be pentecostal. There is no indication that the poem was to treat of attitudes to the historic past as well as of the poet's attitude to his personal history.

Winter scene. May.

Lyric. air earth water end & &
daemonic fire. The Inferno.

　　They vanish, the individuals, and
our feeling for them sinks into the
flame which refines. They emerge
in another pattern & recreated &
　　reconciled
redeemed, having their meaning to-
gether not apart, in a union
which is of beams from the central
fire. And the others with them
contemporaneous.

Invocation to the Holy Spirit.

LITTLE GIDDING

Text of *Four Quartets* (1944)

(1–11)

I

Midwinter spring is its own season
Sempiternal though sodden towards sundown,
Suspended in time, between pole and tropic.
When the short day is brightest, with frost and fire,
The brief sun flames the ice, on pond and ditches,   5
In windless cold that is the heart's heat,
Reflecting in a watery mirror
A glare that is blindness in the early afternoon.
And glow more intense than blaze of branch, or brazier,
Stirs the dumb spirit: no wind, but pentecostal fire   10
In the dark time of the year.

No manuscript exists for Part I. There are typescripts and drafts in M1, M2, D1/M3, M4, M5, D2/M9,
D4/M12, D5/M13

1–11   Midwinter summer is its own season
                                    towards
                 Sempiternal though sodden ~~at~~ the day's end
                                        pole   tropic
                 Suspended in time, between cold and heat,
                          brief   *with frost*
                 When the ~~short~~ day is lightest, ‸ ~~ice~~ and fire
        ⟨*Of*⟩   Windless cold that is the soul's heat.
                          brief
                 The ~~short~~ sun flames the ice, on pond and ditches,
                                              mirror
                 ~~Not melting, but~~ making a watery ~~film~~
                     glare
                 Of light that is blindness, in the early afternoon,
                          ~~blaze~~ *glow*   *fire blaze*
                 And ~~fire~~ more intense than ~~that~~ of branch, or brazier,
                 Stirs   *numbed   ~~mind~~*
        10   ~~Warms~~ the animated spirit: no wind, but pentecostal fire
                              awakened
                 In the dark time of the year.   (M1)

                                                                              sundown
                                                                              sunfall
                     spring   *sun's*
1 spring] summer M2   2 sundown] the day's end M2, D1/M3, M5; the day's end M4
                                                              heart
3 and 4] *for punctuation variants, see opposite*   6 heart's] soul's M2   8 afternoon.]
afternoon, M2–M5; *no stop in* D2; *period supplied* M9   10 Stirs] ⟨?⟩ ⟨Which⟩ stirs M2

The manuscript draft for Part I was probably written on the seven torn-out leaves that originally followed the leaf on which Eliot wrote his notes for the poem. They probably also contained his first draft of Part II, for Part II, which begins on the next surviving leaf, is nearer to a fair copy than a first draft. The earliest version of Part I in M1 has a good deal of alteration in manuscript, particularly in the opening lines. In his second typescript (M2) Eliot had arrived, with insignificant exceptions, at the text he sent to Hayward in July 1941 (D1/M3).

Hayward wrote that his 'general impression' was that Part I was 'all right'. His queries on 'niggling details' were few. Eliot made a few alterations and suggestions in M4 and M5, his retypings of M3, before sending his 'slightly altered' version to Hayward at the end of August 1942. The main interest of the drafts of Part I lies in lines that Eliot dropped rather than in changes in wording.

Hayward made no comment in his letter to Eliot on these opening lines, but he referred in his letter to Morley to 'a lovely vision of Spring in mid-Winter' as one of the 'prodigiously fine things' in the poem. It seems strange that Eliot originally wrote 'Midwinter summer', since the passage is so clearly a reminiscence of the speech of the First Tempter in *Murder in the Cathedral*:

> Spring has come in winter. Snow in the branches
> Shall float as sweet as blossoms. Ice along the ditches
> Mirror the sunlight.

The reversal of lines 5 and 6 of the first typescript (M1) in the second (M2) necessitated some changes in punctuation. Eliot changed his mind, at first proposing a period after line 3 and then reverting to a comma and putting a period after line 4 (M2). But in his first revision (D2/M9) he changed his mind again and ended his opening sentence at line 3 as he had first thought of doing in M2.

(11–20)

Between melting and freezing
The soul's sap quivers. There is no earth smell
Or smell of living thing. This is the spring time
But not in time's covenant. Now the hedgerow
Is blanched for an hour with transitory blossom   15
Of snow, a bloom more sudden
Than that of summer, neither budding nor fading,
Not in the scheme of generation.
Where is the summer, the unimaginable
Zero summer?   20

covenant
14* covenant] recurrence M1–D2; ~~recurrence~~ M9   15 Is blanched] Glitters M1–M4;
    Is blanched
⟨*Blanches*⟩ Glitters   M5   for an hour] for a moment M1
19–20*   Where is the summer, the unimaginable
           Summer beyond sense, the inapprehensible
           Zero summer?   M1–D4/M12, NEW

The close of the first paragraph has no manuscript alterations in M1. Only one insignificant change was made in the typing of M2 ('hour' for 'moment') and there were no changes in the typing of D1/M3.

In the margin of D1 Hayward pencilled against the word 'Glitters' (l. 15) two suggestions: 'Glisters' and 'Whitens'; but he did not explain his objection in his letter. He possibly disliked 'Gli*t*ters' in the same line as 'trans*i*tory'. His only comment was on line 20: '"Zero summer": Is this an allusive reference to the Absolute Zero of physics? I feel a little uneasy about the epithet—slightly Clevelandish?' Eliot did not answer this query. He might have saved his exegetes much trouble had he done so.[1] But he remarked that 'Geoffrey', that is Faber, 'found that the comparison of may blossom and snow on the hedges did not ring true' adding 'but I am awaiting his written comment which I hope will make clear why he feels thus'. I suspect that Faber objected that although snow can glitter in the sun,

---

[1] Whenever I am so rash as to agree to answer questions after a lecture of *Four Quartets*, I know that 'Garlic and sapphires in the mud' and 'Zero summer' will turn up.

may-blossom can hardly be said to 'glitter'. In M5, a second retyping of D1/M3, Eliot has pencilled above the word 'Glitters' the suggestion 'Is blanched' and has written 'Blanches' in the margin. In the first revision (D2/M9) Eliot adopted 'Is blanched'.

The reading 'Not in time's recurrence' (l. 14) remained in the first revision (D2/M9). Eliot hit on the change to 'covenant' in working on M9 and incorporated it into his typescript in his second complete draft (D4/M12). The Biblical word, with its echo of the covenant of God with Noah—'While the earth remaineth, seedtime and harvest, and cold and heat, and summer and winter, and day and night shall not cease'—was an inspired improvement on the tame 'recurrence'.

The line between lines 19 and 20

Summer beyond sense, the unapprehensible

stands in all drafts from M1 to D4/M12, is undeleted in the NEW proof, and appears in the text in NEW. It was omitted in the 'Final Recension' (D5/M13). Hayward has pencilled it in the margin of D5, as if he suspected its omission was accidental. As has been said, the text sent to the editor of NEW was not the 'Final Recension' but a text lying between D4 and D5 which Eliot corrected in proof to the readings of the latter. It seems odd that, if Eliot had deliberately removed this line in his final version, he did not strike it out in either his first or second proof. The top copy of the 'Final Recension' (M13) was the copy sent to the printer of LG in which the line is missing, as it is in *Four Quartets*. It is possible that Eliot overlooked the fact that in this version the line had been omitted and failed to restore it. Any future editor would have to consider seriously whether it should be restored. Without it the paragraph ends rather abruptly. There are two other occasions on which NEW agrees with D4 against LG, FQ, which read with D5; see lines 23 and 217.

(20-39)

If you came this way,   20
Taking the route you would be likely to take
From the place you would be likely to come from,
If you came this way in may time, you would find the hedges
White again, in May, with voluptuary sweetness.
It would be the same at the end of the journey,   25
If you came at night like a broken king,
If you came by day not knowing what you came for,
It would be the same, when you leave the rough road
And turn behind the pig-sty to the dull façade
And the tombstone. And what you thought you came for   30
Is only a shell, a husk of meaning
From which the purpose breaks only when it is fulfilled
If at all. Either you had no purpose
Or the purpose is beyond the end you figured
And is altered in fulfilment. There are other places   35
Which also are the world's end, some at the sea jaws,
Or over a dark lake, in a desert or a city—
But this is the nearest, in place and time,
Now and in England.

22* to come from] to start from M1-D4/M12, NEW
24-6*   White again, in May, with voluptuary sweetness/ ⟨.⟩
                              In the may time, the play time of the wakened senses
                                                      rapture
                                                      rejoicing
                              There is human joy, but no greater ~~glory.~~
                              If you came. . . .   M1

                              White again, in May, with voluptuary sweetness.
                              In the may time, the play time of the wakened senses
                              It would be the same at the end of the journey.
                              If you came. . . .   M2, D1/M3, M5 (*underlining* play time), M4 *cancels*
In the . . . senses *and the period after* journey *for a comma*   26 at night] by night M1, M2
                not knowing
27 not knowing] ~~and knew~~ M1   28 when] where M1   29 pig-sty] pig-stye M1-NEW
32 fulfilled] summoned M1, M2   36 sea jaws] sea's jaw M1   37* in a desert or
                within
                concealed in   *transcending*
a city] ~~or dominating~~ a city M1   39 Tragedy and glory. ⟨Now & in England⟩ M1
                in a desert or

Most of the lines in this passage go back to the first typescript (M1). In M2 Eliot substituted for the line contrasting 'human joy' with some 'greater' glory or rapture the line of the final text (l. 25), and accepted the suggestion 'Now and in England' for his original closing half line 'Tragedy and glory'. The text sent to Hayward (D1/M3) differed only in two readings (ll. 26 and 32) from the text of M2.

Hayward, with his usual dislike of 'jingles' wrote: '"in the may time, the play time": this is a rather dangerous conjunction, maytime and playtime (cf. *Baby* & *Maybe*) being a favourite stand-by in Tin Pan Alley. I should feel happier if this jingle were omitted.' Eliot meekly assented: 'I agree about the playtime jingle: I wanted the Children hint again: but perhaps it is too close to the Playbox Annual.' The 'Children hint again' refers back to the opening paragraph of the letter in which Eliot spoke of 'the children in the apple-tree' being meant 'to tie up New Hampshire and Burnt Norton'.[1] Hayward's only other query was at line 38: '"But this is the nearest": nearest to what, or to whom? I think I understand you, but I am puzzled to know what an American reader would make of it.' Eliot ignored this; but in his first revision the 'jingle' had disappeared. Two minor alterations were made for the final text. In line 22 'start from' remained until the 'Second Complete Draft' (D4/M12). The 'Final Recension' (D5/M13) reads 'come from'. The NEW proof and NEW, as in lines 19–20, read with D4, while LG and *Four Quartets* read with D5. It was not until LG that 'pig-sty' lost its final 'e'. It is odd that Hayward did not notice it.

Hayward in a note to *Quatre Quatuors* identified the other places which 'also are the world's end', and Professor Kenner reports that the same identifications were given by Eliot in a 'note for his brother'.[2] The 'sea jaws' he associated with Iona and St. Columba and with Lindisfarne and St. Cuthbert: the 'dark lake' with the lake of Glendalough and St. Kevin's hermitage in County Wicklow: the desert with the hermits of the Thebaid and St. Antony: the city with Padua and the other St. Antony. This last identification can hardly have been in his mind when he originally wrote 'over a dark lake, or dominating a city'. Padua cannot be said to be 'dominated' by 'Il Santo', nor is this large building with open space around 'concealed in a city'. It seems a strange companion for humble shrines such as the church of Little Gidding and the huts of hermits.

[1] See p. 29 where the passage is quoted as a chapter-heading.
[2] Hugh Kenner, *The Invisible Poet: T. S. Eliot* (1960), 272.

(39-53)

If you came this way,
Taking any route, starting from anywhere,   40
At any time or any season,
It would always be the same: you would have to put off
Sense and notion. You are not here to verify,
Instruct yourself, or inform curiosity
Or carry report. You are here to kneel   45
Where prayer has been valid. And prayer is more
Than an order of words, the conscious occupation
Of the praying mind, or the sound of the voice praying.
And what the dead had no speech for, when living,
They can tell you, being dead: the communication   50
Of the dead is tongued with fire beyond the language of the living.
Here, the intersection of the timeless moment
Is England and nowhere. Never and always.

41*   At any time, the day time or the dark time,
       Or at any season, the dead time or the may time,   M1, M2, D1/M3, M5, M4 *which cancels to*
At any time,/ ~~O~~or at any season   44* Instruct . . . or inform] Inform . . . or cancel, M1, M2,
       instruct
D1; . . . ~~or cancel~~ M3   45-6 You are here . . . valid.] M1 *omits*   47 an order of words]
the meaning of the words learnt M1   48 mind] soul M2   51 is tongued with fire beyond
       does not speak in   *tinged*
the language] ~~exceeds~~ the language M1; is touched with fire . . . M2
                                        tongued
After l. 51*   And the speech of the living is wind in dry grass
               And the living have no communication with each other   M1

               The words of the living are wind in dry grass,
               The communion of the dead is flame ~~beyond~~ on the wind: M2, D1/M3, M5; . . .
on the heart
on the wind M4, *which cancels both lines*   52 Here] And M1

In his second typescript (M2) Eliot adopted the corrections made in M1, and added two explanatory half-lines to his rather censorious warnings to antiquarians and tourists:

> You are here to kneel
> Where prayer has been valid.

They make the transition to the idea of prayer less abrupt. He also rewrote the two lines which expanded the contrast between the 'communication of the dead' and 'the language of the living'.

Hayward, as might be expected, objected to the repetition at the beginning of the paragraph: '"At any time &c . . . or the may time." There is just a faint suggestion here, I think, of your parodying yourself. (*v. supra* Hayward on Jingles).' Eliot struck through the two half lines in his working copy (M4).

Eliot wrote to Hayward on 14 July 1941, during the period he was waiting for his comments, saying he had 'pushed on with Little Gidding' and enclosed 'provisional results'. He must have sent Hayward some pages or passages because he goes on 'You will observe that I have had to remove "cancel" from Part I, because I wanted the word further on'. Hayward has underlined 'cancel' in his draft (D1) and put in the margin 'Deleted T.S.E.' In the top copy he had kept (M3) Eliot wrote 'instruct' above 'cancel' and in M4 he reconstructed the line. He 'wanted the word further on' at the close of the second stanza of the original version of Part IV, in the line 'Or cancelled by the Paraclete'. Eliot was not, like Hayward, averse to deliberate, immediate repetitions but was sensitive to later and accidental occurrences of a word.

Hayward made no objection to the two lines that in the draft sent to him followed on line 51. Eliot cancelled them when he began work again on the poem after a year, possibly feeling that they weakened by expansion the finely worded statement

> the communication of the dead
> Is tongued with fire beyond the language of the living.

Hayward merely noted on D2 '2 lines omitted'.

(54–61)

II

Ash on an old man's sleeve
Is all the ash the burnt roses leave.   55
Dust in the air suspended
Marks the place where a story ended.
Dust inbreathed was a house—
The wall, the wainscot and the mouse.
The death of hope and despair,   60
This is the death of air.

Texts of the lyric are in MS and in M2, D1/M3, M4, M5, D2/M9, D3/M10, D4/M12, D5/M13
54–5*   *an old man's*
                         Dust on a threadbare sleeve
                                   burnt
                 Is ~~all~~ the dust ~~the~~ ᴀ roses leave.   MS
Ash   *ash*   *story*
~~Dust~~ ... ~~dust~~ M2   57 a story] *a history* MS   58–60 *house:* ... *mouse,* ... *despair*— MS,
                                    was
M2, *which corrects to text*   58 was] *is* MS; ~~is~~   M2   59 wainscot] *wainscote* MS

The change of 'Dust' to 'Ash' and the insertion of 'burnt' destroys an echo of *Burnt Norton* ('Disturbing the dust on a bowl of rose-leaves') parallel to the echo of *East Coker* in line 59. The change accords with the poem's central theme of fire and, with the two remaining uses of 'Dust', points forward to the air-raid passage. Eliot said this stanza 'came out of' his experience in fire-watching on the roof of Faber and Faber:

> During the Blitz the accumulated debris was suspended in the London air for hours after a bombing. Then it would slowly descend and cover one's sleeves and coat with a fine white ash. I often experienced this effect during long night hours on the roof.[1]

The stanza had reached final form in the first draft. Hayward queried only the second line:

> Compared with the other lines in the stanza this one seems to me to have too much weight at the end. The heavy stress on 'burnt' could be lightened by omitting the definite article and this would also lay a shade more stress on 'roses'. As it is, this line takes something from the essential 'airiness' of the stanza—dust, breath, air: the death of air—as if the ash of burnt roses was not an imponderable but a tombstone.

Eliot replied 'I am also unhappy about the first two lines of Part II (lyric)'. He bracketed them, with a marginal query, in M5; but whatever it was that made him unhappy he made no attempt to alter.

[1] W. T. Levy and V. Scherle, *Affectionately, T. S. Eliot* (New York, 1968), 15.

(62–69)

There are flood and drouth
Over the eyes and in the mouth,
Dead water and dead sand
Contending for the upper hand.   65
The parched eviscerate soil
Gapes at the vanity of toil,
Laughs without mirth.
This is the death of earth.

Here
62 There are] *There is* MS; Here is M2; There is D1/M3–D4; There is *are* M12   62, 63,
65 drouth . . . mouth, . . . hand.] *drouth: . . . mouth . . . hand* MS   65 Contending] *Competing*
MS, M2   66* parched eviscerate] *scorched and unemployable* MS–M5; annealed and
                                    fruitless   emasculate
unemployable D2; annealed *(and)* unemployable ~~sexless~~ M9   68 Laughs] ~~And~~
                                    eviscerate

s
~~Laughing~~ MS

────────────────────────────────

Hayward commented on lines 66–8:

'unemployable soil': this sounds ugly when read aloud to my ear. (possibilities: acarpous, unavailing, unserviceable). . . . 'Laughs without mirth': I should prefer 'smiles'. It is easier, I think, to conceive of a smile without mirth than a laugh without mirth, for all that people speak of a hollow laugh, &c. And it's easier and more convincing, I feel, to imagine the soil as smiling than as laughing. An inanimate object can appear to be smiling; it can hardly be thought of as laughing. In any case you can't gape *and* laugh at the same time—I've just tried to in the mirror—and you can gape and smile without mirth at the same time. Perhaps I am being too silly!

Eliot replied: 'I like "unemployable" because the word has a special significance in contrast to "unemployed" in relation to "derelict areas" and I wanted the assimilation of the soil to the human material.' He retained 'unemployable' in the first revision sent to Hayward (D2) but replaced 'scorched' by 'annealed'. In his second revision (D3) he adopted 'eviscerate' one of four suggested alternatives to 'unemployable' and abandoned the archaic 'annealed' ('fired, or baked, as earthen ware', *O.E.D.*), which might, by recalling Hamlet's father, have introduced irrelevant religious associations. He did not return to 'scorched', possibly because of the current use of 'scorched earth' for a policy of deliberate destruction.[1] 'Parched', suggested by Hayward in the margin of D1, carried on the 'assimilation of the soil to the human material' which he intended by 'unemployable'. Eliot ignored Hayward's objection to 'Laughs', which persisted. He suggested 'Grins' on D2.

[1] Mr. R. W. Burchfield informs me that the first use of 'scorched earth' recorded for *O.E.D. Supplement* is in 1937, referring to the Sino-Japanese war.

(70–77)

Water and fire succeed   70
The town, the pasture and the weed.
Water and fire deride
The sacrifice that we denied.
Water and fire shall rot
The marred foundations we forgot,   75
Of sanctuary and choir.
        This is the death of water and fire.

71 weed.] *weed* MS; weed; M2
72–6*   *Water and fire deride*
                                         The scarred foundations we denied
                                                    shall rot
                                         Water and fire ~~win by lot~~
                                         The skeletons that we forgot.
                                                maimed the
                                         The broken or entire   MS

                                              marred
                                         The ~~scarred~~ foundations we denied.
                                         Water and fire shall rot
                                         The skeletons that we forgot—
                                         The broken or entire.   M2 *which transposes in pencil*
marred   *crumbled*
~~scarred~~ foundations *and* skeletons that; D1/M3 *with M2 as corrected*; . . . ~~broken~~ . . . M4; . . . The
sacrifice that we denied . . . crumbled . . . D2; . . . forgot+,/The crumbled or entire. ⟨~~Of chantry~~/
    the   *The*
and choir/Of sanctuary/and choir⟩ M9
77* space   *Fire without and fire within*
                                         Expel
                                         Purge the unidentified sin
                                         This is the place where we begin   MS

                                         Fire without and fire within
                                         Shall purge the unidentified sin.
                                         This is the place where we begin.   M2, *which cancels the passage*

A facsimile of the lyric in the Magdalene manuscript, with transcript and
comments, can be found in *Autograph Poetry in the English Language*,
edited by P. J. Croft (1973), ii. 176–7.

Eliot did not arrive at the final text of this stanza until his second revision (D3/M10). The first draft ran

> Water and fire succeed
> The town, the pasture and the weed.
> Water and fire deride
> The skeletons that we denied.
> Water and fire shall rot
> The marred foundations we forgot—
> The broken or entire.
> This is the death of water and fire. (D1)

Hayward made no comment on it. In his letter of 14 July, written while waiting for Hayward's, Eliot said he had had 'some trouble' with 'broken', and on his retyping (M4) he made the suggestion 'crumbled', which he adopted in his first revision (D2) where he also replaced 'skeletons' by 'sacrifice'. In M9 (the carbon of D2) he altered 'forgot—' to 'forgot', and made two suggestions in the margin for the last line: 'Of chantry and choir' (altered to 'The chantry and the choir') and 'Of sanctuary and choir', which he adopted in his second revision.

The three lines that stand as a coda in the manuscript and M2, having been cancelled in M2, did not meet Hayward's eye. He would, no doubt, have complained of their 'nursery rhyme' quality. They seem to belong to Eliot's first conception of the lyric. He wrote in his notes for the poem: 'Lyric. air earth water end & & daemonic fire.' This suggests a three stanza poem on the death of air, earth, and water, followed by a coda on the 'destructive fire' of East Coker. But in the writing he has brought together water and fire in his third stanza. There is nothing in the original notes to suggest that Eliot's experiences in the air raids were to play a part in his poem; they thrust themselves in as he wrote. Anyone who lived through the London raids must link water and fire as equally destructive, remembering the charred and sodden ruins and their smell the morning after as the great hoses played on the flaming and smoking ruins. The coda was rightly cancelled as inconsistent with the lyric as written.

Part II(b)

This passage gave Eliot more trouble than any other section of the poem.[1] He was here attempting to sustain a style consistently over a long span, whereas his natural genius was towards the paragraph. He also committed himself to a strict and difficult verse-form, an approximation to the *terza rima* of Dante, a metre in which few English poets have been successful. Here, again, he was writing against his natural bent which was towards a rhythmically flexible verse. Many lines, phrases, and words were revised again and again, and argued over. Right up to the last proof Eliot was hesitating over whether he had found the exact word needed. The amount of revision, and the numerous suggestions Eliot made in his working copies, which lie between the versions he sent to Hayward, make narrative treatment essential, with successive drafts and the discussion of them set out in order.

In this section, therefore, below the final text, which is printed above a rule for reference, the commentary begins with the text of the first draft sent to Hayward (D1) with the readings of the manuscript and of the first typescript (M2) in an apparatus below it. It will be noted that D1 hardly differs from M2. An asterisk marks lines in D1 which differ from the final text.

The earliest draft is in manuscript. It is neatly written and would seem to be a first fair copy rather than a first draft, although it lacks consistent punctuation. It and the first typescript divide the tercets, which in D1/M3 and subsequently are closed up with indentation of their second and third lines. Between the first draft (D1) and the first revision (D2/M9) come Eliot's two retypings of the whole poem (M4 and M5), and the two first attempts to revise this section: M7 (incomplete) and M8. Eliot worked on his copy of the first revision (M9) to produce his second revision (D3/M10). After sending his second complete draft (D4) to Hayward he was still unsatisfied and made many alterations and suggestions on his copy of D4 (M12). Even after the 'Final Recension' (D5/M13) he made alterations in proof.

---

[1] Professor Christopher Ricks has pointed out that there are striking anticipations of this scene in Eliot's 'Note sur Mallarmé et Poe' translated into French by Ramon Fernandez (*Nouvelle Revue Française*, 1 November 1926); see Christopher Ricks, 'A Note on *Little Gidding*', *Essays in Criticism*, January 1975.

(78–88)

In the uncertain hour before the morning
Near the ending of interminable night
At the recurrent end of the unending   80
After the dark dove with the flickering tongue
Had passed below the horizon of his homing
While the dead leaves still rattled on like tin
Over the asphalt where no other sound was
Between three districts whence the smoke arose   85
I met one walking, loitering and hurried
As if blown towards me like the metal leaves
Before the urban dawn wind unresisting.

Texts in MS, M2, D1/M3, M4, M5, M7, M8, D2/M9, D3/M10, D4/M12, D5/M13

---

*At the uncertain hour before daybreak
   *Toward the ending of interminable night
   *At the incredible end of the unending   80
After the dark dove with the flickering tongue
   *Had made his incomprehensible descension
   While the dead leaves still rattled on like tin
Over the asphalte where no other sound was
   *Between three angles whence the smoke arose   85
   I met one walking, loitering and hurried
As if blown towards me like the metal leaves
   Before the urban dawn wind unresisting.   (D1)

                                            Toward   ending
78 hour] *moment* MS   79 *In the final stillness of the restless night* MS; ~~In the final stillness~~ of
interminable night M2   81 dark] *black* MS   82 descension] *revelation* MS
86 loitering and hurried] *hurried & yet unhurried* MS; hurried but . . . M2   87 As if blown
                                                                                          urban
towards me] *But more as if blown,* MS; . . . toward . . . M2   88 urban] *little* MS; little M2

The manuscript reading 'incomprehensible revelation' relates the falling
fire-bombs to the 'pentecostal fire' of line 10. The change to the astronomical
term 'descension' retains the implication by echoing 'I saw the Spirit descending from heaven like a dove' (John 1. 32).[1] The phrase 'little dawn wind' in
the manuscript occurs also in the drafts for *East Coker*, Part I, where 'little'
was struck out in revision.

[1] Eliot's friend Charles Williams published in 1939 a strikingly original book *The Descent of the
Dove*, a short history of the Holy Spirit in the Church.

Hayward marked on his draft '*end*ing . . . *int*erminable . . . *inc*redible . . . *end* of the un*end*ing' and '*dark* dove'. He commented on the opening lines: 'These lines seem to me to flag a little, particularly lines 2–3, as if the needle of the mind had got stuck in a groove and was faltering. I don't like the mouthful (and earful) "incomprehensible descension".' Eliot replied:

As for 'incomprehensible', I think that can be bettered: re-reading the poem in the train yesterday (with a Three Nuns Vicar peeping over my shoulder: I wonder what he made of it, together with the Giant Umbrella and a volume of Kipling—he probably thought I was what is now euphemistically called an Anglo-Indian) I noticed too many IBLES at the beginning. 'Descension' I mean to clong to cling to: for it means the disappearance of a star or planet below the horizon (the American freshwater college sleuth would here discover some innuendo about Spender & Connolly,[1] but none intended) O.E.D. But I still think that this Part needs some sharpening of personal poignancy: a line or two might do it.

In his two retypings of D1 (M4 and M5) Eliot merely underlined and queried line 85 in M4. In his first typescript after taking up the poem again (M7) he typed 'Towards' for 'Toward' (l. 79) and 'corners' for 'angles' (l. 85). In M8 he typed 'In' for 'At' (l. 78) and 'districts' for 'corners'. The first revision (D2) follows M8. Hayward remained unhappy at 'incomprehensible descension' and suggested 'inexplicable' and 'indescribable'. He also ringed 'dawn' (l. 88) and its recurrence in line 91. He suggested 'morn (cf. morne)'. (It seems doubtful whether anyone would have spotted the pun on 'morne' meaning melancholy.) In M9 (his copy of D2) Eliot cancelled 'daybreak' (l. 78), writing 'morning' above, underlined 'incredible', writing 'recurrent' above, and underlined 'incomprehensible descension'. In his second revision (D3) he adopted 'morning' and 'recurrent' and rewrote line 82 as

Had passed beyond the horizon of his homing.

In the letter he sent with D3, thanking Hayward for his 'letter of the 20th instant', he wrote:

I was sorry to surrender the word 'descension' which you will discover from O.E.D. is an astronomical term but I do think a simpler line at this point is desirable. I hope I have got rid of the unpleasant terminations without any sacrifice of sense.

Hayward's notes on D3 suggested the definite article before 'morning': 'the (cf before the morning watch)', and 'below' for 'beyond': 'below (cf descension)'. Both suggestions were accepted in D4. Hayward here at last noticed the spelling of 'asphalte' and wrote out the Greek with 'cf form of origin'. In D5 Eliot, by substituting 'Near' for 'Towards' and depriving 'asphalte of its "e"', arrived at the final text.

[1] The reference is to the wartime magazine *Horizon*, edited by Cyril Connolly.

(89–98)

And as I fixed upon the down-turned face
That pointed scrutiny with which we challenge   90
     The first-met stranger in the waning dusk
     I caught the sudden look of some dead master
Whom I had known, forgotten, half recalled
     Both one and many; in the brown baked features
     The eyes of a familiar compound ghost   95
Both intimate and unidentifiable.
     So I assumed a double part, and cried
     And heard another's voice cry: 'What are *you* here?'

---

     *And as I scrutinised the downturned face
  *With that pointed narrowness of observation   90
     *We turn upon the first-met stranger at dawn,
     *I drew the sudden look of some dead master
Whom I had known, forgotten, half-recalled,
     Both one and many: in the brown baked features   .
     *The eyes of some familiar compound ghost,   95
  *The very near and wholly inaccessible.
     *And I, becoming other and many, cried
     *And heard my voice: "Are you here, Ser Brunetto?"   (D1)

           that
90 that] *the* MS; the M2   91 We turn upon] *By which we greet* MS; ~~Which w~~*W*e turn upon M2
           drew
92 drew] *met* MS; ~~met~~ M2   some dead master] *the dead masters* MS   93 half-recalled]
                                                                   baked
and recalled MS   94 the brown baked] *those scorched brown* MS; the brown scarred M2
95 *The remoteness of a vague familiar ghost* MS   96 wholly] *very* MS   97 *And I becoming
other, so I cried* MS

The changes between the manuscript and D1 make the encounter more
mysterious. Instead of meeting the look of 'the dead masters', the first
impression is of a single, unidentified 'master' who, it is then realized, is
'Both one and many'. 'A vague familiar ghost' becomes 'some familiar
compound ghost'; the abstract 'remoteness' is replaced by 'eyes'. The over-
friendly 'By which we greet' becomes the cautious 'We turn upon' and the
colourless 'met' becomes 'drew', which suggests a kind of complicity
between the poet and the stranger.

     The lines are modelled on Dante's encounter with Brunetto Latini
(*Inferno* XV), closing with a direct translation of Dante's cry of horrified

recognition: '*Siete voi qui, ser Brunetto?*' The 'pointed narrowness of observation' is an oddly stilted rendering of Dante's description of how the troop of spirits looked at him and his guide: 'As in the evening men are wont to look at one another under a new moon; and towards us they sharpened their brows, as an aged tailor does at the eye of a needle.'[1] The 'scorched brown features' of the MS renders '*il viso abbruciato*'. Eliot probably changed 'scorched' to avoid a repetition of the word from line 66 which, in D1, read 'The scorched unemployable soil'. He first tried 'scarred' and then took 'baked' from another phrase of Dante's: '*lo cotto aspetto.*'

The only comment Hayward made was to query 'at dawn': 'I wish the two stressed monosyllables hadn't got to complete this line; but I don't see how to alter this.' On the draft he drew a line against the first three lines, as if something troubled him, as well as marking 'dawn'. In M4, which Eliot tinkered with while waiting for Hayward's comments, he ringed 'some' (l. 92) and wrote above 'some dead' the words 'a lost'. In line 96, he crossed through 'The' and wrote 'Both' above it. Over the words 'wholly inaccessible' he wrote 'not identifiable' and, in the margin, 'unidentifiable'. In M5, his retyping of M4, he typed

> The very near and unidentifiable.

In his working typescripts for the first revision (M7 and M8) Eliot hit on a proper opposite to 'unidentifiable' and typed

> Both intimate and unidentifiable,

and in M8 he cancelled 'some' and typed 'a familiar compound ghost'. M7 shows the disappearance from the poem of Ser Brunetto:

> And I becoming also many, cried
> altered ~~exclaim   you too?~~   question
> And heard my ∧ voice ∧ : "are you here, ~~Ser Brunetto?~~"

Having struck out 'Ser Brunetto', Eliot underlined 'you'. In the next typescript (M8) the lines had become

> So I assumed another part, and cried
> Hearing another's voice cry: "What! are *you* here?"

With the alteration of 'another part' to 'a double part' and of 'Hearing' to 'And heard', the last seven lines of this passage had reached final form in the first revision sent to Hayward (D2).[2]

---

[1]   come suol da sera
guardar l'un l'altro sotto nuova luna;
e si ver noi aguzzavan le ciglia
come vecchio sartor fa nella cruna.

[2] Except for the hyphen in 'half-recalled' which did not disappear until D4.

Hayward underlined 'And' suggesting 'But or (Hearing)'. He also queried the disappearance of Ser Brunetto. Eliot replied that this was necessary because of the change he had made in the speech of the 'dead master'. There were, he said, two reasons:

> The first is that the visionary figure has now become somewhat more definite and will no doubt be identified by some readers with Yeats though I do not mean anything so precise as that. However, I do not wish to take the responsibility of putting Yeats or anybody else into Hell and I do not want to impute to him the particular vice which took Brunetto there. Secondly, although the reference to that Canto is intended to be explicit, I wished the effect of the whole to be Purgatorial which is much more appropriate.

The first three lines remained as a problem and continued to be so for some time, provoking more correspondence than any other lines in the poem. In the first revision (D2) they read

> And as I scrutinised the down–turned face
> With that pointed narrowness of observation
> We bear upon the first-met stranger at dawn

and differ only from the lines in D1 by substituting 'bear upon' for 'turn upon'.[1] Hayward underlined 'down-turned' and put 'down-cast' in the margin, underlined 'bear' and put the discarded reading of D1 'turn' against it. His wish to restore 'turn' was no doubt his reason for wishing to alter 'down-turned'. In his letter sending Hayward the second revision (D3) Eliot rejected the suggestion: 'I am afraid that "down-cast", that is, with a hyphen between "down" and "cast", would hardly do because the word will be spoken much the same whether there is a hyphen or not.' Hayward also returned to his earlier complaint by ringing 'dawn', and to re-inforce his objection ringed its occurrence three lines earlier in 'dawn wind'. Whether he made any general criticism of the lines or not, Eliot himself was discontented and set to work on his copy of D2 (M9). He wrote 'bent upon' above 'scrutinised', cancelled 'With' in the next line and gave 'that' a capital, and, crossing through 'bear', wrote 'bend' above it. In the margin, against the third line, he wrote 'With which we greet' reverting to the original manuscript version. But above, slantwise, he tried a recast of the second line: 'That pointed scrutiny with which we challenge.' These suggestions resulted in a new version in D3:

> And as I bent upon the down-turned face
> That pointed scrutiny with which we challenge
> The first-met stranger in the first faint light . . .

---

[1] In M8 Eliot temporarily reverted to a variant of the original manuscript version of the line. Beginning to type 'We turn', he went back and overtyped 'We t' to 'With', and produced the line

face

With which we ~~meet~~ the first-met stranger at dawn.

Hayward was not at all happy with this version. He underlined 'bent', writing in the margin 'scrutinised / bend a scrutiny?' and then wrote below 'And as I peered into the . . . / With that pointed scrutiny'. He also did not pass 'first faint light' and put a cross against it with the word 'daybreak'. He no doubt objected to 'first faint' and 'first-met' occurring in the same line. In the next draft (D4) the only change made was in the first line which now read

<blockquote>As I directed to the down-turned face.[1] . . .</blockquote>

In his letter sending Hayward this 'second complete draft' Eliot added in a manuscript postscript: 'I see y^r points about *daybreak* and *waves*[2] but can think of nothing which would not overstress.' Hayward wrote against the first two lines the suggestion 'And as I turned upon / the lowered face / the enquiring look' and for 'first faint light' suggested 'faint half-light'. Eliot took up these suggestions in a long letter of 7 September:

> I had already changed to
>> And as I fixed upon the down-turned face
>
> so that's allright, but you seem to object also to 'scrutiny'? I admit that the sense is late: the first example is from Fanny Burney. Your alternative line is a syllable short.
>
> I am glad you objected to 'First Faint' because it calls my attention to that fact that 'light' will not do either, as it comes too close (being terminal) to 'night' a few lines before. It is surprisingly difficult to find words for the shades before morning; we seem to be richer in words and phrases for the end of day. And I don't want a phrase which might mean *either*. I am inclined to put
>> The first-met stranger after lantern-end
>
> unless it seems to you too quaint. I do mean just the moment at which we should put out a lantern, if we were carrying one. 'End' because 'time' or 'hour' might as well mean 'lighting-up time'. There is very likely some dialect word for this degree of dawn; but even if I could find it it probably wouldn't do.

Later in the same letter he wrote 'I cannot yet improve the daybreak', and in a final paragraph added ruefully:

> No, I don't think 'lantern-end' will do, because there is so much ending at the beginning. Is 'lantern-out' too strained? I reckon it is. But it is better than 'lantern-down'.

Hayward must have replied by return for Eliot's next letter of 9 September thanks him for his of the 8th and goes on:

> This time I accept nearly everything: perhaps it means that my resistance is weakening, at this stage; but chiefly I think because I perceive that these

---

[1] Eliot had made the alteration in M10, his copy of D3, where he also marked 'scrutiny' and scribbled in the margin 'Is this O.K.? only since 1798 (F. Burney) C. Bronte?'

[2] For 'waves', see the discussion of line 251 on p. 223.

belong to that almost inevitable residue of items, in a poem of any length, for
which the ideal is unattainable. I am still however wrestling with the demon
of that precise degree of light at that precise time of day. I want something more
universal than black-out (for even if the blackout goes on forever, I want something holding good for the past also—something as universal as Dante's old
tailor threading his needle. On the other hand, any reference to the reverberes[1]
wd. take the mind directly to *pre-war* London, which would be unfortunate.
It must therefore be a country image or a general one. I have been fiddling with
something like this:

The stranger in the antelucan dusk

The stranger at the antelucan hour

Perhaps it is too self-conscious, and belongs rather to a Miltonic than to a
Dantesque passage? If so, I shall fall back on one of your versions. But I did
rather like 'lantern-end' (more suitable there than a heavy latinism, for the
image should be both sudden and homely, with the precision of country
terminology for these phenomena) if only 'end' hadn't clashed. (What is quite
interesting is to find that this austere Dantesque style is more difficult, and offers
more pitfalls, than any other).[2]

Eliot's 'wrestling' appears on M12, his copy of D4. In addition to altering
'As I directed to' to 'And as I fixed upon', he crossed through 'in the first
faint light' and wrote above 'after lantern-time', and in the margin 'lantern-
end' and below it 'lantern-out', with a tick for the last. At the top of the page
he has written, after ringing the whole line, 'The stranger in / the antelucan
hour' and below 'dark' / 'dusk' / 'dark', then cancelling all three words and
altering 'in' to 'at'. But in the end he had to 'fall back' on one of Hayward's
versions. The Final Recension (D5) reads with the final text:

And as I fixed upon the down-turned face
That pointed scrutiny with which we challenge
The first-met stranger in the waning dusk . . .

In sending D5 to Hayward Eliot wrote: 'You will observe that I have
accepted "waning dusk", and my observation conducted during the last
few days leads me to believe that it will wear. I cannot find words to express
a proper manifestation of my gratitude for your invaluable assistance.'
    Eliot made one other trifling alteration in D5, typing in line 97 'I too
assumed' for 'So I assumed'. Hayward queried 'too' on the draft, pointing
out 'Too strange' in line 104. In the NEW proof Eliot did not alter 'So'.

[1] French for street lamps. Eliot and Hayward had a habit of using French words without signalizing
them by underlining; cf. 'a little insolite' in a letter quoted on p. 191.
[2] Eliot recalled his difficulty here in a talk given at Nice in 1952; see Christopher Ricks, 'A Note on
Little Gidding', *Essays in Criticism*, January 1975.

LG, set from M13, the copy of D5, also reads 'So'. Eliot must have corrected in proof.

(99–107)

Although we were not. I was still the same,
Knowing myself yet being someone other—   100
And he a face still forming; yet the words sufficed
To compel the recognition they preceded.
And so, compliant to the common wind,
Too strange to each other for misunderstanding,
In concord at this intersection time   105
Of meeting nowhere, no before and after,
We trod the pavement in a dead patrol.

---

*Although we were not. I was always dead,
*Always revived, and always something other,   100
*And he a face changing: yet the words sufficed
*For recognition where was no acquaintance
*And no identity, blown by one airless wind,
*Too strange to each other for any cross of purpose
*But intimate at the intersecting time   105
Of meeting nowhere, no before and after,
*Stepping together in a dead patrol. (D1)

99–100   *Although it was not. I was often dead,*
                                Often revived, and always something other, MS

                                                                    a
103 And no identity] *In step together* MS   104 any cross] *cross* MS   105 at the] *as* MS
              nd
106 Of] *A*   MS   107 ~~We~~ *In tacit observance of a shared patrol,* MS; *Stepping together in
a shared patrol.* M2

This passage evoked little discussion but gave Eliot considerable trouble. Changes were made at a late stage: in D5 and NEW proof. Hayward made no mark against this passage in D1 and no comment in his letter, and Eliot made no alterations in his two retypings of D1 (M4 and M5); but he drew a line under 'Always revived' in M4. When he took up the poem again the passage struck him as unsatisfactory. The first typescript of the reworking (M7) shows alterations in the passage as typed and further manuscript suggestions. In the first three lines Eliot typed

Although we were not. I was always dead
And still alive, and always something other,
And he a face changing; . . .

Except that in M8 and D2 Eliot typed 'someone' for 'something' and reverted to 'something' in D3 and D4, to end with 'someone' in D5, these lines remained unchanged up to the second complete draft (D4). M7 goes on

yet the words sufficed

of a new
For recognition ~~where was no~~ acquaintance
Raised from the past   *life*
~~And no~~ identity, blown by one ~~airless~~ wind
Too strange to each other for any cross of purpose,
Accepted
~~Communing~~ at the intersection time
Of meeting nowhere, no before and after,
Stepping together in a dead patrol.

The next typescript (M8) reads

yet the words sufficed

To compel the recognition they pretended.
compliant   And so ~~consenting~~ to the common wind
~~Driven together by~~[1]
Too strange to each other for any cross of purpose,
Consenting
~~Compliant~~
~~Consenting~~ to this intersection time
Of meeting nowhere, no before and after
We strode together in a dead patrol.

The first revision (D2) follows M8 as corrected. Hayward again made no comment and contented himself with supplying a comma after 'so'. Eliot made no change in his second revision (D3) except to revert from 'someone' to 'something'. Hayward's only query was to put in the margin against the word 'pretended': 'portended / (i.e. "presumed") / not profess falsely'. In M10 (his copy of D3) Eliot cancelled 'pretended' and wrote above it 'preceded', the reading of the next draft (D4). Hayward was still unhappy and suggested 'predicted', in addition to his first suggestion 'portended'. In M12, his copy of D4, Eliot wrote 'portended intended?' in the margin, but then crossed them through and in his letter of 7 September wrote:

> I am inclined to stick to 'preceded', because the words you suggest convey a different meaning from what I want. I mean, to be aware that it is someone you know (and to be surprised by his being there) before you have identified him. *Recognition* surely is the full identification of the person.

In M12 Eliot also crossed through 'cross of purpose' and wrote above it 'crossed intention'.

---

[1] Eliot first typed 'Driven together by', overtyped it to cancel and typed 'And so consenting to the common wind' above in the space between two lines.

In the final recension (D5) Eliot rewrote the first three lines, replaced 'cross of purpose' by 'misunderstanding' and 'Consenting to' by 'In concord at':

> Although we were not. I was still the same
> *Knowing*   *yet being*
> ~~Yet recognised~~ myself ~~as~~ someone other—
> And he a face still forming; yet the words sufficed
> To compel the recognition they preceded.
> And so, compliant to the common wind,
> Too strange to each other for misunderstanding,
> In concord at this intersection time
> Of meeting nowhere, no before and after,
> We strode together in a dead patrol.

Hayward put 'trod?' against the last line, but he must have made some objection to 'strode' earlier, since in his letter sending him the final draft Eliot added a postscript:

> I don't like 'strode' and 'patrol' either. But you can't have a verb with a labial termination -ed or -t before 'together', and I don't want to give up 'patrol'. Is 'strode' ever pronounced 'strod'?

Leaving aside Eliot's notion of a 'labial termination', one may assume that Hayward suggested 'trod'. Eliot accepted this in correcting the proof for NEW. He cancelled 'strode together' for 'trod the pavement', writing to Hayward on 22 September:

> Read 'trod the pavement' for 'strode together'. The idea of togetherness is, I think, in the word 'patrol', so that 'together' is superfluous, whereas a reminder of the surface of the Cromwell Road is timely.

The text the printer set for NEW agreed with D4, except in reading 'misunderstanding' and 'In concord with', corrected by Eliot to 'In concord at'. Eliot corrected to the readings of D5 and added the further correction 'trod the pavement'. The text in NEW differs from the final text only in having, with D4, a comma for a dash after 'other'.

(108–119)

I said: 'The wonder that I feel is easy,
  Yet ease is cause of wonder. Therefore speak:
  I may not comprehend, may not remember.'   110
And he: 'I am not eager to rehearse
  My thought and theory which you have forgotten.
  These things have served their purpose: let them be.
So with your own, and pray they be forgiven
  By others, as I pray you to forgive   115
  Both bad and good. Last season's fruit is eaten
And the fullfed beast shall kick the empty pail.
  For last year's words belong to last year's language
  And next year's words await another voice.

I said: "The wonder that I feel is easy
  *And ease is cause of wonder. Therefore speak.
  *I may not understand, may not remember".   110
And he: "I am not eager to rehearse
  My thought and theory which you have forgotten:
  These things have served their purpose: let them be.
So with your own, and pray they be forgiven
  *By others, as I ask you to forgive   115
  *Both good and bad. Last season's fruit is eaten,
And the fullfed beast shall kick the empty pail.
  For last year's words belong to last year's language
  *And next year's words are still an unknown speech. (D1)

108 The] *the* MS, M2   109 Therefore speak] *Speak to me* MS   111 rehearse]
recall MS, ~~recall~~ rehearse M2   113 purpose: let] *turn. so let* MS   117 *Not in* MS

Hayward made no comment on this passage. In D2 Eliot, reverting to
the MS, typed 'the' (l. 108), 'Yet' for 'And' (l. 109), a full stop for the colon
after 'forgotten' (l. 112), and 'bad and good' (l. 116). There were no changes
in the second revision (D3). Hayward suggested a capital for 'the' (l. 108),
which Eliot adopted in D4, where he also typed 'I pray you' for 'I ask you'
in line 115. In the final draft (D5) 'comprehend' replaced 'understand'
(l. 110) and the last line ended with 'await another voice'. These changes
were made after the copy had gone to the printer and Eliot changed the
readings of D4 to those of D5 in proof. The working typescripts show only
one change of mind. In M12 Eliot momentarily reverted to a manuscript
reading, cancelling 'purpose: let' and writing above 'turn so let'; but he
struck out the alteration.

(120–149)

But, as the passage now presents no hindrance   120
. . . .
And faded on the blowing of the horn.

These thirty lines do not appear in the first draft. In their place are twenty-four lines in which the 'visionary figure' offers counsel that has no connexion with the powerful discourse on the 'gifts reserved for age'. The first version, in the manuscript, has some interesting differences from the text in the first typescript (M2) which differs only twice from the text in D1. I give the text in D1, with manuscript readings in an apparatus:

Remember rather the essential moments
   That were the times of birth and death and change
   The agony and the solitary vigil.
Remember also fear, loathing and hate,
   The wild strawberries eaten in the garden,   5
   The walls of Poitiers, and the Anjou wine,
The fresh new season's rope, the smell of varnish
   On the clean oar, the drying of the sails,
Such things as seem of least and most importance.
So, as you circumscribe this dreary round,   10
   Shall your life pass from you, with all you hated
   And all you loved, the future and the past.
United to another past, another future,
   (After many seas and after many lands)
   The dead and the unborn, who shall be nearer   15
Than the voices and the faces that were most near.
   This is the final gift of earth accorded—
   One soil, one past, one future, in one place.

2 the] *your* MS   birth and death] *death & birth* MS, M2   *agony   and the solitary vigil*
3 *The dark night in the solitary bedroom* MS   4 *Remember* ˄ *fear,* ~~and jealousy~~ *even loathing and hate* MS   6 The walls of Poitiers] *Remember Poitiers* MS, M2   9 Such things as seem] *And all that seems* MS   and] *or* MS
10–12 *Remember, as you go this dreary round.*
           So shall time pass from you, & all things hated
                all things
           Or loved, the future and the past MS
13 to another . . . another] *to one . . . and to one* MS   14 *(Borne over many seas and many*
lands) MS   17 of] *on* MS, *on* M2

Nor shall the eternal thereby be remoter
But nearer: seek or seek not, it is here.   20
Now, the last love on earth. The rest is grace."
He turned away, and in the autumn weather
I heard a distant dull deferred report
At which I started: and the sun had risen. (D1)

19 remoter] *less*   MS   21 Now, the last] *This is the last* MS   22 in the autumn
weather] *with his motionvement of dismissal* MS   23 I heard] *There came* MS

Hayward contented himself with adding a comma at the end of line 2,
ringing the definite articles in lines 2–8, suggesting the deletion of one at
the beginning of line 5, writing against line 6 'la douceur angevine', and
putting a cross against 'autumn weather'. In his letter he wrote:

> Sheet 3. Insert comma after 'change' line 18.[1] and so avoid a possible
> Empsonism . . . lines 19–24 are a trifle overpacked with definite articles—
> a difficulty in catalogues—and something might be done to tighten this passage.
> (The first thing that occurred to me—forgive the impertinence—was 'The
> walls of Poitiers, *la douceur angevine*'[2]). . . . 'autumn weather': I do not get the
> significance of *autumn*? It struck me as having a greater significance than you
> may have intended it to have.

Eliot replied: '"Autumn weather" only because it *was* autumn weather—
it is supposed to be an *early* air raid—and to throw back to Figlia che piange.'
In his general remarks Hayward had said he thought Parts I, II, and V
were 'all right'; but Eliot, in reply wrote that he had 'been particularly
unhappy about Part II' and, later in the letter, analysing the 'defect of the
whole poem' as 'the lack of some acute personal reminiscence', wrote
'I can *perhaps* supply this in Part II.' In his first retyping of D1 (M4)
he typed

Remember rather the unchanging moments
That were the times of birth and death and change,

and then underlined 'changing' and 'change', crossed through 'on' and
wrote 'is' above in line 21 and made a squiggle against the last three lines.
In his second retyping (M5) he typed 'unchanging moments' and 'the last
love is earth' and made no corrections. When he went back to M4 he struck
through the whole passage in heavy pencil.

[1] Hayward was counting the lines on the sheet.
[2] The quotation is the conclusion of Du Bellay's sonnet 'Heureux qui, comme Ulysse, a fait un beau
voyage':

Et plus que l'air marin la doulceur Angevine.

Eliot's dissatisfaction with the passage was justified. It is slackly written and the 'essential moments' lose their individual poignancy and are trivialized by being set in a catalogue. The 'strange meeting' deserved a better revelation at its climax than this.[1] It is impossible to hazard a guess as to what 'dead masters' or 'master' Eliot had originally in mind; but the obvious debt to the *Inferno* (Canto XV) suggests he had in mind masters to whom he owed reverence and gratitude but from whom he felt himself severed. Eliot thought of Hell and Purgatory as eternal states known to men here in time,[2] and in this scene of 'meeting nowhere, no before and after' the distinction between the dead and the living is blurred. The ghost is 'compound' but so is the speaker. Right up to the second complete draft (D4) Eliot retained the eerie lines

> Although we were not. I was always dead
> And still alive, and always something other
> And he a face changing; . . .

In this No Man's Land, between two worlds, Eliot may well have had in mind, mingling with the dead, others, still living, from whom he was divided by 'thought and theory' but from whom he had learned to cherish 'essential moments' or 'epiphanies'. Both in the first and the second version, the ghost speaks with Eliot's own voice. It is, in a profound sense, a meeting with himself when he encounters 'a familiar compound ghost' who is 'Both intimate and unidentifiable'.

Whether in the first draft, where he seems to be remembering the masters of his youth, or in the second, where he recognized in the poetry of his greatest contemporary sentiments that cannot be 'entirely alien' to any 'honest man, old enough',[3] Eliot, at the close found an Eliotian meaning in experiences he had shared with the visitant: 'the use of memory' for 'liberation' in the first draft; the acceptance of 'pain for pain', by which fire is not the fire of Hell but the fire of Purgatory, in the second.

---

[1] At the same time, as one critic has shrewdly noted, the tension and ferocity of the second version, one of the most powerful and painful passages in Eliot's poetry, in which the 'acute personal reminiscence' that Eliot thought the first draft lacked is only too nakedly present, fits rather oddly on to the leisurely movement of the first part of the passage with its 'easy' wonder and exchange of forgiveness for things 'forgotten'. See A. M. Charity, 'The Dantean Recognitions', '*The Waste Land*' *in Several Voices*, ed. A. D. Moody (1974), 144.

[2] 'In this life one makes, now and then, important decisions; or at least allows circumstances to decide; and some of these decisions are such as have consequences for all the rest of our mortal life. Some people find themselves consequently in circumstances such that the whole of their mortal life *must* be a torment to them. And if there is no future life then Hell is, for such people, here and now.' Eliot to Paul Elmer More, quoted by B. A. Harries, 'The Rare Contact', *Theology*, March 1972.

[3] See p. 66 supra.

Eliot began the re-casting of the passage by a prose draft:

> [*Th*]*en, changing face and accent, he*
> *declared with another voice:*
>
> *These events draw me back to the*
> *streets of the speech I learned early*
> *in life. I also was engaged in the*
> *battle of language. My alien people*
> *a dying?*
> *with an unknown tongue claimed*
> *me. I saved them by my efforts—*
> *you by my example: yet while I*
> *the darkness*
> *fought* ~~*some evil*~~ *I also fought the*
> *light*
> ~~*good*~~, *striving against those who*
> *false   true*
> *with the* ~~*wrong*~~ *condemned the* ~~*right*~~.
> *Those who have known purgatory*
> *here know it hereafter—so shall you*
> *learn when enveloped by the coils*
> *of the fiery wind, in which you*
> *must learn to swim.*

The first two lines are an afterthought, added above the line at the top of the page. They show that Eliot intended the 'familiar compound ghost' to change personality at this point and become a definite person. Comparison with Eliot's lecture on Yeats shows he clearly had Yeats in mind and the close of the draft shows that, while his original inspiration for the passage had been Canto XV of the *Inferno*, he now wished, as he wrote to Hayward, 'the effect of the whole to be Purgatorial which is much more appropriate'. There is nothing here about old age, nor is there in Eliot's first attempt to versify his summary. On another two leaves from the same pad there is a very rough draft:

> *and becoming*
> ~~*becoming*~~
> *Then changing form and feature* ~~*he continued*~~
> *he spoke   a foreign*
> ~~*As a*~~*Another man,* ~~*speaking*~~ *with an alien voice*
> *mode*
> ~~*On*~~*In another* ~~*theme*~~ *and to another purpose:*
>
> *bring my footsteps back*
> *These desolations draw my pilgrimage*
> *To streets* { *I never thought I should* } *revisit*
> { *and doors I thought not to* }
> *I* ~~*left*~~ *buried my body on a distant*
> *When* ~~*my spirit parted from the southern*~~ *shore*

the passage
this time   ~~transit~~
But at ~~these times the path~~ is short & easy
To the spirit unappeased and peregrine,
Between conditions⌉   ~~closer~~
~~For the two worlds~~⌊draw ⁿ ~~nearer to~~ each other
                    ⌊~~so~~ much alike

                                   should
I also was engaged as you ~~must~~ know,
     the fight battle of both
In ~~fighting~~ for language: ⌃ here, where I was | tutored
                                                phrase
In the strength and weakness of the English ~~tongue~~

                                    flame   dampened
And elsewhere: when the political fire had | [?] regressed
    Another
~~My~~ alien people with an archaic tongue
Claimed me. I, and another, saved them

(at foot)   As you should know, I spent my life contending by my efforts

(sideways)   I spent my life in that unending fight
              To give ~~the~~ people speech:
                     a
              I too was one of those in that unending fight | who for a lifetime strove

                                                          (new leaf)

    From which   for your
~~As you,~~ by my example, you may learn.
                the
Yet while I fought ~~with~~ darkness, fought the light
As who, in imperfection, can avoid,

Striving with those who still defend the darkness
                    real
Asnd even with the ~~true~~ defend the false
                          maintain
And with the eternal truth the local error?

Those who knew purgatory here shall know
    The same
Purgation hereafter: so shall you learn also,
Caught in the coils of that strong
In the embraces of that fiery wind
                          ~~swim rejoicing~~
Where you must learn to swim & better nature."

At the foot of the page Eliot wrote slantwise an alternative to his final line

~~swim rejoicing~~
Where you must learn to swim & better nature."

Moving like a
   dancer through
     the desolation

On the verso of the leaf containing the prose summary Eliot has written an alternative line to 'Another alien people with an archaic tongue':

company   ~~*an alien*~~
Another ~~group of men~~, with another / chime of tongue.

The first typescript of the revision of Part II (M7) is incomplete, or more probably Eliot broke off after two pages having changed his mind. It runs

> ~~Then changing form and feature, and becoming~~
> ~~Another company, speaking in another chime~~
> ~~In another mode and to another purpose:~~
> "This interruption brings my footsteps back
>   To streets I never thought I should revisit,
>   *left*
> When I ~~buried~~ my body on a distant shore.
> But at this time the passage is brief and facile
>   To the spirit unappeased and peregrine,
>   Between two states so much alike each other.
> ~~I also was engaged (as you should know)~~
> ~~To give the people speech: both here where I was tutored~~
> ~~In the strength and weakness of the English tongue~~

The specific reference to Yeats's career as a poet in England and then in Ireland disappears after this, leaving only the reference to his death abroad. But a rough verse-draft on a leaf of the same pad, originally pinned to the leaf containing the prose summary of the speech, plainly derives from the poem 'The Spur' which Eliot quoted in his lecture on Yeats, expatiating on the theme of lust in old age.

> [Y]ou shall know
> ~~For the~~ old rooted sin puts forth again
> Even in exhausted soil, after many seasons,
>   unflowering
> When the starved ˄ growth shows still more foul
>
> Without luxuriance. All time is in a moment
> ~~And a moment is all time.~~
> When all is won or lost. Therefore success
>   ⎧ precipitation   ⎫
> Is ⎨ ~~preparation~~ towards ⎬ a greater danger
>   ⎪ preparation for   ⎪
>   ⎩ the introduction to ⎭

This metaphorical treatment of impotent desire gave place in the final version to a direct and more austere three lines and the moralization was not developed.

The next stage would seem to have been a redraft in prose of the speech. Here Yeats as the poet of old age replaces Yeats as the 'fighter for language'. The draft is on a leaf from the small pad (MS C), which was once pinned to the leaf on which Eliot made his first attempt at the second stanza of Part IV.

> Consider what are the gifts of age—
> the cold craving when the sense is
> gone which kept soul & body to-
> gether; the angry impatience with
> human folly & turpitude & pusillanimity
> with the knowledge of the futility
> of protest; the doubt of self which
> springs from retrospection of past
> motives, the awareness of the
> fact that one was moved while
> believing oneself to be the mover
>
> For all these ills that the enraged
> spirit strives to overcome by pro-
> gressing into new and greater sin—
> there is only the one remedy, pain
> for pain, in that purgative fire
> which you must will, wherein
> you must learn to swim and
> better nature.

The first extant verse draft is in M8, which contains only the Dantean section of Part II. It is the best example among the typescripts of Eliot composing on the typewriter. The amount of discussion of certain lines is so great that the passage needs to be divided into sections to facilitate comparison of readings. The text of D2, the first revision, sent to Hayward on 17 August 1942, is given at the beginning of the commentary with the readings from M8 in an apparatus to it.

(120–130)

But, as the passage now presents no hindrance   120
    To the spirit unappeased and peregrine
    Between two worlds become much like each other,
So I find words I never thought to speak
    In streets I never thought I should revisit
    When I left my body on a distant shore.   125
Since our concern was speech, and speech impelled us
    To purify the dialect of the tribe
    And urge the mind to aftersight and foresight,
Let me disclose the gifts reserved for age
    To set a crown upon your lifetime's effort.   130

---

*But as the passage now is brief and facile,   120
    To the spirit unappeased and peregrine,
    Between two worlds become so like each other,
So I find words I never thought to speak
    In streets I never thought I should revisit
    When I left my body on a distant shore.   125
Since our concern was speech, and speech impelled us
    To purify the dialect of the tribe
    *And urge the conscious mind to be more conscious
Let me disclose the gifts reserved for age,
    *The final prizes of your lifetime's effort. (D2)   130

             become much   ⟨*Now*⟩ ~~So~~ I find
122 become so like] ~~now so~~ like ~~to~~   M8   123 So I find]   ~~I now find~~ M8   126 concern]

                                                                                              final
regard M8   129 Let me disclose] ~~Reflect~~   M8   130 final] ~~utmost~~ M8   your
                                         Let me disclose
          lifetime's effort
lifetime's effort] the ~~life for language~~ M8

Apart from the insignificant change of 'so like' to 'much like' (l. 122), made in D5, the first draft differs from the final text only in three lines. The adaptation of Mallarmé's line[1] (l. 127) balances the reference to Yeats's early days in London and his death abroad to preserve the idea of the ghost as 'compound'.

Hayward made no mark against these lines and Eliot made no alterations in them in his second revision of Part II (D3). Hayward marked 'brief' (l. 120), commenting 'cf brief sun I'. On his copy of D3 (M10) Eliot cancelled 'brief' and wrote 'quick' above. In the next draft (D4) Eliot typed 'short and facile' and altered line 128 to

    And urge the conscious mind to thought more conscious. . . .

    [1] 'Donner un sens plus pur aux mots de la tribu', *Le Tombeau d'Edgar Poe.*

Hayward got to work on D4. He suggested 'swift' for 'short', underlined the repetition of 'thought' in

> . . . I never thought to speak
> . . . I never thought I should revisit

and noted its repetition four lines later in the new version of line 128, writing above 'thought' the suggestion 'be', and adding 'original version / but weak'. He put a cross against the last line, marked assonance in 'final prizes . . . lifetimes', and put in the margin 'crowning / finis coronat opus'. Eliot wrote on 7 September:

> 'Swift' might do: but it suggests great rapidity of movement, as if in a car. What about 'quick' or 'soft', or the more colloquial 'quick and easy'?
> Thought: This I have not solved yet.
> In any case, I now think 'prizes' is rather heavy-handed after 'gifts'.
> I propose
> > Let me disclose the gifts reserved for age
> > That put a period to your lifetime's effort.

Hayward in his reply of 8 September appears to have proposed 'easeful' in line 120, for Eliot wrote on 9 September:

> 'Easeful' will never be any use until Keats's trade-mark has worn off. Also it means something else. There was nothing ease-giving about this transit.

In the final recension (D5) Eliot had arrived at the final text, except in line 120. He 'solved' the problem of 'Thought' by banishing it from line 128, rewriting the line as

> > > > sight
> > And urge the mind to afterthought and foresight

and took up Hayward's suggestion for the last line with an ironic reminiscence of the Latin tag. Line 120 read

> > > But, as the passage now presents no barrier . . .

Hayward wrote in the margin '?hindrance'. Eliot replied on 2 October:

> I changed 'barrier' to 'hindrance' but I am thinking of changing it back again, because it seems a little insolite to speak of a *hindrance between* two points, doesn't it? And the freedom of movement was not in one direction only, but to and fro.

In the NEW first proof Eliot corrected 'barrier' to 'hindrance', but he changed his mind at the last minute and NEW reads 'barrier'. He wrote on 10 October:

> You will find that in the N.E.W. next week I have retained 'barrier' and 'conscious' but in view of your consistency I am not absolutely confident; and one of the purposes of this interim publication is to give an opportunity for alterations in the Faber text. But are you still assured that it is proper to speak of a hindrance *between* two termini?

Apparently Hayward was able to 'assure' him that it was proper and the Faber text (LG) and *Four Quartets* read 'hindrance'.

(131–143)

First, the cold friction of expiring sense
Without enchantment, offering no promise
    But bitter tastelessness of shadow fruit
    As body and soul begin to fall asunder.
Second, the conscious impotence of rage   135
    At human folly, and the laceration
    Of laughter at what ceases to amuse.
And last, the rending pain of re-enactment
    Of all that you have done, and been; the shame
    Of motives late revealed, and the awareness   140
Of things ill done and done to others' harm
    Which once you took for exercise of virtue.
    Then fools' approval stings, and honour stains.

First, the cold friction of expiring sense
*For what, if given, would give no more pleasure,
    But bitter tastelessness of shadow fruit
    When body and soul begin to fall asunder.
*Second, the growing impotence of rage   135
    *At human baseness, lethargy and folly,
    *And of laughter at what ceases to amuse.
*And last, the doubt of self in retrospection
    *Of all that you have been and done, the shame
    Of motives late revealed, and the awareness   140
Of things ill done and done to others' harm
    *Which once you thought were exercise of virtue.
    Then fools' approval stings, and honour stains. (D2)

                                     ing
                friction   expired
131 friction] craving M8   expiring] exhausted M8   133 But] The M8   134 fall]
                        lethargy   _of_
fade M8   136 lethargy] turpitude M8   137 And of] And   M8   141 Of things
        and   to others' harm   Then
ill done then done in all assurance M8   143 Then] And   M8

Hayward contented himself with writing on D2, against line 137, some words from Swift's epitaph on his tomb in St. Patrick's Cathedral, Dublin: 'ulterius cor / lacerare nequit.' On his own copy of D2 (M9) Eliot made an alteration in the preceding line which appears in the draft of his second revision (D3):

> Second, the growing impotence of rage
> At human baseness, and the rending pain
> Of laughter at what ceases to amuse.

In D3 Eliot also typed 'and honour shames' for 'and honour stains' (l. 143), but he reverted to 'stains' in his own copy of D3 (M10), no doubt recognizing that 'shame' appears only five lines earlier. Hayward on D3 queried 'more' in line 132, suggesting 'further', and suggested the transposition of lines 133 and 134. He put a tick of approval against 'rending pain'.

In the next draft (D4) Eliot rewrote the weak line 132 as

> Without enchantment, with no expectation

and altered 'When body and soul' to 'As body and soul'. In his letter sending Hayward D4 Eliot wrote in a postscript: 'I am sorry that *rending pain* can't stand. My metric requires a feminine termination there.' Hayward, on the draft, made the brilliant suggestion 'laceration?'; and Eliot, in his letter of 7 September wrote 'Laceration: yes, I like this.' So, in the final draft (D5) Swift was added to the company that made up the 'familiar compound ghost' of Eliot's dead masters. Hayward, also on D4, called in question the weak line 'And last, the doubt of self in retrospection' (l. 138), and suggested 'and last in retrospect self-doubting'. He also queried 'thought' in line 142, feeling, no doubt, that the word was being rather overworked in the new version of the speech. He suggested 'felt?/took?'

Eliot's struggles with the passage in these final stages can be seen on his copy of D4 (M12). In line 132 he crossed through 'with no expectation' and wrote above 'offering no prospect', crossed through 'no prospect' and wrote in the margin 'the enjoyment' and in the next line altered 'But' to 'Of'. Then crossing through 'the enjoyment' and indicating that 'But' was to stand, he rewrote 'no prospect' in the margin. In line 136 Eliot crossed through 'rending pain' and suggested 'dying spasm', crossed this through and put Hayward's suggestion of 'laceration' in the margin. In line 138 he crossed through 'doubt of self in retrospection' and wrote above it 'pain of memory's re-enactment' while below he wrote 'rending pain of', bracketing the readings as if he were undecided between them. He had previously written 'recollection' in the margin, scored it through and written below it 'the pain of memory's re-enactment'. Then he saw he could salvage 'rending pain' from line 136. In line 139 he crossed through 'been and done' and wrote below 'done, and been' and in line 142 he accepted Hayward's suggestion of 'took for' for 'thought were'.

Eliot wrote to Hayward in reply to his suggestions, accepting 'laceration' and adding: 'I find "self-doubting" rather weak. The best I can do, at the moment is

> And last, the rending pain of re-enactment. . . .

Felt is not strong enough: I mean not simply something not questioned but something consciously approved.' Two days later he wrote again:

And by the way, we both missed something I have just picked up—

> Of all that you have been and done . . .

Why whatever was I thinking of, to have been and done that? Read

> Of all that you have done, and been . . . .

In the final draft (D5) Eliot adopted the corrections made in M12, but altered 'no prospect' to 'no promise'. He had arrived at the final text, except for 'growing impotence' in line 135. Hayward's only comment on D5 was to suggest 'allurement' in place of 'promise'.

In sending his final recension of 19 September Eliot wrote: 'I am still unsatisfied: "enchantment" and "re-enactment" in the same passage are unpleasing.' Three days later he was still troubled and sent a note to Hayward:

> I cannot find any alternative for either 'enchantment' or 're-enactment' which does not either lose or alter meaning. 'Re-enacting' is weak as a sub-stantive; and I want to preserve the association of 'enact'—to take the part of oneself on a stage for oneself as the audience.

On 2 October he wrote: 'I think of changing "growing impotence" to "conscious impotence" as being rather stronger, and having removed "conscious" elsewhere it is possible.' He made the change in NEW proof at the same time as he changed 'barrier' to 'hindrance'. Hayward seems to have disapproved, for in his letter of 10 October Eliot wrote that Hayward would find 'in N.E.W. next week' that he had 'retained "barrier" and "conscious"', which suggests Hayward had objected to both. His objection to 'barrier' is understandable. It suggests some solid, physical impediment inappropriate to movements in and out of time; but it is difficult to see what his objection might have been to 'conscious'.

(144–149)

> From wrong to wrong the exasperated spirit
>   Proceeds, unless restored by that refining fire   145
>   Where you must move in measure, like a dancer.'
> The day was breaking. In the disfigured street
>   He left me, with a kind of valediction,
>   And faded on the blowing of the horn.

> From ill to worse the exasperated spirit
>   Proceeds, unless restored by that refining fire   145
>   Where you must learn to swim, and better nature.
>   *know*
> This you shall ~~learn~~." Down the dismantled street
>   *on,*
>   He passed me, with a kind of salutation,
>   And vanished on the blowing of the horn.   (D2)

                In   decaying street
148–9 This you shall learn." ~~And down~~ the ~~shabby road~~/He left me, M8

Hayward underlined 'swim' and 'better nature'. He suggested 'demolished' for 'dismantled' and queried Eliot's correction of 'He passed me' to 'He passed on', objecting also to 'vanished on' in the last line. He proposed 'passed along' and 'vanished with'. He also wrote below the last line the concluding words of Eliot's first draft—'and the sun had risen'—as if he preferred them to the new ending. On his copy of D2 (M9) Eliot wrote 'move' above 'swim', but then cancelled the suggestion. He crossed through 'dismantled' and wrote above it 'disfigured'. Without cancelling 'with a kind of salutation' he wrote above it 'as the sun was near its rising'. At the foot of the page he tried out a new line to replace line 146: 'Where you must / learn your measure, / like a dancer.', and 'Where you / must move / in measure.'

The text in the second revision (D3) ran:

> From wrong to worse the exasperated spirit
>   Proceeds, unless restored by that refining fire
>   Where you must move in measure, like a dancer."
>   *breaking*
> The day was ~~glimmering~~. Down the disfigured street
>   He passed me, with a kind of salutation,
>   faded
>   And ~~vanished~~ on the blowing of the horn.

In his letter of 27 August, sending the second revision, Eliot replied to Hayward's comments on D2. Explaining that he wished the effect of the whole passage to be Purgatorial, he went on:

> That brings us to the reference to swimming in fire which you will remember at the end of Purgatorio 26 where the poets are found. The active co-operation is, I think, sound theology and is certainly sound Dante, because the people who talk to him at that point are represented as not wanting to waste time in conversation but wishing to dive back into the fire to accomplish their expiation. However, I have for the moment discarded the whole image and rather like the suggestion of the new line which carries some reminder of a line, I think it is about Mark Antony.
>
> I don't understand in the least what you mean about the repetition of 'on'. I cannot find any second 'on' unless you mean the last syllable of 'salutation' and that does not seem to me close enough to require an alteration which would mean my losing the allusion to Hamlet's ghost.

Hayward queried 'The day was breaking' and also put a cross against 'salutation'. Against the last line he wrote 'vanished (also Hamlet) / & fading already / "neither budding / nor fading" I'. At the foot of the page he wrote 'passed on v passed me' and 'The $\begin{cases} \text{day} & \text{lightning} \\ \text{east was brightening} \end{cases}$'.

In his next revision, D4, Eliot typed 'In the disfigured street' and 'He left me'. When he sent Hayward the final recension, D5, by the alteration of 'from wrong to worse' to 'from wrong to wrong' and by the substitution of 'valediction' for 'salutation' he had achieved his final text. In his letter, referring particularly to the Dantean section of the poem he wrote he was 'still unsatisfied' but added:

> I think that there is a point beyond which one cannot go without sacrifice of meaning to euphony, and I think I have nearly reached it. . . . There will still be the possibility for alterations in proof. But to spend much more time over this poem might be dangerous. After a time one loses the original feeling of the impulse, and then it is no longer safe to alter. It is time to close the chapter.

Part III

Part III gave Eliot much less trouble than the second section of Part II. The interest of the MS, typescripts, and drafts lies in what Eliot added and deleted rather than in changes of wording and there is much less discussion in the correspondence. All the same, the process of expansion is better represented by setting out successive drafts than by means of a critical apparatus.

The prose summary of the material for Part III is on the untorn-out leaves of MS A and follows immediately on the close of the fair copy of Part II. On the next page Eliot wrote a single line, presumably intended for the first line of Part V.

V
To make an end is to make a beginning

On the next four pages he wrote a verse draft of Part III. This is freely written with few corrections.

The prose summary runs

> *The use of memory. to . detach oneself*
> *ones own*
> *from the past.—they vanish & return*
> *in a different action. a new relation-*
> *ship. If it is here, then, why regret it?*

> *If I think of three men on the*
> *scaffold it is not to revive dead political*
> *issues, or what might have happened—*
> For *Can a lifetime represent a single mo-*
> *tive? The symbol is the fact, and*
> *one side may inherit the victory, another*
> *the symbol. This means the moment*
> *of union, an eternal present.*

> *Detachment*
> *& attachment*
> *only a hair's width*
> *apart.*[1]

Air—air[2]
earth—   *Anima*
water—   *Christi*
fire & perfect fire

[1] A line is drawn to indicate this should come between the two paragraphs.
[2] Eliot has drawn a line to connect, it would seem, 'air' with 'Anima/Christi'.

(150–165)

III

There are three conditions which often look alike   150
Yet differ completely, flourish in the same hedgerow:
Attachment to self and to things and to persons, detachment
From self and from things and from persons; and growing between them,
   indifference
Which resembles the others as death resembles life,
Being between two lives—unflowering, between   155
The live and the dead nettle. This is the use of memory:
For liberation—not less of love but expanding
Of love beyond desire, and so liberation
From the future as well as the past. Thus, love of a country
Begins as attachment to our own field of action   160
And comes to find that action of little importance
Though never indifferent. History may be servitude,
History may be freedom. See, now they vanish,
The faces and places, with the self which, as it could, loved them,
To become renewed, transfigured, in another pattern.   165

Texts in MS, M2, D1/M3, M4, M5, M6, D2/M9, M11, D4/M12, D5/M13

---

                  three
There are three conditions, which differ | completely, | ~~yet grow~~
                  Very
~~Yet grow very~~ close together, like the | affinities ~~life~~ of the hedgerow
Attachment to things or to persons, detachment
                        third,
From things & from persons, and ~~last~~ | indifference
Which resembles the others as | death resembles life
Being between two lives. This is the use of | memory,
In liberation, not less of love but extension
Of love in the death of desire, so, liberation
From the future as well as the past. | So love of a country
Begins in love of our own activities | but reaches completion
In finding their unimportance—and this | is not indifference

                                            (new leaf)

So, they vanish, the faces & places,
        with the self which we loved and which loved them
To be seen to be represented, in another pattern.   (MS)

The first draft sent to Hayward hardly differs from the first typescript
(M2) and is very near the final text:

There are three conditions look very much alike,   150
Differ completely, flourish in the same hedgerow:
Attachment to things and to persons, detachment
From things and from persons; and growing close by them, indifference
Which resembles the others as death resembles life
Being between two lives. This is the use of memory: 155–6
For liberation—not less of love but expansion
Of love in the end of desire, and so liberation
From the future as well as the past. Thus, love of a country
Begins as dependence upon our own field of action   160
And comes to find that action of little importance
Though never indifferent. History is servitude:
History is also freedom. See, now they vanish,
The faces and places, with the self which—as it could—loved them:
To become renewed, transfigured, in another pattern. (D1)   165

comes

150 look] which look M2   151 Differ] And differ M2   161 comes] grows M2
162–3 *History is servitude,/History is also freedom. (inserted in pencil above half-lines)* M2   163 See]
So M2

Hayward wrote on the draft '1st para. Too didactic?/needs fusing'. In
his letter of 1 August 1941 he put his objections as tactfully as he could.

The first fifteen lines of Part III—the didactic passage—strike me as being
imperfectly resolved into poetry, in fact rather laboured and prosy. I think
I appreciate the difficulty of this kind of expository writing. It may be that it
is too easy to cast such philosophic and ethical statements into the kind of long,
fluid lines you use so ingeniously. But this particular passage does seem to me
to drag; to need fusing: possibly to be presented to the reader in a less didactic
and uncompromising form.

Eliot replied laconically on 5 August: 'I agree that the first part of Part III
needs thorough re-writing.' But, whether because when he came back to
the poem a year later he had forgotten Hayward's complaint, or whether he
had not really assented to it, no 'thorough re-writing' took place. He did
nothing to it in his copy of D1 (M3) and very little in his two re-typings
(M4 and M5). In M5 he drew a line down the side of the passage, as if to
remind himself to reconsider it; in M4, the typescript he worked on when
he took up the poem again, he only tinkered with a few words and phrases,
making suggestions, some of which he incorporated in the first typescript
of the revision of Part III (M6). The first revision sent to Hayward (D2)
differs in only one reading from the typescript M6 and only three times,
insignificantly, from the final text. The most striking difference from D1

was the insertion of two half-lines, expanding on the image of 'the life of the hedgerow':

> Being between two lives—unflowering, between
> The live and dead nettle.

Hayward did not take up again his general attack on the passage. He merely suggested 'Yet differ' for 'And differ' at the beginning of line 151 and the inversion of 'the live nettle and the dead'. Eliot accepted 'Yet' in his next draft (D3), but rejected the other suggestion in a 'what every schoolboy knows' manner:

> I am sorry that I cannot fall in with your suggestion of an inversion of 'dead nettle'. You know as well as I do that the dead nettle is the family of flowering plant[s] of which the White Archangel is one of the commonest and closely resembles the stinging nettle and is found in its company. If I wrote 'the live nettle and the dead' it would tend to suggest a dead stinging nettle instead of a quite different plant, so I don't see that anything can be done about that.

I suspect that Hayward, along with many readers of the poem was ignorant of 'the White Archangel'[1] and had taken it that the 'unflowering' plant of 'indifference' grew between a live and a dead specimen of the same plant. The image is very apt, when explained: indifference, that neither stings nor bears a flower, being between selfish love that stings and unselfish that bears a white flower. Eliot did do something about it, by inserting 'the' before 'dead nettle', although I doubt if this protected readers from misapprehension. He made the change in D4. He altered 'expansion' (l. 157) to 'expanding' and replaced dashes by commas in line 164 in D5.

---

[1] Mrs. Ridler pointed out to me that Eliot has confused two plants of the same family: White Deadnettle (*Lamium album*) and Yellow Archangel (*Galeobdolon luteum*). I suppose he would have rejected the suggestion of a hyphen in 'dead-nettle' on the same grounds as he rejected Hayward's suggestion of 'down-cast': that the word would be spoken much the same whether there was a hyphen or not.

(166–184)

Sin is Behovely, but
All shall be well, and
All manner of thing shall be well.
If I think, again, of this place,
And of people, not wholly commendable,   170
Of no immediate kin or kindness,
But some of peculiar genius,
All touched by a common genius,
United in the strife which divided them;
If I think of a king at nightfall,   175
Of three men, and more, on the scaffold
And a few who died forgotten
In other places, here and abroad,
And of one who died blind and quiet,
Why should we celebrate   180
These dead men more than the dying?
It is not to ring the bell backward
Nor is it an incantation
To summon the spectre of a Rose.

If I think last of this place,
And of people, not wholly commendable
But some of peculiar genius,
And touched by a common genius,
It is not to ring the bells backward
It is not an incantation
To summon the ghost of a rose

If I think of a king at nightfall
              , and more,
Of three men in turn on the scaffold
Why should a man lament
The dead any more than the dying?   (MS)

Eliot drew a line on the manuscript to indicate that the last four lines
should be moved to precede 'It is not to ring the bells backward'. In his
first typescript (M2) he has made the transfer and begun a process of
expansion. The first draft sent to Hayward (D1) differs very little from M2.

If I think, last, of this place,
And of people, not wholly commendable,   170
Of no immediate kin or kindness,
But some of peculiar genius,
All touched by a common genius;
If I think of a king at nightfall   175
Of three men, or more, on the scaffold
And two or three who died quietly
In other places, here or abroad,
                    we celebrate
Why should a man lament   180
The dead men
Dead people more than the dying?
It is not to ring the bells backward
Nor is it an incantation
To summon the ghost of a rose.   (D1)

174 All] And M2   176 men, or more] men and more M2   177 two or three] one or
                              or
two M2   178 here or] here and M2   180 a man lament M2   181 The dead
men   *Nor is it*
any more M2   183 It is not M2

Hayward underlined 'summon' and wrote in the margin 'raise up' and in
his letter wrote

> PART III. 'To summon the ghost of a rose': I can't resist expressing a regret
> that, having quoted so far, you didn't follow Sir T.B. and put 'raise up the
> ghost of a rose'.[1] I do wish you would consider making this alteration. It is an
> exquisite evocation.

Eliot replied:

> Damn Sir T. Browne, a writer I never got much kick from: I suppose it *is*
> a reminiscence, though I was thinking of the Ballet, and perhaps it would be
> better to go all out for the quotation, as the reference back to the Royal Rose
> must be retained because of the two or three other rose connotations.

The 'reference back' refers to the 'Royal Rose' of *The Dry Salvages* (l. 126).
It is odd that Eliot did not capitalize 'rose' in his first draft, since in his
letter to Bonamy Dobrée[2] he said that of the three roses in the poem the
'socio-political Rose' always appeared with a capital. In M3, his copy of D1,
he put 'R?' in the margin. Eliot was much devoted to the Russian Ballet
in his early years in London and the words of Sir Thomas Browne blended
in his memory with the ballet of *Le Spectre de la Rose* in which Nijinsky
made his famous leap.

[1] 'Nor will the sweetest delight of Gardens afford much comfort in sleep; wherein the dulness of
that sense shakes hands with delectable odours; and though in the Bed of *Cleopatra*, can hardly with
any delight raise up the ghost of a Rose.' Sir Thomas Browne, *The Garden of Cyrus*, V.
[2] Quoted on p. 137 supra. It was probably one of Eliot's re-typings of his first draft that he sent to
Dobrée. In these 'Rose' has its capital.

In his two re-typings of his first draft (M4 and M5) Eliot merely gave
'Rose' its capital and substituted 'These dead men' for 'The dead men'.
On M5 he pencilled Hayward's suggestion 'raise up' above 'summon'. He
appears to have abandoned M5 and, when he took up the poem again, to
have worked on M4. The pencilled corrections and suggestions made on
the typescript are made in a light and a dark pencil, as if they were made at
different times. At the head of the page that begins 'If I think last of this
place' he scribbled in the light pencil 'Sin is behovely, but / All shall be well,
and / All manner of thing / shall be well'. It looks as if he thought of using
these words, recognizing their metrical fitness, but was not certain where
they were to go. Below he has written 'Julian' with an arrow pointing to the
head of the paragraph. (This is in the dark pencil.) In light pencil he crossed
through the word 'quietly' and wrote 'obscurely' above it and in the margin
'(One who died blind and quiet)'. In light pencil he wrote 'spectre' above
'ghost', though without cancelling 'ghost', and he put a line under 'immediate'
with a cross against the line in the margin.

The typescript of the revised version (M6) differs only twice from the
first revision sent to Hayward:

> Sin is behovely, but
> All shall be well, and
> All manner of thing shall be well.
> If I think, again and last, of this place,
> And of people, not wholly commendable,   170
> Of no immediate kin or kindness,
> But some of peculiar genius,
> All touched by a common genius,
> United in the strife which divided them;
> If I think of a king at nightfall,   175
> Of three men, and more, on the scaffold
> And a few who died forgotten
> In other places, here or abroad,
> And of one who died blind and quiet,[1]
> Why should we celebrate   180
> The dead men more than the dying?
> It is not to ring the bell backward
> Nor is it an incantation
> To summon the spectre of a Rose.   (D2)

169 ~~But i~~If I think, last M6   179 And one M6

Hayward made no mark against this passage on the draft, but he must
have queried 'behovely' in his letter. Writing on 2 September, to send him
a 'new fair copy' (D4), Eliot wrote 'I forgot in my previous letter to give an

[1] This line is inserted between two lines in the first typescript of the revision (M6), as an afterthought.

explanation which bears on your query of *behovely*'. He explained that 'This
line and the two which follow and which occur twice later constitute
a quotation from Juliana of Norwich' and explained also that 'The beautiful
line the presence of which puzzles you' in Part V 'comes out of *The Cloud of
Unknowing*'. He added that there was 'so much 17th century in the poem'
that he was afraid 'of a certain romantic Bonnie Dundee period effect' and
he wanted 'to check this and at the same time give greater historical depth
to the poem by allusions to the other great period, i.e. the 14th century'.[1]
He concluded by asking 'Does it seem to you possibly that the passages in
question ought to be put in inverted commas?' Hayward appears to have
written back suggesting capitalization, for Eliot wrote on 7 September:

> I am afraid I don't like capitalising the quotes. Too much like headlines:
> slightly comic. I thought better of restoring the spelling; but I read the texts
> in modern versions. . . . I now incline to put between guillemets
>
> 'Sin is behovely,' etc.
>
> on its first appearance, but *not* the two repetitions. This means putting 'With
> the drawing of this love . . .' in quotes also. *Or not?*

Eliot tried out quotation marks on M12, his copy of D4; but a letter from
Hayward provided a more acceptable solution. Eliot wrote on 9 September,
acknowledging 'Yours of the 8th': 'I accept the more limited capitalisation.'

I was always slightly puzzled by 'ring the bell backward' (l. 182), but
took it to be a metaphorical way of saying 'reverse the course of history',
on the model of 'turn the clock back'. The original reading 'ring the bells',
unaltered until the revision of the passage in M6, along with the 'drum' of
line 187 and Eliot's reference to a 'romantic Bonnie Dundee period effect',
makes it clear that Eliot was remembering one of those 'thumpers' for which
he once confessed his affection in a broadcast talk: Scott's famous song[2] that
begins

> To the Lords of Convention 'twas Claver'se who spoke,
> 'Ere the King's crown shall fall there are crowns to be broke;
> So let each Cavalier who loves honour and me,
> Come follow the bonnet of Bonny Dundee.
>
> 'Come fill up my cup, come fill up my can,
> Come saddle your horses, and call up your men;
> Come open the West Port, and let me gang free,
> And it's room for the bonnets of Bonny Dundee!'
>
> Dundee he is mounted, he rides up the street,
> The bells are rung backward, the drums they are beat. . . .

Eliot's alteration to the singular and Hayward's failure to comment on it
show that neither of them realized the meaning of 'ringing the bells back-

---

[1] The passage is quoted in full in the discussion of sources on p. 70 supra.
[2] The song is sung in *The Doom of Devorgoil*, II. ii.

ward'. This is to ring a peal in reverse, or 'over the left', that is to begin with the bass bell and not with the treble. This is a signal of distress or alarm, to give warning of fire or invasion, or, as here, to call out the citizens. It is impossible to ring a single bell backward, so Eliot's alteration to the singular means we must give a metaphorical meaning to the words. One can understand why Eliot attached some such meaning as I have suggested above to a phrase in a poem on Dundee's forlorn hope in 1689 to undo the 'Glorious Revolution', by setting up the standard for King James II at Stirling.

The text of D2 is virtually the final text. In his next draft (D4) Eliot reverted to 'here and abroad', and substituted 'These dead men' for 'The...'. In D5, as well as supplying a capital for 'Behovely', he dropped 'and last', preferring the shorter line

> If I think again of this place.

On D5 Hayward, a stickler for 'correct English', queried 'which' following the definite article in the fine line Eliot had added in the first revision

> United in the strife which divided them.

Eliot wrote on 10 October 'I have definitely accepted your THAT (was it Swift or Defoe who wrote a plea for WHICH?)'. He corrected 'which' to 'that' on the NEW proof and the text in NEW reads 'that'. But his conversion to 'correct English' did not last. He made no correction of the text of D5 for the printing of LG and *Four Quartets*, which both have the idiomatic 'which'.

(185-199)

We cannot revive old factions   185
We cannot restore old policies
Or follow an antique drum.
These men, and those who opposed them
And those whom they opposed
Accept the constitution of silence   190
And are folded in a single party.
Whatever we inherit from the fortunate
We have taken from the defeated
What they had to leave us—a symbol:
A symbol perfected in death.   195
And all shall be well and
All manner of thing shall be well
By the purification of the motive
In the ground of our beseeching.

No one is wholly alive
No man is free from sin
And sordid or petty weakness.
We cannot revive old factions
We cannot restore old policies
Or follow the antique drum.
These men and those who opposed them
And those whom they opposed
⌈*Are folded in a common party.*
⌊*Consenting to a common silence,*
The victory no longer a victory
But only a neutral fact.
No life had a single motive
We have our bequest from the victors,
Receiving from the defeated
What they had to leave us—a symbol
The symbol created by death
The life only death can bequeathe
In death the perfection of the motive
Which the moment of death attained.

                                          (*new leaf*)

Soul of Christ, inspire them
Body of Christ, make their bodies good soil
Water from the side of Christ, wash them,
Fire from the heart of Christ, incinerate them. (MS)

The text of the first typescript (M2) differs so much from that of the first draft that it has to be set out in full:

> No one is wholly ~~alive~~ *right*
> No one is free from sin
> And sordid or petty weakness.
> We cannot revive old factions
> We cannot ~~revive~~ restore old policies
>   *n antique*
> Or follow a ~~broken~~ drum.
> These men and those who opposed them,
> And those whom they opposed,
> Accept the
> ~~Consent to~~ constitution of silence
>   single
> And are folded in a ~~common silence~~ party.
> ~~No longer defeat and victory~~
> ~~But only a neutral fact.~~
> Whatever we inherit from the victors,
> We have taken from the defeated
> What they had to leave us—a symbol:
> The symbol created by death,
> The life only death transmits,
> The perfection of the motive
> Which the moment of death brings to life.
> Soul of Christ, sanctify them,
> Body of Christ, let their bodies be good earth,
> Water from the side of Christ, wash them,
> Fire from the heart of Christ, incinerate them. (M2)

Eliot has boxed in the first three lines in pencil and has cancelled, also in pencil, the lines in the centre of the passage. His prose summary for Part III shows that he intended to adapt the prayer '*Anima Christi sanctifica me*' to the theme of the four seasons and in the manuscript draft he relates its first clause to 'air'. He probably used in his own devotions the version in a popular Anglo-Catholic manual *St. Swithun's Prayer Book*, which begins

> Soul of Christ, sanctify me
> Body of Christ, save me
> Blood of Christ, inebriate me
> Water from the side of Christ, wash me. . . .

In the typescript he has reverted in the first line to the wording of the prayer. There is no clause to parallel Eliot's 'Fire from the heart of Christ, incinerate them'.

With the deletion of the first three lines and the alterations made in the typing and in pencil, Eliot had reached the final text of lines 185-91 in his first typescript. His difficulty was to refine on the concept of the 'symbol' which was the legacy of the defeated. The first draft sent to Hayward of lines 192-9 ran

> Whatever we inherit from the victors,
> We have taken from the defeated
> What they had to leave us—a symbol:
> The symbol created by death
> (Created by such a death)
> The life only death transmits,
> The perfection of the motive
> Which the moment of death brings to life.
>   Soul of Christ, sanctify them,
>   Body of Christ, let their bodies be good earth,
>   Water from the side of Christ, wash them,
>   Fire from the heart of Christ, incinerate them. (D1)

Hayward put a cross in the margin against the line 'And are folded in a single party', but he made no comment to explain his difficulty in his letter. He bracketed the last four lines and put against them 'Cut by T.S.E.' Eliot must have made the cut while waiting for Hayward's letter. He wrote on 14 July, a week after sending the first draft to say he had 'pushed on with Little Gidding', and to 'enclose provisional results'. Hayward, in his letter, wrote: 'I approve of the omission of the last four lines of Part III.' Eliot had meanwhile been working on M3, his copy of D1. He did not cancel the last four lines but attempted to improve the two preceding ones:

>   *purification*
> The ~~perfection~~ of the motive
>   *assent to*   *perfects*
> Which ~~the moment of~~ death ~~brings to life~~. (M3)

In his first re-typing of D1/M3 (M4) he typed the text in M3 as corrected, but in light pencil he bracketed and struck through the last four lines and put a query against them. He also altered 'assent' to 'consent'. In his second re-typing, M5, he omitted the last four lines and typed for conclusion

> The purification of the motive
> Which consent to death perfects. (M5)

When he came back to work on the poem, on M4, he struck through, with the same heavy pencil he had used to strike through the conclusion of Part II, all that followed the line

> What they had to leave us—a symbol:

and, actuated by the same desire to 'give greater historical depth to the poem' as had made him turn to the fourteenth-century mystics, thought of including with the defeated Royalists other figures who had fought for lost causes. Against the cancelled passage he wrote:

The symbol of the defeated | the crown on the | hedge—the Duke with | his iron shutters. We | must keep the symbol | but not confuse it | with the use we | make of it. | Who survives the | test of victory?

On the back of the preceding page he cast this into verse:

battered
The ~~damaged~~ crown on the/thornbush
The Duke with his iron shutters
Have the dignity of the defeated
In a world in which, as it happens,
~~Only the defeated have dignity~~
The victors seldom keep dignity.

The chroniclers report that the crown which Richard III wore on the battle field at Bosworth was found with the spoil of battle by Lord Stanley, who crowned the victor, Henry Tudor, there and then. The legend that the crown was found hanging in a thornbush arose in the sixteenth century.[1] In a television programme on Eliot his friend Miss Hope Mirrlees reported that he always wore a white rose on the anniversary of Bosworth in memory of 'the last English king'.[2] Even his enemies owned that Richard died bravely, the only English king to die in battle, except Harold, the last of the Saxons; but, even so, he seems an odd companion for Charles I.[3] The most devoted adherents of his cult would hardly propose that churches should be dedicated to him. I suppose Eliot thought of Bosworth as 'the end of the Middle Ages' and of Richard as representing an old order that was passing. In the same way, Wellington, with the windows of Apsley House twice

---

[1] Ironically, it probably arose from a Tudor emblem, celebrating the union of the Roses, which showed a rosebush growing through a crown with the interlaced initials H and E entwined above.

[2] I suppose Normans and Angevins having stayed a long time had become 'English'. The cult of Richard III is more fervent in the United States than in England, particularly in California. Societies dedicated to the rehabilitation of this maligned monarch were much in evidence during the exhibition of 'The Reign of Richard III' at the National Portrait Gallery recently, coming over on charter flights. The learned catalogue of the exhibition provided me with the explanation of the thornbush legend given in the note above.

[3] They were brought together by Mr. George Every in his play about King Charles's visit to Little Gidding which Eliot read in 1936. John Ferrar, in his discourse with his niece reminds her

King dead, the crown
One day was plucked by a crafty hand from a thornbush

and Charles links himself with Richard:

one man, one king
Knew not to live, only knew how to die,
Richard, the King, and I.

broken by the London mob, which regarded him as the chief opponent of
the Reform Bill,[1] represented pre-industrial England.

In his first typescript of the revised version of Part III (M6) Eliot reduced
the reference to Richard III and Wellington to two lines, which he then
cancelled, and concluded with another quotation from Julian of Norwich:[2]

> Whatever we inherit from the fortunate
> We have taken from the defeated
> > leave
> What they had to ~~give~~ us—a symbol, /
> The symbol of the defeated—
> ~~The crown hanging in a thornbush~~ +
> ~~The Duke with his iron shutters~~ +
> *with*
> ~~In~~ the purification of the motive
> In the ground of our beseeching.

In the first revision sent to Hayward (D2) Eliot abandoned his attempt to
enlarge on the 'symbol' and contented himself with a repetition of Julian of
Norwich's words:

> Whatever we inherit from the fortunate
> We have taken from the defeated
> What they had to leave us—a symbol:
> And all shall be well and
> All manner of thing shall be well
> By the purification of the motive
> In the ground of our beseeching.

The text in D4 was unchanged; but in the final recension (D5) Eliot reverted
to the conception of death as perfecting life by adding to 'a symbol':

> A symbol perfected in death.

In a lecture 'On the Notion of a Philosophy of History' Professor Donald
Mackinnon singled out this section of *Little Gidding* for 'a quality of poetic
meditation, a curious precision of language bringing out exactly the distinctions we have to draw in a spiritually disciplined approach to the pain
of the past'.

> We cannot be partisan and follow an antique and silent drum. There is
> a kind of make-believe in trying to fight the battles of the past as if they were
> our own. Yet the answer to this attitude is not found in a sort of superior
> detachment, altogether disdainful of issues for which good men were prepared
> to die. And so we have to commit ourselves, but in such a way that we are ready
> to see how much we owe to those who were on the other side from that to which

[1] The windows were broken by the mob on 27 April 1831, three days after the death of the Duchess,
though her body was still lying in the house. They were broken again on 12 October. Wellington left
them unmended and put up iron shutters, which remained until his death.

[2] In her Fourteenth Revelation, on prayer, Julian heard the words 'I am Ground of thy Beseeching'.

in some sense we have given our allegiance. Yet to talk in this way is not to commit ourselves to some vision of a synthesis in which reconciliation is achieved. Men died; others were banished and knew the loneliness of exile. These sufferings were real enough; yet, if we recall their reality, it is not to summon up our animosity. Rather it is a remembrance that must have an ascetic quality. . . . I would suggest that in this poem we have an example of the attempt to present 'the meaning of history'. If that phrase has any sense, it may be the sort of thing that can only achieve its definition in poetry.[1]

[1] *On the Notion of a Philosophy of History*, L. T. Hobhouse Memorial Trust Lecture, No. 23, delivered 5 May 1953 (1954).

Part IV

Part IV demands the same kind of narrative treatment as is necessary for dealing with the second part of Part II. As with the speech of the 'dead master', Eliot abandoned his first conception. The manuscript drafts are particularly interesting here, showing the first very rough beginnings of both the version in the first draft and the revision. They need to be set out in succession. It was Eliot himself who was dissatisfied with the dead master's advice to remember 'essential moments'; Hayward made no criticism of the passage. The contrary happened with Part IV. Hayward was baffled by the first version and, as tentatively as was possible, suggested it really would not do. Eliot's first reaction was slightly pained and puzzled. But, with characteristic humility, he came to recognize that the attempt to write a 'conceited' poem had been a misjudgement and was a distraction from the poem's underlying theme of Pentecost.

(200–213)

IV

The dove descending breaks the air   200
With flame of incandescent terror
Of which the tongues declare
The one discharge from sin and error.
The only hope, or else despair
    Lies in the choice of pyre or pyre—   205
    To be redeemed from fire by fire.

Who then devised the torment? Love.
Love is the unfamiliar Name
Behind the hands that wove
The intolerable shirt of flame   210
Which human power cannot remove.
    We only live, only suspire
    Consumed by either fire or fire.

Texts in MS, M2, D1/M3, D4/M12, D5/M13

The version of Part IV sent to Hayward in July 1941 consisted of three stanzas. The third of these became, without alteration, the first of the two stanzas of the final version. Eliot's original plan was to repeat the 'metaphysical' manner of the lyric in *East Coker*, using the language of financial transactions as he had there used medical imagery. The first brief draft is scrawled on the verso of the leaf on which he had written his versification of petitions from the *Anima Christi*.

> *This death shall call the bailiffs in*
> *With all our patrimony spent*
> *Or lost in worthless shares, we win*

On the next and final leaf of MS A he drafted two stanzas

> *The dove descending breaks the air*
> > *breath*
> *With ~~tongues~~ of crepitative fire*
> *Where*   *Of which the*
> *While*   *~~Its~~ tongues declare*
> *The culmination of desire,*
> *Expectancy, hope,*
> *~~Of expectation,~~ doubt, despair.*
> > *Beneath those never resting feet*
> > *All aspirations end and meet.*

> *The marked invisible watery cross,*
> *The*   *~~unseen impress~~*
> *touch*   *The ~~forgotten mark~~ of delegated hands,*
> *But emphasise our loss,*
> *Transformed into the sign that brands*
> *~~The miserable athanatos~~*
> > *~~The votaries of thanatos~~*
> > *The votary of Soledos*
> *Who gambled*
> *~~The gambler between~~ death & birth*
> *Whose[1] climax is a pinch of earth*

I presume the 'miserable athanatos', 'the votaries of thanatos', and 'the votary of Soledos' are rather despairing attempts to find rhymes for 'cross'. The first two would seem to refer to those who deny their baptism and face a miserable immortality, or have chosen death rather than life. The 'votary of Soledos' baffles me and all upon whom I have tried it. The reading is confirmed by Professor Bennett and Mrs. Eliot. It may be that Eliot who did not know Spanish wrote 'Soledos' for '*Soledad*', solitude.

---

[1] Eliot has written 'Whose' over the beginning of another word.

Having crossed through the whole of the second stanza, Eliot tried again on the verso, choosing a less difficult rhyme word:

> *Between the invisible watery sign*
> *And climax of a pinch of earth*
>   *false accounts*
> *Our ~~slippery hearts~~ decline*
> set   ~~square~~   *show*
> *To pay the dues of death & birth*
> *And mark the debt beneath the line*
> *The deficit which is complete*
> *Or cancelled by the Paraclete*

The next stage can be seen on the first typescript (M2), which has two versions of a poem in three stanzas. The first runs

> Between the invisible watery sign
> And ~~the~~ climax of a pinch of earth
> 2 ~~We in o~~Our false accounts decline
> To square the dues of death and birth
> And mark the debt below the line:
> The deficit that is complete
> Or cancelled by the Paraclete.

>   audit
> Till death shall bring the bailiffs in
>   hoarded
> To value all our worthless treasures:
> <u>Unprofitable</u> <u>Sin,</u>
> 1 <u>Comforting</u> <u>Thoughts,</u> and <u>Sundry</u> <u>Pleasures,</u>
>   ventures
> The ~~assets~~ that we think ~~w~~to[1] win
> By <u>Prudence,</u> and by <u>Worldly</u> <u>Cares</u>
> Figure as <u>gilt-edged</u> stocks and shares.

> The dove descending breaks the air
>   flame
> With ~~breath~~ of crepitative terror
> Of which the tongues declare
>   *one restorative from error.*
> The ~~culmination of desire.~~
> The only hope, or else despair
>   Is, like the bird upon the pyre   *Lies in the choice of pyre*
>   To be ~~revoked~~ from fire by fire.   *or pyre*
>   redeemed

---

[1] Eliot began to type 'we' and altered to 'too' for 'to'.

The second version in M2 is, with a few exceptions noted below, the text
sent to Hayward:

<blockquote>

2   Till death shall bring the audit in   *Perhaps*
    To value all our hoarded treasures∤   -∕   *omit 2?*
    The <u>Profitable Sin</u>,

    Cos*n*se*n*ting [1] <u>Thoughts</u>, and <u>Sundry</u> Pleasures;   :∕
    The prizes that we think to win
    By <u>Prudence</u>, and by <u>Worldly Cares</u>,
    Figure as gilt-edge stocks and shares.

1   Between the initial[2] watery sign
    And climax of a pinch of earth,
    Our false accounts decline
    To show the dues of death and birth
    Or[3] mark the debt below the line:
    The deficit that is complete,
    Or cancelled by the Paraclete.

3   The dove descending breaks the air
    With flame of incandescent[4] terror
    Of which the tongues declare
    The one discharge from sin and error.[5]
    The only hope, or else despair
      Lies in the choice of pyre or pyre—
      To be redeemed by fire from fire.[6] (D1)

</blockquote>

	initial		*incandescent*	
1 Cosseting M2	2 ~~invisible~~ M2	3 And M2	4 crepitative ⟨?⟩ M2	5 from
mortal error M2	6 from fire by fire M2			

It is difficult to understand why Eliot ever wished to use the coinage
'crepitative' for fire from heaven, since its connotations are medical and
'crackling' seems hardly apposite. The substitution of 'incandescant' may,
as has been suggested,[1] derive from a memory of Mallarmé's '*Le Cantique
de Saint Jean*':

<blockquote>

Le soleil que sa halte
Surnaturelle exalte
Aussitôt redescend
Incandescent.

</blockquote>

It is possible to regret the dismissal of the phoenix, 'the bird upon the pyre'
in the first draft in M2. Perhaps Eliot felt one symbolic bird in the stanza
was enough, and that the mythical did not blend with the Scriptural here.
Hayward bracketed the first stanza and wrote against it 'Cut by T.S.E.'

<hr>

[1] See E. J. H. Greene, *T. S. Eliot et la France* (Paris, 1951), 138.

Eliot must have written to him during the time he was waiting for his letter to tell him to cut this as well as the '*Anima Christi*' lines at the close of Part III. Hayward also drew a bracket against the two other stanzas and wrote against them 'IV / obscure / & too little of it / non sequiturish?' In his letter of 1 August he wrote 'Part IV seems to me to break down', and later in the letter went on to express his feeling of bafflement:

> As for Part IV, I can't fit it into the scheme of the poem as a whole. Now that you have discarded (and rightly so, I think) the 2nd. stanza ('Till death shall bring the audit in . . .') it consists of only two short stanzas and their point has escaped me. This is more than likely to be due to my own obtuseness. But the point I should like to make is that these two stanzas seem to me scarcely to justify a section to themselves. My own view, for the little that it is worth, is that this section should be extended rather than rewritten, or if this is not possible, that it should be so reorganized as to be capable of being incorporated in some way either at the end of Part III or at the beginning of Part V. In its present form it has an obfuscating effect—rather as if you had thrown out a smoke-screen to prepare for the next stage. This, at any rate, is how it affected me.

Eliot replied:

> I am specially puzzled about Part IV. It may be that the attempt to give a XVII century flavour is a mistake (having previously done it successfully) but I feel that some explicit attack on the Descent of the Holy Ghost (which is an undertone throughout) is necessary at this point.

The last stanza 'The dove descending breaks the air' had reached final form in the first draft, D1. It splendidly 'attacks' the poem's underlying theme of the Descent of the Holy Ghost, and Eliot's problem was to write a matching stanza. His first attempt is on one of four leaves from a pad of smaller size than the pad he used for other rough drafts (MS C). The leaf on which it is written was pinned to another leaf containing a prose draft of the new close of the speech of the 'dead master'. It runs

> *Who heaped the brittle roseleaves? Love.*
> *Love put the match; and blew the coals.*
> *Who fed the fire? Love.*
> *To torture and to temper souls*
> *With*
> *In that consumption from above*
> *   Where all delights & torments cease*
> *   The will is purified to peace.*
>
> *Endless consumption, which is love*

The next two attempts are on the versos of two leaves on which Eliot made notes for his lecture on Yeats delivered in Dublin in June 1940 (MS D). The reminiscence of the 'bowl of rose-leaves' in *Burnt Norton* is

abandoned and the drafts work towards making the stanza's central image
the 'shirt of flame':

designed
Who then devised the torture? Love.   (f. 1)
fuel
He laid the ~~train and~~ fixed the cure.
~~He also wove~~
And ~~h~~He it was who wove
The insupportable shirt of fire
~~He set the ambush~~
He kindled the encircling fire

Who then designed the torture? Love.
Love is the unfamiliar name
Of ~~Him~~ what, below, above,

torment?
Who then devised the torture? Love.   (f. 2)
unspeakable
Love is the unfamiliar name
in the beginning
Of what, ~~before Eden,~~ wove
before time
The insupportable shirt of flame
human kind cannot
Which ~~we must wear, and not~~ remove
We only   only
~~But always~~ live ~~and still~~ expire,
Consumed by either fire or fire.
Behind
Written by the hands that wove
loom
Behind the ~~power~~ that wove

The first revision sent to Hayward (D2) did not include Part IV and the
second revision (D3) was a revision of Part II only. In sending the second
complete draft (D4) on 2 September Eliot wrote 'As for Part IV, which
I now include, I am as yet too close to this new version to be able to tell
whether it is fundamentally right or fundamentally wrong'. Hayward made
no comment on D4 where the second stanza ran

Who then designed the torture? Love.
Love is the unfamiliar Name
Behind the hands that wove
The intolerable shirt of flame
Which human power cannot remove.
We only live, only suspire
Consumed by either fire or fire.

In a postscript to his letter of 9 September Eliot wrote 'From your silence on the point, am I to infer that you are satisfied with Part IV? I had hesitated already between "torture" and "torment" (first draft "devised" rejected as too self-conscious)'. The phrase 'I had hesitated already' suggests that Hayward, though not commenting approvingly on the lyric as a whole, had in his letter queried 'torture' and suggested 'torment' and proposed 'devised' for 'designed'. At any rate in the final recension (D5) Eliot adopted 'devised the torment'.

Part V

Having sketched out in prose the matter of Part III, Eliot, on the next
leaf of his pad, wrote a single line

V

To make an end is to make a beginning

and, having thus noted the gist of his concluding part, went on with a verse
draft of Part III and with his attempts at Part IV. This brought him to the
end of his pad, and the first rough draft of Part V, which hovers between
verse and prose, is on two leaves from a smaller pad.

> *What we think a beginning is often an end*
> *And to make an end is to make a | beginning.*
> *The end is where we start from. | For every moment*
> *Is both beginning and end. | So every phrase*
>   *the   one*
> *When it is ˄ right, ˄ when every | word has power*
> *To sustain the others, to do its part*
> *In subservience to the phrase—*
>
>   *epitaph*
> *Is the end and the beginning. | The only ~~obituaries~~*
> *Is written in every word of | the man who | writes it.*
> *Every poem is its own epitaph | every action*
> *A step on the scaffold, to the fire, | to the sea,*
> *And that is the beginning.*
>
>   *(new leaf)*

>   *The dying die for us*
> *And we die with them. | But to speak of regret*
> *Is to outlive regret. | The moment of | the rose*
> *And the moment of the yew tree | are equally moments*
> *And so must vanish to become | eternal*
>   *these*
> *So, they return: and the winter | sunlight*
>
>   *from*
> *Freedom past and future*
> *Is union with past & future*

(214–227)

V

What we call the beginning is often the end
And to make an end is to make a beginning.   215
The end is where we start from. And every phrase
And sentence that is right (where every word is at home,
Taking its place to support the others,
The word neither diffident nor ostentatious,
An easy commerce of the old and the new,   220
The common word exact without vulgarity,
The formal word precise but not pedantic,
The complete consort dancing together)
Every phrase and every sentence is an end and a beginning,
Every poem an epitaph. And any action   225
Is a step to the block, to the fire, down the sea's throat
Or to an illegible stone: and that is where we start.

Texts in M2, D1/M3, M4 (ll. 214–29 are on a missing page), M5, D2/M9, D4/M12, D5/M13

                      mark as   *call?*   *call*
214* call] think M2–D2; ~~think~~ M9; (mark as) D4; ~~mark as~~ M12   the end] an . . . M2
                           where
217* And] Or M2–D4/M12, NEW (~~which~~ every word is at home, ~~in~~ M2   218 Taking its
place] Doing its part M2–D2/M9   support] sustain M2
                      common precise   *exact*   *precise?*
221–2*   The ~~new~~ word ~~simple~~, without vulgarity,
                  formal   ~~*exact*~~   *precise*
             The old word ~~formal~~, without pedantry M2
                                               but not pedantic
222* precise but not pedantic] precise without pedantry D1–D2; precise ~~without pedantry~~ M9
223 *Not in* M2
                          and sentence
224–5   ~~So e~~Every phrase ∧ is an end and a beginning/
             ~~So e~~Every poem ~~is~~ its own epitaph
                          And
             ~~And that of the writer,~~ ~~E~~every action M2
224 and every sentence] or sentence D1/M3; and sentence M5   225 an epitaph] its own epitaph
    an   *any decision*
M2–D4; ~~its own~~ . . . M12   any action] every action M2–D4; ~~every action~~ M12   226 Is a step
                                                     May be
to the block] ⟨Is⟩ A step on the scaffold M2; Is a step up the scaffold D1–M5; Is . . . M12   down]
to M2

The interest of the typescripts and drafts for Part V lies less in minute changes in wording than in expansions. The first draft (D1) adds thirteen lines to the first typescript (M2) and D2 adds three to the version in D1. The most interesting lines in M2 in this passage are the first draft of the famous definition of the diction of poetry (ll. 220-4) where Eliot began by simply expanding, with chiasmus, 'the old and the new'. In D1 he added line 224.

> The complete consort dancing together)

to his long parenthesis.

Hayward made no comment on Part V in D1 and in his letter referred to it as 'all right'. In sending him his revision (D2) Eliot referred to it as being, like Part I, only 'slightly altered'. In these lines the only change was from 'Every phrase or sentence' to 'Every phrase and every sentence' (l. 224). On D2 Hayward queried 'think' (l. 214) and suggested 'suppose?' Eliot tried 'mark as' on his copy of D2 (M9) and typed 'mark as' on his next revision (D4); but he bracketed it and suggested 'call?', which he settled on in D5. Against the line

> The formal word precise without pedantry

Hayward suggested an inspired improvement: 'but unpedantic'. His marks suggest it was the rhythm as much as the repetition—'without vulgarity . . . without pedantry'—that troubled him.

In the second revision (D4) 'Taking its place', which fits better the 'complete consort dancing', replaced 'Doing its part' which has a slight hint of the 'team spirit'. On D4 Hayward woke up to the repetitions of 'every': 'Every phrase and every sentence . . . Every poem . . . every action'. He suggested 'All our actions / Are steps' with a note 'cf all our exploring'. Eliot tried 'And any decision' on his copy of D4 (M12), and in his letter of 7 September suggested 'And any decision / Is a step . . . (or, May be a step)'. He wisely settled for 'any action' and rejected the timid 'May be'.

Line 217 is the third example of Eliot's not correcting in proof a reading of D4 to the reading of D5 for publication in NEW.

(228–251)

We die with the dying:
See, they depart, and we go with them.
We are born with the dead: 230
See, they return, and bring us with them.
The moment of the rose and the moment of the yew-tree
Are of equal duration. A people without history
Is not redeemed from time, for history is a pattern
Of timeless moments. So, while the light fails   235
On a winter's afternoon, in a secluded chapel
History is now and England.

With the drawing of this Love and the voice of this Calling

We shall not cease from exploration
And the end of all our exploring   240
Will be to arrive where we started
And know the place for the first time.
Through the unknown, remembered gate
When the last of earth left to discover
Is that which was the beginning;   245
At the source of the longest river
The voice of the hidden waterfall
And the children in the apple-tree
Not known, because not looked for
But heard, half-heard, in the stillness   250
Between two waves of the sea.

                                     We die with the dying,
228 We die with the dying:] ~~The dying die to us,~~   M2; ... dying, D1/M3   229 them.]
                                                      are born
them; D1/M3   230-1 *Not in* M2   230 are born] ~~return~~   D1/M3   230-1 dead: ...
them.] dead, ... them: D1/M3   233 people] nation M2   234 for] and M2   236 winter's]
                                              's
winter M2-D2; winter M9   238* *Not in* M2-M5   ... love ... calling D2-D4/M12
239 shall] must M2   241 Will be] Is M2   242 *Not in* M2   244 last of earth]
last place M2   245 that which] that where M5   beginning;] beginning M2, D1/M3; ...:
M5   248* *Not in* M2
250-1*
                                     in the silence
                        Of distant lands and seas.   M2-M5

                                     in the silence
                    Between two waves of the sea.   D2/M9, D4

                                  stillness
                                in the silence
                                 on the shore   ?
                    Between two waves ~~of the sea.~~ M12

Eliot expanded from his first typescript (M2) in D1 by adding to 'We die with the dying . . .' the beautiful variation (ll. 230–1) 'We are born with the dead . . .'; by enriching the notion that we shall 'arrive where we started' by the line

> And know the place for the first time;

and by adding to 'The voice of the hidden waterfall' a line meant, as he wrote to Hayward, 'to tie up New Hampshire and Burnt Norton':

> And the children in the apple-tree.

The most striking addition was the final eight lines of the poem. In M2 the poem ends:

> At the source of the longest river
> The voice of the hidden waterfall
> Not known, because not looked for
> But heard, half-heard, in the silence
> Of distant lands and seas.

The last line echoed a line in the original speech of the 'dead master' in Part II: 'After many seas and after many lands.'

Hayward made no comment on D1. On D2 he suggested 'winter's' for 'winter' and was puzzled by the line from *The Cloud of Unknowing* as he had been by the quotation from Julian of Norwich in Part III.[1] Against line 241 Eliot had written in the margin 'or whence?' and Hayward added 'at where'. He seems to have objected to the word 'waves' in the new version of line 151, for Eliot in a postscript to the letter in which he explained the quotations from Julian and *The Cloud of Unknowing* wrote 'I see yr points about *daybreak* and *waves* but can think of nothing which would not overstress'.

On the next draft (D4) Hayward queried 'Will' (l. 241), putting 'shall' in the margin. He put a cross against 'silence' (l. 250) and against 'Between two waves' he wrote 'Between the' and, below, the words 'trough' and 'valley'. Eliot wrote back:

> I *think* silence will have to stand, because I was using a line from the Family Reunion.[2] And surely the (relative) silence between two waves is when they are breaking *on* something. Should I say 'Between two waves on the shore'?

All the same, in D5 he adopted 'stillness', but, although he tried 'on the shore' in his copy of D4 (M12) he decided against it.

---

[1] See p. 70 supra for Eliot's letter explaining the presence of fourteenth-century mystics in the poem and discussion over the desirability of capitalizing the quotations or using quotation marks.

[2] The line from *The Family Reunion* comes in Harry's speech to Mary:

> And I hear your voice as in the silence
> Between two storms, one hears the moderate usual noises
> In the grass and leaves, of life persisting.

(252-259)

Quick now, here, now, always—
A condition of complete simplicity
(Costing not less than everything)
And all shall be well and   255
All manner of thing shall be well
When the tongues of flame are in-folded
Into the crowned knot of fire
And the fire and the rose are one.

condition   utter

252-9 *Not in* M2   253 condition] ~~matter~~   D1/M3   complete] ~~complete~~ M4   255-6* Omit
                                                                                     final
D1-M5;? *And all manner of/thing shall be well?* M4 (*written after the conclusion*)   257 tongues
     burning tongues?   *rose* ?
of flame] tongues of flame D4   258 knot] knot M4   259 *are one]* are the same D1-4

For his coda to the poem and to the whole series Eliot took a line from the
close of *Burnt Norton*. Hayward made no comment on D1 or on D2,
apparently thinking the repetition of Julian's words did not need to be
signalized as a quotation. In D4 he put a query against the penultimate line,
presumably being doubtful of the image of a 'crowned knot'. Eliot had
shown some doubt about 'knot', writing 'rose?' above it in M4. The reminiscence of the vision of the Trinity[1] at the close of the *Paradiso* is perhaps
not sufficiently obvious. Hayward also queried the last line, writing against
'the same' the word 'as one'. Eliot accepted the criticism and wrote on
7 September: 'Very well then,
                    And the fire and the rose are one.'

[1] La forma universal di questo nodo
     credo ch'i vidi. . . .

1. The first draft of *Little Gidding* sent to John Hayward, 7 July 1941

[Sheet 1]

(7th July, 1941)

(LITTLE GIDDING)[1]

I.

Midwinter spring is its own season
Sempiternal though sodden towards the day's end,
Suspended in time, between pole and tropic,
When the short day is brightest, with frost and fire.
The brief sun flames the ice, on pond and ditches,
In windless cold that is the heart's heat,
Reflecting in a watery mirror
A glare that is blindness in the early afternoon,
And glow more intense than blaze of branch, or brazier,
Stirs the dumb spirit: no wind, but pentecostal fire
In the dark time of the year. Between melting and freezing
The soul's sap quivers. There is no earth smell
Or smell of living thing. This is the spring time
But not in time's recurrence. Now the hedgerow

Glisters   Glitters for an hour with transitory blossom
whitens   Of snow, a bloom more sudden
Than that of summer, neither budding nor fading,
Not in the scheme of generation.
Where is the summer, the unimaginable
Summer beyond sense, the inapprehensible

X   Zero summer?

             If you came this way,
Taking the route you would be likely to take
From the place you would be likely to start from,
If you came this way in may time, you would find the hedges

---

[1] Hayward's pencilled marks and suggestions are printed in red.

[Sheet 2]

I.2

White again, in May, with voluptuary sweetness.
In the may time, the play time of the wakened senses,   X
It would be the same at the end of the journey.
If you came at night like a broken king,
If you came by day not knowing what you came for,
It would be the same, when you leave the rough road
And turn behind the pig-stye to the dull façade
And the tombstone. And what you thought you came for
Is only a shell, a husk of meaning
From which the purpose breaks only when it is fulfilled
If at all. Either you had no purpose
Or the purpose is beyond the end you figured
And is altered in fulfilment. There are other places
Which also are the world's end, some at the sea jaws,
Or over a dark lake, in a desert or a city—
But this is the <u>nearest</u>, in place and time,   to what?
Now and in England.
                If you came this way,
Taking any route, starting from anywhere,
At any time, the day time or the dark time,   X
Or at any season, the dead time or the may time,   X
It would always be the same: you would have to put off
Sense and notion. You are not here to verify,
Inform yourself, or <u>cancel</u> curiosity
Or carry report. You are here to kneel
Where prayer has been valid. And prayer is more

§ T.S.E.

[Sheet 3]

I.3

Than an order of words, ~~or~~ the conscious occupation
Of the praying mind, or the sound of the voice praying.
And what the dead had no speech for, when living,
They can tell you, being dead: the communication
Of the dead is tongued with fire beyond the language of the living.
The words of the living are wind in dry grass,
The communion of the dead is flame on the wind:
Here, the intersection of the timeless moment
Is England and nowhere. Never and always.

II.

Ash on an old man's sleeve
Is all the ash the burnt roses leave.   X
Dust in the air suspended
Marks the place where a story ended.
Dust inbreathed was a house—
The wall, the wainscot and the mouse.
The death of hope and despair,
        This is the death of air.

There is flood and drouth
Over the eyes and in the mouth.
Dead water and dead sand
Contending for the upper hand.
parched   The scorched and unemployable soil   X acarpous
Gapes at the vanity of toil,   unavailing
smiles   Laughs without mirth.   unserviceable
        This is the death of earth.

Water and fire succeed
The town, the pasture and the weed.
Water and fire deride
The skeletons that we denied.
Water and fire shall rot
The marred foundations we forgot—
The broken or entire.
        This is the death of water and fire.

At the uncertain hour before daybreak
    Toward the ending of interminable night
    At the incredible end of the unending
After the dark dove with the flickering tongue
    Had made his incomprehensible descension   X
    While the dead leaves still rattled on like tin
Over the asphalte where no other sound was
    Between three angles whence the smoke arose
    I met one walking, loitering and hurried
As if blown towards me like the metal leaves
    Before the urban dawn wind unresisting.

And as I scrutinised the downturned face
With that pointed narrowness of observation
   We turn upon the first-met stranger at dawn, _____ X
I drew the sudden look of some dead master
Whom I had known, forgotten, half-recalled,
   Both one and many: in the brown baked features
   The eyes of some familiar compound ghost,
The very near and wholly inaccessible.
   And I, becoming other and many, cried
   And heard my voice: "Are you here, Ser Brunetto?"
Although we were not. I was always dead,
   Always revived, and always something other,
   And he a face changing: yet the words sufficed
For recognition where was no acquaintance
   And no identity, blown by one airless wind,

[Sheet 6]

II.3

Too strange to each other for any cross of purpose
But intimate at the intersecting time
   Of meeting nowhere, no before and after,
   Stepping together in a dead patrol.
I said: "The wonder that I feel is easy
   And ease is cause of wonder. Therefore speak.
   I may not understand, may not remember".
And he: "I am not eager to rehearse
   My thought and theory which you have forgotten:
   These things have served their purpose: let them be.
So with your own, and pray they be forgiven
   By others, as I ask you to forgive
   Both good and bad. Last season's fruit is eaten,
And the fullfed beast shall kick the empty pail.
   For last year's words belong to last year's language
   And next year's words are still an unknown speech.
Remember rather the essential moments
   That were the times of birth and death and change ∧   ,//
? ᛚ ———— ¹ The agony and the solitary vigil.
Remember also fear, loathing and hate,
   The wild strawberries eaten in the garden,
   The walls of Poitiers, and the Anjou wine, —la douceur angevine
The fresh new season's rope, the smell of varnish
   On the clean oar, the drying of the sails,
Such things as seem of least and most importance.
So, as you circumscribe this dreary round,
   Shall your life pass from you, with all you hated

¹ Squares represent Hayward's ringing of the definite articles.

[Sheet 7]

II.4

And all you loved, the future and the past.
United to another past, another future,
  (After many seas and after many lands)
  The dead and the unborn, who shall be nearer
Than the voices and the faces that were most near.
  This is the final gift of earth accorded—
  One soil, one past, one future, in one place.
Nor shall the eternal thereby be remoter
  But nearer: seek or seek not, it is here.
  Now, the last love on earth. The rest is grace."
He turned away, and in the <u>autumn</u> weather   X
  I heard a distant dull deferred report
  At which I started: and the sun had risen.

[Sheet 8]

(7th July 1941)

III.

There are three conditions look very much alike,   1st para. Too didactic?
Differ completely, flourish in the same hedgerow: needs fusing.
Attachment to things and to persons, detachment
From things and from persons; and growing close by them, indifference
Which resembles the others as death resembles life
Being between two lives. This is the use of memory:
For liberation—not less of love but expansion
Of love in the end of desire, and so liberation
From the future as well as the past. Thus, love of a country
Begins as dependence upon our own field of action
And comes to find that action of little importance
Though never indifferent. History is servitude:
History is also freedom. See, now they vanish,
The faces and places, with the self which—as it could—loved them:
To become renewed, transfigured, in another pattern.

If I think, last, of this place,
And of people, not wholly commendable,
Of no immediate kin or kindness,
But some of peculiar genius,
All touched by a common genius;
If I think of a king at nightfall
Of three men, or more, on the scaffold
And two or three who died quietly
In other places, here or abroad,

III.2

we celebrate
Why should ~~a man lament~~
The dead men
~~Dead people~~ more than the dying?
It is not to ring the bells backward
Nor is it an incantation
To <u>summon</u> the ghost of a rose.   raise up
We cannot revive old factions
We cannot restore old policies
Or follow an antique drum.
These men and those who opposed them,
And those whom they opposed,
Accept the constitution of silence
And are folded in a single party.   _____X
Whatever we inherit from the victors,
We have taken from the defeated
What they had to leave us—a symbol:
The symbol created by death
(Created by such a death)
The life only death transmits,
The perfection of the motive
Which the moment of death brings to life.

> Soul of Christ, sanctify them,
> Body of Christ, let their bodies be good earth,
> Water from the side of Christ, wash them,   cut by T.S.E.
> Fire from the heart of Christ, incinerate them.

IV.

Perhaps
omit 2 ?

② Till death shall bring the audit in
To value all our hoarded treasures/   — /
The Profitable Sin,
Consenting¹ Thoughts, and Sundry Pleasures/ : / cut by T.S.E.
The prizes that we think to win
By Prudence, and by Worldly Cares,
Figure as gilt-edge stocks and shares.

① Between the initial watery sign
And climax of a pinch of earth,
Our false accounts decline
To show the dues of death and birth
Or mark the debt below the line:
The deficit that is complete,
Or cancelled by the Paraclete.

IV
obscure
& too little of it
non sequiturish?

③ The dove descending breaks the air
With flame of incandescent terror
Of which the tongues declare
The one discharge from sin and error.
The only hope, or else despair
        Lies in the choice of pyre or pyre—
        To be redeemed by fire from fire.

¹ Corrected by Eliot from 'Cosseting'.

[Sheet 11]

V.

What we think the beginning is often the end
And to make an end is to make a beginning.
The end is where we start from. And every phrase
Or sentence that is right (where every word is at home,
Doing its part to support the others,
The word neither diffident nor ostentatious,
An easy commerce of the old and the new,
The common word exact without vulgarity,
The formal word precise without pedantry),
The complete consort dancing together)
                              and
Every phrase or sentence is an end ~~or~~ a beginning,
Every poem its own epitaph. And every action
Is a step up the scaffold, to the fire, down the sea's throat
Or to an illegible stone: and that is where we start.
We die with the dying,
See, they depart, and we go with them;
        are born
We ~~return~~ with the dead,
See, they return, and bring us with them:
The moment of the rose and the moment of the yew-tree
Are of equal duration. A people without history
Is not redeemed from time, for history is a pattern
Of timeless moments. So, while the light fails
On a winter afternoon, in a secluded chapel
History is now and England.

[Sheet 12]

V.2

We shall not cease from exploration
And the end of all our exploring
Will be to arrive where we started
And know the place for the first time.
Through the unknown, remembered gate
When the last of earth left to discover
Is that which was the beginning
At the source of the longest river
The voice of the hidden waterfall
And the children in the apple-tree
Not known, because not looked for
But heard, half-heard, in the silence

Of distant lands and seas.
Quick/ now, here, now, always—
   condition
A ~~matter~~ of complete simplicity
(Costing not less that[1] everything)
When the tongues of flame are infolded
Into the crowned knot of fire
And the fire and the rose are the same.

[1] Typing error uncorrected by Eliot.

2. John Hayward's letter commenting, 1 August 1941[1]

MERTON HALL

CAMBRIDGE   1 August 1941

My Dear Tom: I'm sorry there's been this long delay in writing to you about 'LITTLE GIDDING'. I sent off the last of the marks and the reports on the 700 vile little bodies last Tuesday; the following day I had to write answers to letters received during the previous week; Victor was here all day yesterday. To-day I feel free at last, though still a little stupefied. I mention this because I am sure that whatever critical faculty I possess is momentarily distempered by the work it has [had] to do in the past fortnight. So please bear this [in] mind as you read the following observations. . . . I agree with you that the poem, in the *unfinished and unpolished* state in which you have allowed me to see it, is not quite up to the standard of the others in the group. But it does not seem to me to be, potentially, inferior to them; nor do I think that it shows signs of fatigue or that, as you seem to fear, it is merely a mechanical exercise; I am sure that it only requires to be revised and perhaps rewritten in certain passages, to which I shall refer, to be brought to perfection as the culminating poem of the series. I need hardly say that it has given me intense satisfaction and pleasure to read it even in its present unfinished condition. As a whole, it has moved me no less than its predecessors. My general impression is that Parts I, II, V, and all but the first paragraph of Part III are all right. Part IV seems to me to break down. The first fifteen lines of Part III—the didactic passage—strike me as being imperfectly resolved into poetry, in fact rather laboured and prosy. I think I appreciate the difficulty of this kind of expository writing. It may be that it is too easy to cast such philosophic and ethical statements into the kind of long, fluid lines you use so ingeniously. But this particular passage does seem to me to drag; to need fusing: possibly to be presented to the reader in a less didactic and uncompromising form. As for Part IV, I can't fit it into the scheme of the poem as a whole. Now that you have discarded (and rightly so, I think) the 2nd. stanza ('Till death shall bring the audit in . . .') it consists of only two short stanzas and their point has escaped me. This is more than likely to be due to my own obtuseness. But the point I should like to make is that these two stanzas seem to me scarcely to justify a section to themselves. My own view, for the little that it is worth, is that this section should be extended rather than rewritten, or if this is not possible, that it should be so reorganized as

---

[1] Hayward's erratic use of points to separate his 'niggling details' (varying in number from four to thirteen) is not reproduced, nor his failures to separate words and occasional mistypings.

to be capable of being incorporated in some way either at the end of Part III or at the beginning of Part V. In its present form it has an obfuscating effect—rather as if you had thrown out a smoke-screen to prepare for the next stage. This, at any rate, is how it affected me. I approve of the omission of the last four lines of Part III.

[Page 2]

Now for a few niggling details. PART I.—'Zero summer'. Is this an allusive reference to the Absolute Zero of physics? I feel a little uneasy about the epithet—slightly Clevelandish? . . . 'in the may time, the play time': this is a rather dangerous conjunction, maytime and playtime (cf. *Baby* & *Maybe*) being a favourite stand-by in Tin Pan Alley. I should feel happier if this jingle were omitted. . . . 'But this is the nearest': nearest to what, or to whom? I think I understand you, but I am puzzled to know what an American reader would make of it. . . . 'At any time &c . . . or the may time'. There is just a faint suggestion here, I think, of your parodying yourself. (*v. supra* Hayward on Jingles) . . . PART II. 'Is all the ash the burnt roses leave': Compared with the other lines in the stanza this one seems to me to have too much weight at the end. The heavy stress on 'burnt' could be lightened by omitting the definite article and this would also lay a shade more stress on 'roses'. As it is, this line takes something from the essential 'airiness' of the stanza—dust, breath, air: the death of air—as if the ash of burnt roses was not an imponderable but a tombstone. . . . 'unemployable soil': this sounds ugly when read aloud to my ear. (possibilities: acarpous, unavailing, unserviceable). . . . 'Laughs without mirth': I should prefer 'smiles'. It is easier, I think, to conceive of a smile without mirth than a laugh without mirth, for all that people speak of a hollow laugh, &c. And it's easier and more convincing, I feel, to imagine the soil as smiling than as laughing. An inanimate object can appear to be smiling; it can hardly be thought of as laughing. In any case you can't gape *and* laugh at the same time—I've just tried to in the mirror—and you can gape and smile without mirth at the same time. Perhaps I am being too silly! . . . Sheet 2, lines 2–5: these lines seem to me to flag a little, particularly lines 2–3, as if the needle of the mind had got stuck in a groove and was faltering. I don't like the mouthful (and earful) 'incomprehensible descension' . . . 'stranger at dawn': I wish the two stressed monosyllables hadn't got to complete this line; but I don't see how to alter this. It's not important. . . . Sheet 3. Insert comma after 'change' line 18. and so avoid a possible Empsonism. . . . lines 19–24 are a trifle overpacked with definite articles —a difficulty in catalogues—and something might be done to tighten this passage. (The first thing that occurred to me—forgive the impertinence—was 'The walls of Poitiers, *la douceur angevine*'). . . . 'autumn weather': I do not get the significance of *autumn*? It struck me as having a greater significance than you may have intended it to have. . . . PART III. 'To summon the ghost of a rose': I can't resist expressing a regret that, having quoted so far, you didn't follow Sir T.B. and put 'raise up the ghost of a rose': I do wish you would consider making this alteration. It is an exquisite evocation. . . . These are all my comments. Please let me know if they are helpful in the slightest degree; but more particularly, assure me that you intend to add 'LITTLE GIDDING' to the group. You *must not* discard it just because you have the natural misgivings of a poet bringing a movement to its close—misgivings doubtless exacerbated by the miserable time you have had with your teeth. I sympathize with you most keenly and closely, but hope that your general health will greatly benefit from now on. I saw a copy of POINTS OF VIEW at the booksellers yesterday. Perhaps F. & F. will shortly send me an editor's copy or *copies! Topicks must be postponed until our next.*

Love from y^r old creating critick : John.

Manuscript material in Magdalene College, Cambridge

Eliot gave to Magdalene College, Cambridge the remains of a scribbling pad, along with leaves torn out of two, or possibly three, other pads, some of which were pinned together. The main pad, MS A, contains drafts of parts of *The Dry Salvages*, and of the first version of *Little Gidding* II–IV. The other, odd, leaves contain the first draft of *Little Gidding* V and drafts in prose and verse of Eliot's revisions of Parts II and IV. All the drafts are in pencil.

MS A

The original brown cover of the pad has been preserved and reads 'W. Straker Ltd./"Rekarts" (Regd.) Series No. 6/The/EMPIRE/Scribbling Pad/Ruled Feint and Perforated'. A count of the stubs of leaves which have been torn out shows that the pad had originally a hundred leaves. The leaves, when torn out on the line of perforation, measure $18 \cdot 1 \times 16 \cdot 1$ cm. Only the last nine leaves are still in place (ff. 92–100). The first sixty-four leaves have been neatly torn out; but the next twenty-seven have been roughly torn, leaving irregular stubs behind. The destroyer, presumably Eliot, stayed his hand and preserved thirteen of these last, putting them with the untorn-out remnant and the torn-off cover. By matching the stubs against the torn-out leaves, it is possible to reconstruct the pad.

ff. 1–64	Removed neatly and destroyed
f. 65	Summary notes for *The Dry Salvages*
ff. 66–7	Missing
f. 68	Suggested rhymes for the lyric of *The Dry Salvages* II
f. 69	Missing
ff. 70–1	Verse draft of *The Dry Salvages* III, to top of f. 71
ff. 71–2	Verse draft of *The Dry Salvages* IV
ff. 73–6	Missing
f. 77	Summary notes for *Little Gidding*
ff. 78–84	Missing. These leaves probably contained drafts of *Little Gidding* I
ff. 85–6	Verse draft of the lyric of *Little Gidding* II
ff. 87–9	Verse draft of *Little Gidding* II, 'At the uncertain hour . . .' to 'last season's fruit is eaten' (ll. 80–116)
ff. 90–1	Draft of a tribute to Evelyn Underhill (died 15 June 1941)
ff. 92–3	Verse draft of the first version of *Little Gidding* II, ll. 118 to close of Part II
f. 94	Prose draft of *Little Gidding* III

f. 95   'V/To make an end is to make a beginning'
ff. 96–8   Verse draft of *Little Gidding* III
f. 99   Four lines versifying *Anima Christi*
f. 99ᵛ   Three lines of an attempt at the first version of *Little Gidding* IV
f. 100   Verse draft of two stanzas for the first version of *Little Gidding* IV
f. 100ᵛ   Another attempt at a stanza for *Little Gidding* IV

The pad thus reconstructed shows Eliot, having planned the matter of his poem, beginning at the beginning and composing the parts in sequence, except for the single line for Part V on f. 95. It shows also how rapidly he composed when the fit was on him. He breaks off his draft for the speech of the 'dead master' to draft a letter, perhaps to *The Times*, to supplement an obituary notice for Evelyn Underhill. As she died on 15 June, her obituary cannot have appeared before 16 June at the earliest. By 7 July the complete first draft of *Little Gidding* was sent to Hayward.

MS B

This consists of four leaves from another pad of the same type but measuring 18·4 × 16·1 cm. The leaves have been coupled by being pinned together.

f. 1   Prose draft for the revised ending of Part II
f. 1ᵛ   One line of the above versified
f. 2   (Pinned to f. 1) Verse draft of lines on 'the old rooted sin' intended for the speech of the 'dead master'
ff. 3–4   (Pinned together) Verse draft (very rough) of the first attempt at the revised speech

The verse drafts of ff. 3–4 present an early stage of composition. They suggest that, on the whole, the comparatively finished drafts of Part II in MS A do not represent Eliot's first attempts to cast his thoughts into verse and were preceded by various attempts on rough paper which found their way into the waste-paper basket.

MS C

This consists of four leaves from a smaller pad (18·1 × 12·6 cm).

ff. 1–2   Verse draft of *Little Gidding* V
f. 3   (Pinned to f. 4) Prose draft for the final version of the close of the speech of the 'dead master': 'Consider what are the gifts of age'
f. 4   First attempt at the concluding stanza of the final version of *Little Gidding* IV: 'Who heaped the brittle roseleaves? Love.'

MS D

This consists of two leaves from a pad of the same size as MS A. They could be leaves from the beginning of the pad. They contain Eliot's notes for his lecture on 'The Poetry of W. B. Yeats', delivered in Dublin in June 1940. On the back of both leaves are verse drafts for the final version of the second stanza of *Little Gidding* IV.

Like the rough drafts for the first version of *Little Gidding* IV on ff. 99^v, 100, and 100^v of MS A, and the rough drafts for the revised ending of Part II on ff. 3–4 of MS B, and the draft for the second stanza of Part IV on f. 4 of MS C, these drafts on the back of his old lecture notes allow us to see Eliot shaping his conceptions into verse.